I hope reading this book as much as I did writing it.

Love,
Carol

SOUTHERN DECEPTION

BY
CAROL GREENBAUM
& RICH TOWSLEY

Designed by EllEss Design, Inc.
Creative Director: Laurie Straus
845-268-3995

Cover photo by Carol Greenbaum
Back cover photo by Eric Bern Studio

Southern Deception was designed and printed in the USA

ISBN: 9780615413907-52495

SOUTHERN DECEPTION

This book is dedicated to Daddy.
The source of my values, morals and beliefs.
Who taught me that through God
all things are possible.

INTRODUCTION

T rust is a precious gift we are seeking to
find, needing to share. Our hearts naturally
reach out to find someone we can trust,
someone with whom we can share our real selves.
We cannot buy trust, but we can choose to give our
trust to another. A child instinctively learns trust
from its mother, as a mother freely gives herself to her
child and models trust for her child. Faithful words
and actions can strengthen trust, but trust is always
a choice. I must choose to trust you, and you must
choose to trust me. Trust is the ultimate expression of
faith.

Like interest compounding over time, trust
that is freely given and received grows deeper and
wider, drawing two hearts together in a strong, clear

bond. Trust is as clear and strong as a crystal glass, a sparkling and beautiful work of art. But trust is also as fragile as a crystal. Like crystal, trust can be shattered into a thousand sharp and broken pieces that cut if you try to pick them up and put them back together. When trust is broken, the aftermath can be devastating and the emotional scars can last a lifetime.

But sweeping up the crystal splinters, throwing them away and letting go of the treasure we have lost is like choosing to forgive someone who has broken our trust. On that rare occasion that the person forgiven truly accepts and understands this powerful human act, the resulting positive change can last a lifetime. Only then can we come back to the relationship and begin again. But if we can begin again, if we can truly forgive, we can share the hope we all need… that we can really change, that we can grow to become the persons we want to be.

1

There would be no valentine on Valentine's Day. After 25 years as a loving wife and mother, Carol Greenbaum was 49, and she felt so alone. Laying down her mascara, Carol examined her reflection in the mirror. Her delicate facial features were attractive and vivid within the gilded frame of honey blonde hair falling straight and stylish around her shoulders. Her slender body was toned by morning walks and daily tennis. Her experienced eye and refined taste had selected luxurious, designer clothing to accent her sleek figure.

Carol had lived the life of the genteel Southern woman. Soon after graduating from Mercer University, she had married her college sweetheart. They had built an idyllic life in the Atlanta suburbs, in a spacious, elegant home in the Atlanta Country Club where they were long-standing members. Their two daughters, now in their twenties, had grown up with all the best Atlanta had to offer. Everything seemed perfect. But as any good Southern girl knows, perfection was an image she had always hoped they would live up to, to make their reality. This was not to be, for her husband had chosen to walk down a destructive path. She smiled wistfully as she thought of her marriage … the disappointment … the years she'd spent building a life with a man who had made bad decisions and thrown it all away … but that was in the past, not now.

She picked up her mascara and swiped the wand across her eyelashes one last time. Perfect. With eyes a shade of blue that bordered on violet, she'd always been told that her eyes were one of her best features. In spite of the pain and sadness her crumbling marriage had brought, her eyes remained clear and wide. She was a strong woman, and she would trust again one day, she thought. Examining her jewelry box, Carol selected a pair of diamond-encrusted hoops. She carefully put them on, with her diamond bracelet and necklace. The light from the setting sun crept through her bedroom window, making the diamonds blaze with fire.

Satisfied with this choice, Carol turned to her closet. Her refinement and taste spoke from each article of clothing, carefully selected to complement her features and outfit her for the many social occasions where she was part of the beauty and tradition she loved so well. She scanned the racks carefully, her fingers tracing lightly over rich textures and fabrics of every color until she found what she was looking for: a sapphire blue satin dress, with an empire waist and three-quarter length sleeves. She bought it recently, and it fit her as if it were custom made just for her. She'd been dying for an occasion to wear it. She slipped into the dress and did a little half-turn in the mirror. She looked fine, just fine. As she turned, her phone quickly drew her to the bedside table where it rang.

"Carol? Are you ready?" asked Sherry's familiar voice. "Our reservations are for 8:00 – are you coming?"

"I'll be there soon. Don't worry." Carol smiled as

she set down the receiver. Over the last twelve years, Sherry had become one of Carol's dearest friends. She had been encouraging Carol to try dating again, and to have some fun. With no dates for Valentine's Day, they'd decided to spend the evening together at The Blue Ridge Grill on West Paces Ferry, one of their favorite Atlanta restaurants. A glass or two of a fine wine and engaging conversation over a delicious dinner shared with a trusted friend ... Carol really had been looking forward to the evening. And, she thought, who knows? She might even meet someone interesting there. You never know.

She quickly drove the familiar route to pick up Sherry at her home, enjoying the familiar sights of her neighborhood: lush, green lawns leading to meticulously landscaped shrubbery, framing grand homes rising gracefully above the dogwood and oak trees. The clear, bright February sky was growing dark, and Carol could see lights glowing from kitchens and dining rooms – inside, she thought, some families were sitting down to dinner, sharing a meal, talking about the day's events, maybe even bickering over whose night it was to do the dishes. She sighed, remembering the pleasure she had enjoyed cooking a gourmet meal for her family. But times had changed, and so had she. She sometimes ate dinner at the country club with friends, but she often ate alone. Most of the time, she really didn't mind. Her girls were happy where they were in their lives, and she was naturally sunny. After her divorce, she really did enjoy some of the independence she had gained. She stayed actively involved in charity work; she faithfully attended an urban Christian church; and she had enough money to maintain her elegant lifestyle. But when she thought about the days and years ahead, about another Valentine's Day ... she would like to find someone to spend time with, to enjoy a meal, to talk and laugh with her ... someone to share her life again.

Turning onto Sherry's street, she pulled into the driveway to wait for her friend. Carol checked her reflection and touched up her lipstick in the rear-view mirror. A moment later, Sherry opened the passenger door and slid into the front seat opposite Carol.

"You look simply gorgeous!" Sherry exclaimed, tilting her head to admire her friend. "Is that a new dress?"

"I found it at Sak's and I couldn't pass it up," Carol replied with a grin. "You look great, too! I just love the color of that sweater – it looks so perfect on you!"

"Thanks." Sherry smiled and smoothed the front of her silk sweater. It was a deep, emerald green and the scooped neckline was adorned with delicate, emerald-green beads. Set against Sherry's dark, wavy hair and deep brown eyes, the effect was stunning.

"Let's go – we look too beautiful to sit in the driveway, and I'm starving!"

They giggled like schoolgirls as Carol backed down the driveway. On the way to the Blue Ridge Grill, they chatted happily, exchanging the latest news: Carol's older daughter Malinda had just accepted a job at MTV in New York; her younger daughter, Caroline was having a great time in Australia on a college exchange program. As the valet parked her car, Carol turned to her friend with sparkling eyes. "Thanks so much for getting me out of the house, Sherry. You're right – I do need to get back out there. I mean, just look at us! Two great friends out on the town! Who needs a date? This will be the best Valentine's Day ever!"

Carol was relieved that Sherry had made their reservations so many weeks in advance as she stepped inside and went to the reservation desk. The Blue Ridge Grill had long been one of the most popular fine restaurants in Atlanta – usually crowded, and even more so tonight. The hostess led them through a softly lit dining room filled to capacity. Carol noticed couples holding hands and looking deep into each other's eyes, their faces aglow in the soft candlelight. Someday, she told herself, she'd be there as well, sitting across from a handsome man who would tenderly gaze into her eyes and gently ask to hold her hand.

That would be another day.

"So, what do you think?" Sherry opened her menu and scanned the contents. "Salmon or chicken? Or the crabcakes? So many great choices, I can never decide! What are you getting?"

Carol laughed. She hadn't really seen the menu she held in front of her. "Oh, I don't know, Sherry – I think I'll get the salmon; they really do it best here." She took a sip of her wine, and began to study the menu thoughtfully. "Yes. Definitely the plank-grilled salmon. With the steamed asparagus."

Sherry put down the menu and looked across the table to her friend. "So, have you met anyone interesting on that dating website? What was it again, 'Meet a Millionaire'?" The waiter came to take their orders, giving Carol a moment's pause. She had felt a little silly when Sherry had suggested online dating; surfing the Internet for a date felt strange, and went against her somewhat old-fashioned manners. But with Sherry's encouragement, Carol had agreed to try it and see what happened. Sherry helped her create a profile on a couple of dating sites, and she had even taken Carol's picture. They had gone into her front yard on a bright November afternoon. It was a simple, pretty picture of Carol, with a happy smile on her face and standing in front of her beloved home. Carol thought her personality would really shine through this picture on the dating website.

"It's 'Millionaire Match,'" Carol corrected. "Yes, I've met a couple of men, but no one I've really connected with, you know what I mean? They seemed nice enough, and they were well educated – good looking, too. But I just didn't feel that spark. Not yet."

"Don't get discouraged," Sherry said. "You might just meet someone when you least expect it. It might be at church or even at the grocery store. You never know! But I just know you'll meet someone if you keep looking."

With a more serious look, Carol turned her deep blue eyes to Sherry. "It seems like I've asked God so many times about His plan for me – you know, with the divorce, and everything – and I just feel like He has something wonderful waiting for me; I just don't know what it will be or when I'll find it. I'm not sure about this Millionaire Match. On one hand, it seems nice enough – the men are upper class, so they're not interested in my money. But, I haven't found anyone I'm really interested in meeting – isn't that terrible?"

Sherry's response was interrupted as their food arrived. It looked delicious: Carol's salmon was the perfect shade of deep pink, glazed in a light, white wine sauce, and complemented by the lovely, bright green asparagus. After some deliberation, Sherry had chosen the filet mignon, and it was grilled to perfection. The food was almost too gorgeous to eat.

Carol looked at her plate, because something was missing. She lightly motioned to their waiter. "Excuse me, may I please have some ketchup? Just a little dish on the side?"

"You and your ketchup!" Sherry teased her friend. For as long as she'd known Carol, she'd rarely seen her eat a meal without a healthy side of ketchup. Steaks, salads – about the only thing Carol had never eaten with ketchup was her coffee. "You just leave my ketchup alone!" Carol huffed in mock indignation as the waiter placed a tiny silver dish of ketchup next to her plate. She smiled widely and tossed her golden hair. She looked like a giddy teenager without a care in the world. Her sorrows were far away right now. Happily, she dipped a stalk of asparagus in her ketchup and giggled.

The evening's conversation turned to happy times. Carol talked about the charity ball she was working hard to organize. They both talked about their children enjoying where they were and what they were doing. They reminisced about other Valentine's Days, and swapped funny dating stories. Carol enjoyed the evening more than any she could remember in a long time.

At the close of the evening, Carol dropped Sherry off at home and returned home alone. She paused in the kitchen to admire the beautiful things that surrounded her: The bright, artistic floral pattern of her china and the handmade crystal chandeliers; the hand-painted living room end tables and the rich, imported tapestries. Carol's personal imprint was evident in every room of the house; she'd spent 25 years making it her own. The antique, gilded mahogany credenza in the formal living room was crowded with pictures of her daughters smiling at her. All at once, she felt at home again in this house that had seemed to be too empty. Once again, she found herself at home.

A mug of steaming coffee in her hand, Carol slid out of her shoes and padded to the living room – after all the talk about dating, she wanted to check her email and see if she had a message. The hour was late, but Carol didn't feel tired. Entering her password and clicking into her mail, she was delighted to see a new email in her inbox.

A man named Rich had emailed her. She read

the subject line, "Saw your profile on MM; I'd like to meet you." Carol was surprised to feel a smile growing in spite of herself. She read the subject line one more time. The first thing in the morning, she would read Rich's email. Maybe she'd even write back to him. Suddenly tired, she shut down her computer and turned to go to bed.

Snuggling down under her satin sheets, Carol considered her life. She thought about her daughters, pursuing their dreams in different parts of the world. She thought of her father, who must be asleep by now in the family home down in Macon. She smiled as she remembered her evening with Sherry, and how she appreciated her wonderful friends at the Atlanta Country Club.

As she did every night, she thanked God for these precious blessings. She had so much to be thankful for.

Drifting off to sleep, Carol remembered the message from Rich and wondered if he might be interesting.

2

ich Towsley leaned back in his desk chair and rubbed his eyes: just a few more papers to review for tomorrow's meeting. It was getting late, and he had to finish packing before his big move to Atlanta in the morning. Maybe he was procrastinating, he thought, checking his watch for
the third time in a half hour. It was already 7:45 PM. He needed to get moving, but his thoughts wandered off to Millionaire Match.

Rich heard about Millionaire Match a few months earlier from John, a longtime friend and business associate. Rich was surprised when John confided that he had recently decided to try online dating. When Rich and John met for golf at the country club, John had brought a date. John was a little older than Rich and had been single for several years.

Through online dating, John met Glenda. With long, auburn hair and a bright smile, Glenda was tall and tanned, a stunning woman. While the trio played golf, Rich saw that Glenda was educated and interesting, and successful, as well. She owned her own catering company and had just bought a condo at the beach. She was obviously crazy about John, as he was about her. Throughout the afternoon the two giggled and held hands like teenagers. Rich was surprised to feel envious … he'd been alone for years and realized he'd almost given up on dating. Watching John and Glenda made him feel that something … or someone… was missing from his life. Not long after the golf game, he opened his mailbox to find a thick, cream-colored envelope with his name engraved in elegant, silver script: It was an invitation to John and Glenda's wedding.

Rich sighed and returned to his computer, hoping he might find that storybook ending like John and Glenda. How silly! He was 44 years old, and very successful as a network marketing professional. He enjoyed living in a large, tastefully decorated home in an exclusive community in Sarasota, Florida. He was a confident man who lived the American dream. He had worked hard to put the past behind him, and he wanted everything his success had to offer. With a touch of amusement, he realized the terror he faced in putting himself out there dating again. After 16 years alone, Rich felt really out of practice.

The Millionaire Match homepage displayed a smiling couple at the prow of a sailboat and another couple strolling hand-in-hand in the surf of some faraway beach at sunset. Hesitating, Rich clicked on Create Profile. It seemed easy enough: he began to type in his name, age, education and profession, and income. This was not too painful, he thought. The doorbell broke the silence and Rich glanced at his watch.

It was eight o'clock and Mark had come by to check on him. Rich stretched, and got up to answer the door. Mark stood on his front steps, holding a small bag. "I brought you some dessert! Melanie and I went out for dinner tonight, and I know you love their cheesecake." Mark warmly clapped his friend on the back and they moved into the living room. "You should have come with us! Melanie said to tell you hi. Did you eat, or have you been working all night?"

"No," Rich replied. "I mean, no, I didn't eat. I lost track of time." Rich walked into the kitchen and pulled a fork from the drawer. "How's Melanie? You two have a nice dinner?"

"Yeah, it was nice." Mark opened the refrigerator and tossed Rich a bottle of water, then helped himself to one. "I'll be out of town for our usual date night, so I wanted to make it up to her."

Rich opened the box and took a bite of the cheesecake. "Man, this is good! Thanks! I didn't realize how hungry I was."

"Anytime," Mark replied, shrugging. "It does look good. I'd ask you for a bite, but I've known you too long to think that would happen."

Rich smiled. Mark was right. After their 25 years of friendship, Rich really didn't have to explain. Mark wasn't offended that Rich didn't share his dessert. Not that Rich was greedy – far from it. Some things he just didn't do, not even with his best friend … sharing his food was one of them. He had to avoid things that would remind him of a painful past that he needed not to remember. Too many bites of friends' sandwiches when he had no lunch money in grade school … too many soiled and worn old school clothes … too many times he had done things to escape a past he'd vowed to forget. Rich wished he could change his past – but, at least with Mark, he didn't' have to explain or dig up the painful memories again.

"So, are you all packed?" Mark asked.

"What?" Rich shook his head; he looked haunted, and the sparkle had gone out of his dark brown eyes. He'd been deep in thought, and Mark's words had jarred him out of his reverie. "Oh – yeah. Almost. I just have a few papers to go over, but I'm ready. Come on, we can talk while I finish up."

As they walked into the study, Mark noticed the computer screen. "What's Millionaire Match?" he asked. "Some kind of dating site?"

"It is. John told me to try it," said Rich. "He said that successful, single people like me have had some success in finding each other through the site. John has. Did I tell you he's getting married?"

"I got an invitation, too," said Mark. "Good for him. It's about time. And, I could say the same for you, Rich. You're young, good-looking and successful enough –

I'm surprised you're still single." Mark gestured toward the screen. "So, show me how it works!"

"First, you have to make a profile – I was just starting mine when you got here. Want to help me?" Rich sat down and studied the screen. "This whole thing seems sort of silly, but who knows, right? Maybe I'll meet someone. I thought it might be nice to have someone to go to dinner with – and I don't know anyone in Atlanta. I'll be there for a while, at least until I get the new business on its feet. I might meet a woman who I could spend some time with, take on a date, you know. Like you and Melanie?" Rich paused and turned to ask Mark, "Would you say I am more 'athletic', or do you think 'muscular build' sounds better… or 'stocky'?"

Mark pulled up a chair. "Muscular. Definitely muscular."

With Mark's help, setting up his dating profile was easier, almost fun. Rich had broad shoulders and a muscular build. His hair was shiny, dark brown and well-cut, and he was clean-shaven – as a businessman, he liked a clean, professional look. He dressed the part, too: with an eye for good tailoring and confidence in his choices, Rich knew he looked good in the fine business casual clothing he chose to wear. This part of the profile was simple, Rich thought. He just tried to describe what he saw in the mirror. Not so hard. Rich read the physical description out loud, adding, "Hey, this makes me sound like quite a catch!" Mark laughed.

"What's next?" asked Mark. "Income and net worth? Hey, I've got an idea – we can have some fun with this, don't you think?" Mark poked at his friend as a mischievous grin spread across his face. "Just for laughs, put something really out there on this part. You're so picky about what you like, you probably won't find someone there anyway."

"Hey, I'm not that picky," retorted Rich. "I'm just careful about who I get involved with."

"Right ... you're so careful that you haven't seriously dated a woman for, what, about a decade?" Mark pointed out. "Man, you're turning 44 – why not make your net worth $44 million?"

Rich laughed. "It'd be a lot more fun if I actually had $44 million. That would make a great birthday present!" He hesitated at Mark's suggestion. In truth, he was a millionaire. But $44 million was more than a little exaggeration. How funny. He was worried about representing himself with an exaggerated income on a dating website, when he'd spent years representing himself as… but that was the past, not now. At any rate, Mark was probably right – what harm was there in having some fun, when he just wanted some practice, to see what kind of women might be out there? "$44 million it is," he said. "This is fun. Now, what other assets do I have? A yacht? A private jet?"

"There you go!" Mark said, laughing. "What about a collection of cars? You've always liked cars. That's it! You have, say, eleven cars."

"That's good!" Rich replied. He was smiling now, and typing quickly. "Hey, Mark – do you want to borrow one of my cars? I mean, I've got eleven of them, so you can have your pick. Do you want the Ferrari or the Lamborghini? … or the Porsche?"

They were really getting into the game now. "What, I'm not good enough for the Rolls? Rich, man, I thought we were friends!" Mark was laughing so hard that he had to wipe the corners of his eyes. "That's too funny." He wiped his eyes again, but then remembered to check his watch. "Oh, man – is it that late already?

I've got to get going or Melanie's gonna kill me. I told her I was just going to swing by your place for a minute to drop off some dessert."

"Blame it on me," Rich said. "Tell her you had to give me some dating advice." He got up from the computer and walked Mark to the door. "So, are you still game to help me tomorrow?"

"I'll pick you up at seven tomorrow morning," replied Mark. "Melanie has your key. She said she'll come over here and check on the house while we're gone."

"Thanks, Mark. That's great. And tell Melanie thanks for me, too."

Closing the door behind Mark, Rich turned back to his computer. He went over his profile information one last time, chuckling softly at his 11 cars and $44 million net worth. His profile was complete. Now he got to search for profiles he wanted to see. He knew exactly what he wanted … the problem was, he'd never found her. He had to admit he had always been rather particular about who he dated. She should be 45 to 50, and had to be a non-smoker. He enjoyed intelligent conversation, so he thought she should have some education; even a college degree would be nice. Rich hummed to himself as he checked the boxes, narrowing the search criteria to find his perfect match. He continued working his way down the list until he came to the question about his religious preferences.

Rich backed away just a little. He didn't consider himself to be a believer; in fact, even the sight of a church made him uncomfortable … always had, ever since he was a kid. Something just bothered him about seeing happy families, dressed up in their Sunday clothes … Rich checked "religion unimportant" and then "start searching."

He waited.

Unbelievable! Just in the Atlanta area, 1,508 women matched his search criteria. He couldn't believe there were that many! Rich started scrolling down through the profiles. The ten women who had profiles on the first page had a "preferred" status next to their names – they'd paid extra to be listed first. None of them caught his eye. He clicked on the next page. A few of the women were attractive; some he might even say were beautiful; almost all claimed to be wealthy. But, to Rich, they all looked nice, just so much the same.

Maybe Mark was right, Rich thought. Maybe he was too picky. Maybe online dating wasn't for him. Rich yawned and decided to finish that page, and then stop for the night. He had a flight to catch in the morning, and it was almost 10:30. He scrolled past three more women ...

And there she was.

His mouth fell open, and he gazed in wonder at the beautiful face he saw. Her sparkling, deep blue eyes seemed to be looking at him, even to really see him. Her honey blonde hair gleamed in the sunlight. Her screen name was "HappyLark", which matched her carefree and laughing smile. She seemed to be beckoning Rich to come and walk with her. How strange that such a comfortable feeling made Rich wonder if he'd known HappyLark all his life, even if they had not yet even met. Rich skimmed down to read that her name was Carol, but he couldn't concentrate on the rest. His eyes kept going back to her face – and her eyes. How could this happen in a moment, through a picture on the Web? This woman named Carol – with her cheerful screen name and deep, blue eyes – had stirred something in him that he hadn't felt in many years.

Rich's hands quivered as he typed.

Dear Carol, he began. "*My name is Rich. This is my first time to try an online dating service. Your picture caught my eye. I am actually moving to the Atlanta area this week, and I am looking forward to speaking with you. Please call me at 941-879-3646. I look forward to hearing from you. Thanks, Rich.*"

He'd never done this before, so he anxiously wondered if she would respond. He hoped she would …

Crawling into bed, his thoughts returned to those deep, blue eyes. How did they touch him so easily, when he had so carefully hidden his heart for so long? He had good reason to be guarded. He recalled what he had worked so hard to forget: 25 years guarding a separate identity, living a double life … in this world, things weren't always what they had appeared to be. He could still keep things straight. It could be dangerous if he didn't.

As Rich's head touched the pillow, he thought once more of Carol's eyes … and then he thought of the demons that haunted him. As he drifted off to sleep, he thought about how lucky he was to be alive …

3

Carol opened her eyes slowly, and stretched as she slipped out of bed. After a wonderful night's sleep, it was back to the same morning routine: Putting in her contact lenses, starting the coffee, and getting ready for her daily tennis game. It was a routine that Carol loved, and she smiled as she poured her first cup of coffee. She made herself a bowl of cereal and carried her breakfast into the sunny living room and sat down at her desk. It was time to read Rich's email. She thought that this customary routine would calm her excitement, but her excitement just seemed to grow. Carol noticed that her heart beat a little faster as she entered her password. She reminded herself that she didn't know anything about the man who had sent her a message, so she ought to wait before letting her heart get involved. Still, Carol sipped her coffee and waited as the computer powered up. She smiled as she admitted to herself that she enjoyed savoring the anticipation.

Rich's message was at the top of her inbox. She was relieved to see the message was still there, and she was curious to find out more. Carol took a deep breath and clicked "read."

Hi Carol, My name is Rich. This is my first time to try an online dating service. Your picture caught my eye. I am actually moving to the Atlanta area this week, and I am looking forward to speaking with you. Please call me at 941-879-3646.

I look forward to hearing from you.

Thanks, Rich

As she reread the email, Carol thought she really liked Rich's tone. He seemed honest and confident, and she was happy to learn that he was as new to online dating as she was. Carol took a bite of her cereal and read the message again. There were so many things the email didn't say. Her mind was filled with questions: Where in Atlanta was Rich moving? Had he been married before? What did he do for a living?

She looked at his phone number and sighed. As much as she wanted to speak with Rich, her traditional, Southern upbringing would not allow it. She may have found Rich on the Internet, but that didn't mean that she would be first to call. Rich would have to call her. She would have to let him know.

Looking at her watch, Carol realized she was due at the Atlanta Country Club for her tennis match in 20 minutes. After reading Rich's message once more, she typed a quick response. She thanked Rich for his email and said that she was looking forward to talking with him. She asked when he'd be in Atlanta and what neighborhoods he considered moving into ... She hesitated for a moment, and then she slowly typed her phone number at the end of her message.

Satisfied, she clicked "send" and headed out the door for tennis, hoping that Rich would call her soon.

✦✦✦✦✦✦

Rich looked down through the plane window at the beautiful, green Georgia landscape below him. In the seat next to him, Mark flipped through the pages of a magazine.

"How long until we land?" Rich asked. "Are we almost there?"

"And good morning to you, too," Mark said. "Were you up late last night after I left?"

"Yeah, I guess it was late. After I finished my profile, I wanted to see if they would match me with anyone. There were more than fifteen hundred matches! I began to glance through them, and, well, I – I think I found her." *Did I just really say that?* Rich wondered. "I mean, I think I found *someone*. In Atlanta. Her name's Carol. And she's got this amazing smile and long, honey blonde hair – and her eyes ... Man, if you could see her eyes ... "

"Whoa, Rich, are you serious?" Mark looked at his friend in disbelief. "You already found someone? I can't believe it! I've never even seen you *look* at a woman for more than a few minutes, much less remember her deep blue eyes, or her hair, or her smile. Who are you, and what have you done with my friend Rich?"

Laughing, Rich had to admit Mark's point. To Rich, the whole dating scene had seemed like a pointless charade – he never felt a connection with any of the women they met on these nights out. Truthfully, Rich had been more than a little relieved when Mark finally settled down with Melanie and lost interest in the nightlife.

"It's still me, your friend Rich! I'm fine. Really!" Rich replied. "I just … I don't know, Mark. How did you feel the first time you saw Melanie? I have to say I wasn't really looking expecting to find someone, but when I saw her … I just felt so good, so different. Like I could imagine how great it would be to see her again, maybe even see her every day. I can't explain it, and you might think it sounds crazy, but I just felt at home, and so comfortable the way she looked at me in that photo. I hope I get to meet her soon."

Mark raised an eyebrow. "You do sound a little crazy, but maybe that's okay. You remember the first time I saw Melanie, that I couldn't take my eyes off her. She was different, to me. Hey, Rich, that's great! Maybe my old friend has finally found his match!"

Rich smiled. It felt good to tell Mark how he felt, and he was glad Mark didn't give him too much of a hard time about it. "I sent her an email last night," he confided. "I didn't say much, but I gave her my phone number and I asked her to call me. Do you think she'll call me?"

Mark shrugged and opened his magazine. "I don't know. You're the one trying the online dating! I guess you'll just have to wait and see what happens."

The conversation was interrupted as the pilot announced the final descent into Atlanta. As the plane banked to the left with its engines whining, Rich looked out the window as the quilt squares of tree-lined fields below were replaced by neighborhood streets faced with small homes. The large ribbons of highways drew his eye to clusters of taller buildings. As the plane approached the airport, Rich could see rolling hills dotted with houses, a golf course, and shopping centers with large parking lots. He leaned closer to the window, thinking about his new home. He could see cars on the highways now. Some of the houses had swimming pools and tennis courts. The bare trees of winter made the whole picture look like a miniature, like something not quite real.

But maybe it would be real, Rich thought. Maybe he would find that place he could call home in Atlanta.

And although he couldn't see her ... he knew that somewhere down there, Carol was waiting for him.

◆◆◆◆◆◆

Anxiously, Carol went back to her car to get the rest of her groceries. Here she was, a woman her age waiting by the phone like a teenager hoping her boyfriend would call. She had to admit that it felt good. She picked up the rest of her grocery bags and walked back to the kitchen, humming softly. It was nice to have something to look forward to. As Carol opened the door to the house, she could hear her cell phone ringing.

"It's him!" Carol exclaimed as she set her bags on the kitchen floor and ran to the counter where she'd left her Chanel handbag. "Oh, where *are* you? I can never find anything when I need it ..." Carol rummaged through her purse, following the sound of her ringtone until she found her tiny, pink phone. A quick glance at her caller ID revealed an unfamiliar 941 area code. It had to be him. She flipped the phone open, hoping that he hadn't hung up.

"Hello?"

"Hi – Carol?" The deep voice was cheerful and pleasant. "Carol? This is Rich. Rich Towsley. From Millionaire Match?"

Carol's smile broke into a wide grin. "Yes, Rich, this is Carol. It's so *nice* to speak with you. How *are* you?"

"I'm doing well, thanks. I just got in to Atlanta a few hours ago, and I – well, I have to be honest; the first thing I did was check my email after I got to my hotel. I saw you wrote back with your phone number, and I wanted to talk to you right away – is this a good time?"

"Of course," Carol replied. "I'm so glad you called! So, Rich, what brings you to Atlanta?"

Carol was delighted that talking with Rich felt relaxed, and their conversation flowed easily and naturally. Rich was a businessman, he told her, and he was in Atlanta to start a new enterprise. He was looking for a house, but for now he was staying with a business associate at the Ritz-Carlton in Buckhead. Rich was energetic and positive; right away, she liked his sense of humor and easy laugh. When he asked

Carol a question, she noticed how good it felt that he was genuinely interested in what she had to say. His voice was rich and deep, and Carol found herself wondering what he looked like … Carol already knew she would meet him if Rich would ask her. She couldn't remember the last time she'd had this much fun just talking on the phone. She didn't realize that they'd been talking for over an hour until her stomach growled. Her groceries were still on the counter where she'd left them, and she had forgotten all about her salad. It was past 2:00 in the afternoon, she was really hungry, and she remembered the work for the charity ball that she had to finish that day.

"Rich, I've enjoyed our conversation so much," said Carol. "But, I have some things I really have to finish. I'm so glad we got to talk. Could we can talk again later?"

"How about tomorrow?" Rich asked. "I'd love to meet you. We could have lunch."

"I'd love to meet you, too, but I'm sorry to say that I already have plans for tomorrow. I have church in the morning, and afterwards I'm going to lunch with friends. What about Monday?" Carol suggested hopefully.

"Monday is fine," Rich replied. "Around noon? Since I'm new to Atlanta, would you like to pick the restaurant? We can go anywhere you choose."

Carol smiled with delight. "That sounds wonderful. I'll have fun taking you to one of my favorite restaurants. I'm looking forward to it, Rich."

Rich said he would pick her up, so Carol gave Rich her address and thanked him again for calling. After they said good bye, Carol quickly dialed Sherry's number – she just had to share her exciting news.

"Hi Carol!"

"Hey, Sherry! I'm so excited. You'll never believe who I was talking with on the phone just now …"

Carol told Sherry the important details of her conversation with Rich.

"He is picking you up at your home?" Sherry said surprised.

"Yes," Carol said.

"Why would you not meet him in a public place like you have with your dates in the past? I'm not sure if your decision is a safe one," said Sherry.

"You know Sherry that I have not given anyone

I have dated in the past my home address until I had went out with them at least a few times. I know that this is going to sound strange, Sherry, but I trusted him immediately. I can't explain the overwhelming sense of peace I felt when I was talking to Rich over the phone. His voice was soothing and reassuring."

"Well, when he comes to get you that afternoon for lunch, I would like to be at your house if you don't mind. At least that way, I can see who he is and what he looks like. Sorry, Carol, I am just trying to protect you as my dear friend."

"I appreciate your thoughtfulness and that really means a lot to me," Carol said.

✦✦✦✦✦✦

On Monday morning, Rich glanced at his watch again, and looked at Mark sitting across from him at the dark mahogany table. The room was empty now. Rich had checked his watch at least ten times as the meeting came to a close. The event had gone well, and Rich was glad – he knew he was extremely good at what he did, but that day he felt preoccupied …

Sometimes he lost his train of thought completely. He'd found himself at a loss for words more than once; he'd been glad Mark had been there to get him back on track.

Mark gathered his papers and was ready to leave. Rich just sat there, unaware that he was staring off into the distance. He was thinking about those deep blue eyes, and how much he wanted to look into them. He twirled his pen nervously and took out his phone. Mark cleared his throat. Rich dropped the pen on the table, his trance broken by the sudden noise in a silent room.

"Why don't you just call her?" Mark said. "Tell her you finished early and you wondered if you can come a little sooner. No big deal. You're going to wear out that watch if you keep checking it every ten seconds. You saved her number in your phone, didn't you?"

Rich nodded. "I don't want to be too pushy. It might make her nervous."

Mark rolled his eyes and laughed. "Rich, seriously. Relax! You're killing me. Call her. Please. Just call her!"

Rich opened his phone and scrolled down to

Carol's number. He glanced up at Mark once more, and then pressed *Send*. "It's ringing," Rich said. His mouth felt dry, and he was nervously drumming with his fingers on the table. "It's still ringing. Maybe she's not …"

"Hello?"

"Hi Carol! It's Rich. Listen, my meeting finished up a little ahead of schedule, and I was wondering if I could pick you up a little sooner. Could I pick you up in about half an hour?"

Mark grinned and gave Rich a thumbs-up.

Rich continued, "My business partner, Mark, is with me still, and I think the office where we had the meeting is closer to you than to the hotel. Would you mind if he came along?"

Rich shrugged and sheepishly looked at Mark. Had he really just invited Mark on his date with Carol? He had no idea why, but he was nervous, he supposed. Mark could be there for moral support. Mark sighed as he shook his head. He'd never seen Rich this befuddled before.

"That'll be just fine," replied Carol. Her gentle voice seemed almost musical to Rich's ears. "Of course

you should bring your friend. You can't just leave him
at the hotel alone. And I know the perfect place for us
to have lunch. We'll go to Bone's; it's a very popular
place for a business lunch. You'll love it!"

"That sounds great! We'll head out and pick you
up in about half an hour." Rich closed his phone and
looked at Mark apologetically. "I know, I know. A
grown man bringing his best friend on a date. I must
be a little nervous, okay? Let's go. You can help me find
her house."

◆◆◆◆◆◆

"Wow. Nice neighborhood!" Mark whistled
as they drove into Carol's subdivision. The drive
to Carol's house was their first taste of the Atlanta
scenery. Atlanta was known for its lush landscaping
and elegant homes. Even in winter, it was beautiful.
The stately homes of the Atlanta Country Club were
set back on large lots, with smooth green lawns before
variegated colors of shrubs and trees. They noted the
neatly manicured golf course with gently rolling hills.
"Let's see, we're looking for this street." Mark checked

the directions again. "Take a left here."

"How do I look?" Rich asked. "Do I look okay?"

Rich was wearing a black, button-down shirt and tan wool pants. Instead of a sport coat, he'd chosen a simply well-cut black leather jacket that matched his favorite Gucci loafers. He didn't want to be too dressed up, but now he wondered if he should have worn a suit instead. He nervously ran a hand through his hair.

"You look great," Mark replied. "Now keep an eye out for the house so we don't miss it – look, that's it on the left!"

Rich slowed to see a circular drive in front of a graceful, sunny yellow home with white columns and large, welcoming windows. It was simply grand, framed by a beautifully manicured yard with what looked like 100-year-old maple trees. It was beautiful.

"Is that it? I don't see a house number." Rich said. He shielded his eyes and peered at the beautifully carved, leaded glass front door. "Did you see a number?"

"Yeah, it was on the curb," said Mark. "This has to be it. Go and check. Ring the doorbell – I'll wait here so you can have some privacy."

Rich stepped out of the car and walked to the front entryway of the elegant home. He took a deep breath and rang the bell. A woman called from somewhere in the house, and he heard footsteps approaching. He anxiously waited to see Carol … to hear that welcoming Southern voice … to look into those deep, blue eyes …

As the door swung open, Rich was greeted by a rather plain woman with brown eyes and dark brown hair, piled in a messy knot on her head. She was wearing a pair of faded jeans and an oversized, hooded sweatshirt.

"Oh, excuse me," Rich said. "I must have the wrong house." He turned and looked at the mailbox, but the lid was open, and he couldn't make out the number.

The woman smiled with a twinkle in her eye. "You must be Rich! Honey, you're in the right place! You just come right on in!"

"O … kay … thanks," Rich hesitated, but followed her into the foyer. The setting was incredible, with the dark mahogany chest and sparkling Venetian mirror in the marbled entry hallway. Still, his heart sank. This was not the gorgeous woman with the deep blue eyes who had captured his imagination. *This is what I get for trying online dating,* he thought. *Someone can put up pictures that look nothing like them, and you don't know until you agree to meet them in person ...* Rich smiled politely at the woman, taking in her jeans and sweatshirt ensemble again. *This is how she goes on a date? If she brushed her hair, or put on some lipstick ...*

The woman extended her hand. To Rich's surprise, it was beautifully manicured. "I'm Sherry," she said. "Carol's in the living room, finishing up the guest list for the charity ball. You know, the Circle for Children? She's the co-chairperson."

Relieved, Rich shook her hand with real enthusiasm. "Wonderful to meet you, Sherry. Really — *wonderful.*"

Sherry smiled warmly. Her charming Southern accent sounded very much like Carol's had sounded on the phone. "I'm glad to meet you, too, Rich. You'll have to excuse my attire — I'm painting some cabinets for Carol today, so I'm dressed to spill a little paint. And I probably will!" She laughed apologetically and smoothed the paint-spattered pocket of her sweatshirt. "If you'll wait right here, I'll tell Carol you've arrived."

As Rich waited in the entry, he began to look around. The decoration was elaborate, and beautiful. He could see an expansive formal living room, filled with fine Louis XIV French antiques and several oversized, original oil paintings with custom gold-leaf frames. Over the marble fireplace hung an oil portrait of a stunning young woman with large, deep blue eyes. An ornate Italian, crystal chandelier hung above the center of the room, glinting in the sunlight. The effect was quite regal, even breathtaking.

"Hey, Rich!" That familiar, sweet Southern voice almost startled him.

Rich turned, and there she was. Carol looked exactly as she had looked in the online picture. As she approached he thought of an angel – a creation of grace and beauty. She walked toward him with a graceful step that perfectly matched that beautiful picture. Athletic and petite, she had a delicate smile and an air of sophistication about her that reminded him of Audrey Hepburn. A simple black cashmere dress with puffed sleeves and black patent heels perfectly framed her slim figure and set off her long, blonde hair. Rich remembered Carol's profile listed her age as 49, but he was sure that must be wrong. He would have guessed her to be about 38, or 40 at the most. Carol approached with open arms to give him a welcoming hug, and finally looked into those deep blue eyes. The eyes he hadn't forgotten since leaving Florida. They were all he had imagined. Carol glanced at Sherry, who nodded with obvious approval.

Saying goodbye to Sherry, Rich and Carol proceeded to the car. Mark was in the back seat, on the phone with his wife – he smiled and mouthed a *hello* as Carol slid into the passenger seat. As Carol directed and Rich drove to Bones, they happily chatted about the sunny day and how glad they each were to be going to one of Carol's favorite restaurants. They seemed more like comfortable and warm old friends rather than new acquaintances on a first date. The spark between them was obvious to Mark. When they pulled up to the entrance of Bone's, Rich gallantly opened the door for Carol before handing his keys to the valet.

"What a gentleman," said Carol. "Thank you. I hope you like Bone's. I think they have some of the best steaks in Atlanta."

As they entered the restaurant, the host greeted Carol by name and asked her if she would like her usual table. Rich was impressed – Bone's seemed like a very upscale restaurant, and she appeared to be a preferred customer. Rich elbowed Mark, who nodded at him and smiled as they followed Carol and the Maitre'D to an intimate table at the back of the restaurant. The dining room was abuzz with impeccably dressed men and women having lunch and discussing business. Soft lighting on richly paneled walls and Sinatra's melody in the background made a pleasant, relaxed atmosphere. Rich stepped in before the host, pulled out Carol's chair, and she appreciatively took her seat. The host placed Carol's napkin in her lap as Rich and Mark sat down on either side of her.

The three chatted as they began to examine the extensive menu. "Do you see something you like, Rich?" asked Carol. "Mark? What about you? The porterhouse is wonderful here."

"Steak does sound good," Rich replied. "I think I'll start with the French onion soup and have the filet with a baked potato."

"I think I'll have the same," said Mark. "But I'll have a salad instead of the soup."

The server came to take their orders. Carol thought it was a bit unusual when Rich ordered his filet butterflied and very well done. Unbeknownst to Carol, if it was the least bit rare, it somewhat reminded him of blood. Rich had seen his share of blood in his past; a past life that he was trying to forget. Rich and Mark began to tell Carol about their new network marketing venture in Atlanta. Rich was pleasantly surprised at how easily he could talk to Carol about anything – he felt like he could truly be himself, and he enjoyed her conversation. He noticed that Mark wasn't saying much, but that wasn't unusual – Mark had always been the less outgoing of the two.

Their first course arrived, and it made Rich smile with curiosity when the server brought Carol a small dish of ketchup with her house salad. She proceeded to dip her lettuce, carrots, and cucumbers in the ketchup before taking each delicate bite. He tasted his soup – Bone's was famous for its French onion soup, and it was quite delicious.

"Oh, this is fantastic!" Rich exclaimed. "Carol, have you tried this? It's the best I've ever had. Here, you've really gotta try this." Rich dipped his spoon into the bowl, then held it out to Carol. "Really, try it. It's great."

"I'd love to try it, Rich." Carol leaned over, holding back her hair to sip the warm soup from his spoon. "Ooh, that is wonderful. Thank you for sharing."

Carol happily turned back to dip another carrot in the ketchup. Southern traditions are just that – traditions; often passed on from grandparents or parents. In regards to Carol's preferential treatment of ketchup – it was Daddy who passed down the torch. As a young girl, Carol watched Daddy periodically make himself a ketchup sandwich. Though the sandwich choices were abundant in the Williams' home, it was the choice of champions. Carol, often sampling Daddy's delicacy, became accustomed to the taste. By the time she was a teenager, it was her condiment of choice also.

Across the table, Mark dropped his fork and

stared at Rich in utter disbelief. Rich just looked at him and shrugged. What had come over him? They both knew that Rich didn't share his food with anyone: not a dessert or a sip of a drink. Now he had just offered a spoonful of his soup to a woman he had just met. Carol thought this was just a kind gesture, sharing something especially good; but to Rich and Mark, it revealed something more.

The main course was served, and they all enjoyed their selections. Mark was silent during the rest of the meal, but Rich and Carol had so much to talk about that they hardly noticed. By the time they drove back to Carol's house, Rich and Carol gave the impression they had almost forgotten he was with them. Carol was satisfied by the good meal and the engaging conversation, as Rich joked and laughed with her. When they arrived at Carol's house, Mark muttered a quick goodbye and declined Carol's invitation to come inside.

"I'll be right back," Rich said over his shoulder to Mark. "I'm just going to walk Carol to the door."

"Fine." Mark stated, looking in the other direction.

Feeling nervous again, Rich came around the car

to open Carol's door. They were almost timid as they slowly walked between the large planters before the front door. Rich had to admit to himself that he really wanted to kiss her. He hoped she felt the same way.

Carol didn't pause, but quickly opened the front door, and Rich could see Sherry in the living room – she waved cheerfully to Rich, and gave Carol a playful wink before she retreated back to the kitchen. Carol turned to Rich. "Rich, this was a lovely lunch – thank you so much for a wonderful time," said Carol. She was playing nervously with a strand of her blonde hair. She looked like a teenager, Rich thought.

"I had a great time, too, Carol. Thank you. It was so great to meet you. And, I'm sorry about bringing Mark at the last minute like I did." Rich looked over his shoulder toward the car; he saw that Mark was already back in the front passenger seat.

"Oh, bless your heart – it was very nice to meet your friend. It was probably easier to have someone you knew come along since you are in a new town and we had never met in person. I understand… sometimes – it helps to have someone there to break the ice." Carol smiled at him with genuine understanding.

"Thanks, Carol. Well, I better get going. Can I call you? We could go out again sometime, if you'd like. Maybe without Mark?"

"That would be very nice," said Carol, with a shy smile.

Rich took a deep breath. "So, I'll talk to you soon."

He leaned down to kiss her, but she was already reaching up to give him a friendly hug. His kiss landed on her cheek, but her hug was warm and inviting. "Well, bye for now, Carol."

"Bye, Rich. Call me." Carol smiled as she closed the door.

Rich sighed. As he walked back to the car, he knew that he was in store for some serious teasing. Mark was already shaking his head as Rich got into the driver's seat.

"*'Here! Try a bite of my soup! No, really! It's delicious!'* Are you kidding? You actually used your own spoon to give her a bite of your food. Rich Towsley, who keeps everything to himself, shared his food with a complete stranger. Unbelievable!" Mark had a teasing look on his face, but there was a hint of anger in his voice. "I've been your best friend for 25 years, but I would never even ask for so much as a bite of your sandwich or a sip of your Coke. Here you are insisting that she eat from your spoon! I just don't understand you sometimes!"

"I don't know, Mark. She's different," said Rich simply. "I don't know what came over me. She's just ... she makes me feel so different. I've never met anyone like Carol before."

"Oh, and that makes me what? Chopped liver?" the anger in Mark's voice was obvious, but Rich didn't notice. "You know, man, just forget it."

"Did you notice how everyone at Bone's knew Carol's name?" Rich said to himself. Mark was no longer listening. "Did you see how polite she was? You know, she wouldn't even call me the first time; she's got such good, old-fashioned, southern manners. What did you think of that sweet accent? I could just sit and listen to her talk all day long, about almost anything. Just to hear that voice ..."

Mark rolled his eyes as he stared out the window, but his back was all Rich could see. Rich couldn't see the sneer on his face.

"I'm definitely taking her out again ... for a nice dinner, this time ... in the evening, where we can spend some time alone, just the two of us." Rich fumbled with his jacket pocket, steering carefully with one hand, searching for his cell phone. "Right now, I just want to talk to her for a minute, again."

"Are you nuts? You just left her house ten minutes ago!" Mark looked at Rich with amazement. "You can't call yet; you have to wait. If you call before tomorrow, you'll look too desperate, too eager ... Call her in a few days, get your head clear, and ..."

But Rich had already pressed *Send*. Before he had pulled into the parking lot of the Ritz-Carlton, he had a date with Carol on Saturday night.

Rich spent the rest of the evening reviewing paperwork for the next day's meetings. He even went down to the hotel's fitness room and spent a half hour on the elliptical machine. He wasn't sure if he was hoping a little exercise would help him focus, or if he suddenly wanted to be in better shape. But nothing worked ... his mind kept drifting off to her smile, that infectious laugh, and those deep blue eyes. For the first time in his life, Rich couldn't stop thinking about a woman… it was crazy, he thought. It felt so good to think about being with her again. Mark had a point – Rich knew that in the past he would never think of letting himself get attached to someone, never let anybody in. It would just be too complicated, too difficult. Somehow, when he thought of Carol, he just didn't care about all that so much any more. He couldn't explain it, even to himself, but he knew he just had to see her, to be with her again.

4

It was early Saturday evening. Carol sat anxiously on her sofa, waiting for her second date with the tall, dark, and handsome man from Millionaire Match. It was amazing, she thought – she'd only been on one date with Rich, but she hadn't stopped thinking about him since their lunch at Bone's. Where had this man been hiding? He was handsome and worldly, articulate and charming … she'd never enjoyed a date that much. It was refreshing to be with someone so happy, social, and upbeat.

Carol smiled at the thought of Rich. He'd been so attentive, too, opening doors and pulling out her chair for her before she sat down. And he'd been interested – genuinely interested – in what she'd had to say. After more than one awkward first date, Carol had been

delighted that she felt comfortable enough with Rich
to just be herself. It was like they'd known each other
for several years instead of just a few hours, and she
couldn't wait to see him again.

Carol looked at her watch and sighed. It was 7:00;
Rich was picking her up at 7:30. She'd been ready for an
hour; after a morning of tennis at the Atlanta Country
Club, Carol had returned home and spent the rest of
the afternoon carefully selecting the perfect ensemble
for her night out – she'd been looking forward to the
evening for days, and she wanted to make sure that
she looked perfect. And she'd succeeded: Dressed in a
long, crushed-velvet Ralph Lauren skirt and matching
winter-white cashmere sweater, Carol was a vision of
exquisite beauty. She wore knee-high Ralph Lauren
boots in rich, brown leather, and she'd selected a simple
gold-and-diamond necklace with matching diamond
earrings.

She checked her watch again. 7:05.

The phone rang and Carol jumped. Maybe Rich
would be early again, she thought as she hurried to the
kitchen to answer. Her heart beat a little faster at the
thought of speaking to him again. Being on time was

very important to Rich, that much she knew. She was glad he was so conscientious about being prompt. This was one habit Rich had that Carol really appreciated.

"Hello?" Carol hoped she didn't sound as nervous as she felt.

"Hi there Carol, it's Rich." There was something strange about his voice, Carol thought. He sounded flat and a little tired.

"Hey Rich," Carol said, concerned. "Is everything okay? Do you need directions or anything?"

"Well, I think I'm coming down with a cold," Rich said, sniffling. "Is there a pharmacy near your home?"

"Oh, I am so sorry," Carol replied. "Yes, there is a CVS pharmacy actually down the street from my home, on Johnson Ferry Road. You should pick up some sinus cold plus non-drowsy and some vitamin C, too." Growing up in a medical family, doing this was second nature to Carol. "Are you sure you still want to go out tonight, Rich? I'd understand if you wanted to stay in and rest."

"Are you kidding me?" Rich said. "I've been looking forward to this all week. Wouldn't miss it! I'm just going to swing by and get some medicine before I pick you up. I might be a few minutes late, but I'm looking forward to seeing you."

"Me too, Rich," replied Carol. "Take your time, and drive carefully. I'll see you when you get here."

Carol hung up the phone, relieved that Rich hadn't canceled their date. It was unfortunate that he wasn't feeling well, but she was thrilled that he still wanted to see her, even if he was a bit under the weather. Carol dug a tube of lipstick out of her purse and stepped into her powder room to do a quick touch-up. She smiled as she gazed at her reflection – the woman in the mirror looked radiant; happy … she looked, Carol thought, like a woman in love.

The doorbell rang at 7:40. Carol suppressed an excited giggle as she opened the door to greet her date. As Rich stepped into the foyer, the inviting scent of his cologne wafted past Carol, beckoning her to come closer to him. It was nice, she thought, inhaling deeply. She looked at Rich, her blue eyes taking in every detail of his sport coat and beautifully cut wool trousers … their eyes met, and they embraced.

Carol closed her eyes, leaning close to take in the heady scent of Rich's cologne one more time.

They stood that way for a moment; holding each other as if they were long-lost lovers reunited, rather than two virtual strangers who'd known each other for a few days.

"Sorry I'm late – you look fantastic," Rich said as he stepped back to admire Carol's winter white ensemble. "I found the pharmacy and I got some medicine. I'll be feeling like a million bucks in no time. Shall we?" Rich sniffled again, but he seemed confident and in high spirits as he helped Carol put on her cream-colored fur jacket. He opened the car door for her, and they headed off to their second date.

"I'll bet you miss your cars," Carol said, looking around the interior of Rich's car. "I mean, this car is nice, especially for a rental, but you probably have some really wonderful cars back in Florida." Carol paused and smiled shyly. "I read on your profile that you have a car collection. My daddy's always loved cars, too – how long have you been collecting, Rich?"

"I'm sorry?" Rich paused, and a strange look crossed his face; a moment later it was gone. "Oh, my cars – right. Sorry, I think, uh – I think this cold's got my ears plugged up," he stammered. The cars ... He'd been so caught up in his new romance with Carol that he'd forgotten about the 11 cars he didn't have; the 11 cars that were posted on his Millionaire Match profile. Too late now, he thought. What would she think of him if he told her the truth? "Yeah, they're, uh – they're pretty great. It's an expensive hobby, though. I'm thinking of giving it up. It's funny, I hardly drive them. It's almost like I forget I have them sometimes, you know?"

"I understand," Carol replied, nodding earnestly. "One or two is plenty, I think. Which one is your favorite?"

"Oh, well … you know, it's hard to pick just one. They're all classics – beautiful." Rich shrugged casually, but on the inside, he was racking his brain to come up with a new topic of conversation. "But, come on, let's hear about you – I'm sure you don't want to hear a bunch of car talk, right?" They stopped at a red light, and Rich gazed at Carol sitting next to him in the darkness. His eyes took in every inch of her before coming to rest on her wide blue eyes. "So, tell me more about this place we're going tonight. What's it called again?"

"It's called Pastis," said Carol. "Oh, you'll just love it, Rich – it's in Roswell, that's just another suburb about 15 minutes from here, and it's just the quaintest little area. It's where all the antique stores and little boutiques are located. And Pastis is an elegant French restaurant – it's very charming and intimate."

"Sounds great," Rich said. "Your choice of Bone's the other day was perfect, so I trust your judgment."

Carol smiled at him, her red lips parting to reveal a row of perfectly-shaped teeth. "Thank you, Rich. I appreciate that." She motioned to the left. "You'll just want to make a left here on Canton Street – that's the turn for Roswell."

✦✦✦✦✦✦

As they entered Pastis, Rich looked around appreciatively. Carol had very good taste and was obviously accustomed to the finer things in life, he thought, as he took in the sights and sounds around him. It was getting crowded – diners circled the restaurant's first-floor bar, talking softly and sipping glasses of wine. A piano played softly in the background, adding a touch of romance to the candlelit dining room. Carol had reserved a table in the upstairs dining room, and they followed the hostess up the antique, wooden stairway.

Rich watched as Carol walked gracefully up the stairs, her legs and hips moving enticingly beneath her skirt. This was a woman who put a lot of effort into her appearance, he thought, taking another appreciative look at her legs, thin and toned from her tennis games and daily walks. Rich nearly tripped over a step – he was mesmerized by her looks … the rest of the world had slipped away.

He'd never felt that way about a woman, not for a very long time. He knew then that he wanted her. It was that simple.

Rich collected his thoughts and followed Carol to their table. She ordered a glass of white wine, and Rich ordered a beer – he wasn't much of a drinker. In fact, he almost never touched alcohol. But tonight felt special; he raised his glass to Carol's and smiled at her warmly, his brown eyes sparkling in the candlelight.

"To our first real date alone, without Mark," said Rich, as they clinked glasses. Carol giggled at the toast and took a sip of her wine – she looked happy and beautiful. Rich tried to concentrate as their server listed the night's specials, but he found himself staring at Carol's full lips and perfectly manicured hands… and, of course, those eyes. Somehow, Rich managed to compose himself enough to order – though he couldn't remember what he'd ordered until a perfectly cooked filet mignon appeared in front of him. Across the table, Carol took a bite of her salmon.

Rich sniffled again. His head was pounding. But he didn't care. All he wanted was her. They talked easily during dinner. He learned that Carol had two grown daughters, each pursuing their dreams in different parts of the world; and a sister living in Albany, Georgia, who was married to an orthopedic surgeon. Rich listened as she talked about her family with pride and admiration … and he was genuinely interested in regards to the girls' schooling.

"Well we were careful in choosing a school for the girls. Education has always been an important matter to us," Carol said. "We finally settled on Holy Innocents. I wanted to be involved with their education and daily routine. Being in the fortunate position of not having to work, I was able to dedicate quite a bit of my time to helping out at the school."

"I initially started out as a part-time room mother and worked my way up the ladder volunteering as a Vice-president and eventually the President of the Parents' Association. I would like to think that I did my part in helping Holy Innocents' continue being a dominant private educational institution."

They talked about his plans to buy a home in the area, and Carol said that she'd be happy to recommend to him the best Atlanta neighborhoods. "So what made you choose Atlanta?" Carol asked. "Well, I knew that I would need to be in Atlanta for at least a year, the reason being that I had numerous friendships and connections in the Atlanta area from network marketing in the past and it was a practical place to start."

"In addition, being close to the busiest airport in the country allows for convenient access to most airports anywhere in the world." (There was personal business in Atlanta that needed to be attended to as well.)

"I found a home near a very good friend of mine

that would certainly serve its purpose, unfortunately during the inspection process, they found a hole in the roof that had allowed water to enter over a long period of time so I think I am going to get my earnest money back and will need to look elsewhere."

Rich sneezed; his eyes were watering, and his throat felt like it was on fire. He could hardly taste his steak. He sneezed again and looked sheepishly around at the other diners, talking quietly at small tables. Discreetly, he rummaged in his jacket pocket for a tissue. Carol looked at him with genuine concern in her blue eyes.

"Rich, are you feeling bad? You just look miserable, poor thing," Carol touched his hand sympathetically.

"I sound worse than I feel," Rich replied. "But, to tell you the truth, I feel pretty awful."

"Well, let's go, then. We can go to my house -- you can come in and sit for a while, if you'd like. I can make some coffee." Carol said.

Rich nodded. "I'd like that."

After Rich paid the check, they started toward the staircase. Rich followed Carol down, hoping for another chance to admire her shapely legs. Halfway down the stairs, Carol froze – she stopped so suddenly that Rich almost bumped into her.

"You okay?" Rich looked over the staircase. Below them, the restaurant was packed with people. The earlier group at the bar had tripled in size, crowding Pastis' small dining room. The Saturday night crowd had arrived in droves, and there were people everywhere, laughing and talking, sipping drinks and dancing. The soft piano music had been replaced by a live band … the loud music combined with the noise of the crowd made it virtually impossible to hear anything. Rich noticed a waitress with a tray of drinks fighting her way through the masses.

Carol looked at the scene below and turned to Rich. It was obvious: she was scared. At a petite 5'4", Carol was intimidated by the large group. Without a word, Carol took Rich's hand. Rich wrapped his arm protectively around her waist and led her through the bar crowd, which parted easily at the sight of his muscular frame. Carol squeezed Rich's hand, and they moved through the room and out the door. Outside, the sky was clear and cloudless, the night sky lit up with stars. Carol shivered. She didn't let go of Rich's hand.

"Thank you, Rich. I've never liked crowds, and it was so loud in there," Carol said as they walked back to the car. "I'm sorry about that – I don't usually go to Pastis on Saturday night; I didn't think they'd be that busy. And with you having a cold and all, I just hope you had a good time, Rich."

"Don't apologize," said Rich gently. "It's not your fault. And I had a great time."

Rich explained to Carol how he had gotten into the network marketing industry. "I thought that the business model was both practical and ingenious." For a couple of hundred dollars down and about a hundred dollars per month, a person could share the opportunity and product or services that a company had to offer with anyone in America. The business also allowed you to not only get paid on anyone that you brought into the business, but to also get paid on the people that they too brought into the business.

On the drive back to Carol's house, they talked more about their likes and dislikes, their passions and hobbies. They discovered that they both liked asparagus, and neither of them cared much for sushi. Rich wouldn't touch tomatoes, but Carol loved them.

She confessed that she loved ketchup and put it on absolutely everything. Rich laughed and teased her good-naturedly. Much to Rich's relief, Carol seemed to have forgotten about his car collection. Carol told Rich about the Atlanta Country Club and her tennis games, and Rich talked about his life in Sarasota. His cold was getting worse, but he tried to hide his symptoms, sniffling softly and discreetly wiping his nose with a tissue when Carol wasn't looking. As they pulled into Carol's driveway, she took his hand again and smiled brightly.

"Come on in, Rich," she said. "I'll put some coffee on and then I'll give you the grand tour of my house."

"Sounds great," Rich replied, sniffling again.

◆◆◆◆◆◆

The rest of Carol's home was as lavish as her living room. Rich had never seen anything like it, except in magazines or on television. There were beautiful bouquets of fresh flowers everywhere and each room was decorated with the finest furniture money could buy. Carol shyly led Rich from room to room, pointing out some of her favorite pieces, like the imported Italian chandelier in the kitchen to the hand-carved table and chairs in the dining room. Carol was proud of her home, and with good reason. She'd decorated the home herself, painstakingly choosing each piece of furniture and every light fixture … it was a project she was passionate about, and her enthusiasm was obvious.

Carol's demeanor changed as they approached the bedroom – her bedroom. Rich stood in the doorway and admired the room … it reminded him of a palace. The room was dominated by a large, hand-carved, four-poster bed. The satin sheets were a deep, rich aquamarine color trimmed in gold, and her pillows were embroidered with the letter C. A grand window faced the bed, accented with imported draperies. The walls had been faux finished by a local Atlanta artist; they had a stucco texture and were washed in a soft golden hue.

"Wow," Rich said appreciatively. "Really – Carol, this is beautiful. You've done an amazing job here; the whole house, it … it looks like it's fit for a queen."

"Well, thank you, Rich," Carol said, smiling. "I've always loved decorating – you should have seen this

house when we first bought it, years ago. It was so plain.
Everything was beige; the walls, the kitchen, the tiles
in the bathroom. So ordinary. I didn't want this house
to be ordinary. Of course, I never thought that I'd be
in this house this long, we always talked about moving,
you know, but …"

Carol trailed off and looked at the floor. Being in
the bedroom with a man – a new man – had flooded
her with memories. She knew that, to Rich, the
bedroom was simply that: a bedroom. But to Carol, the
bedroom represented a place of disappointment, a place
where her desires had never been fulfilled… in her 25
years of married life, she'd spent many nights weeping in
that bed, wondering why her life as a wife was so lonely.
To Carol, the bedroom wasn't a haven of retreat and
solace; it was a painful reminder of her lonely, loveless
marriage. She felt tears start to well up in her eyes, but
she blinked them back and put on a brave face before
looking at Rich again.

"So, that's it. My house … I think the coffee's
ready." She took a deep breath and smiled. "Would you
like to go sit in the living room, Rich?"

"That would be nice," Rich replied. He followed

Carol to the living room and sat down on the couch while she got the coffee ready. Rich looked down and noticed a crystal bowl of M & M's on the table. They were pink and white. He picked one up and studied it more closely. Each of the candies was customized – some said "I love you, Mom", and some said simply "Carol."

Rich looked up as Carol set a hot mug of coffee in front of him. "These are nice M & M's," he said, popping one into his mouth. "I've never seen them customized like that."

"Aren't they precious? They're from my daughter, Malinda, for Valentine's Day." Carol took a seat next to Rich on the sofa. She smiled as she looked at the bowl of candy. "She lives in New York City."

Carol and Rich sat on the couch until almost 2 A.M., just talking. Finally, after he realized how late it was, Rich stood to go.

"Thank you for a lovely evening, Carol," said Rich. "I know you probably have plans tomorrow, so I should go and let you get some rest."

Carol stood up and took his hand. "Thank you, Rich. I had a wonderful time."

Rich couldn't hold back any longer; he'd contained himself too long. He pulled Carol close to him and kissed her. Carol, he noticed, didn't resist.

They walked slowly to the door, and kissed again. He gently bit her lip and held on as if he didn't want to let her go.

"Rich? I was wondering about something. I usually wouldn't ask something like this, but ..." Carol hesitated, looking slightly flustered. "Would you like to come to church with me tomorrow? I'd love it if you did."

"Of course," Rich replied, without missing a beat. "That would be lovely. What time should I pick you up?"

"I'll pick you up," said Carol. "I know you don't know your way around that well yet, and Buckhead Church isn't very far from your hotel. How's 10:30 sound?"

"Perfect. I'll see you then, Carol." Rich smiled and they kissed one more time before Carol shut the door.

Carol sighed as she watched Rich walk to his car. Two in the morning, she thought. I can't believe it – we're like teenagers. Carol thought about that kiss on the couch ... how much she'd enjoyed being close to Rich, being in his arms.

She walked to the bathroom and proceeded with her usual bedtime routine, washing her face and brushing her hair. She thought again of how he'd walked her through the crowd at Pastis ... she'd felt so safe with him, like nothing could hurt her. And, she thought with a grin, he'd agreed to go to church with her. As Carol drifted off to sleep, she thanked God for the new man in her life; she'd waited so long to meet someone like Rich – someone happy, intelligent, and confident.

✦✦✦✦✦✦

As Rich drove to his hotel, he was flooded with a mixture of emotions: he was thrilled that he'd found Carol, and he replayed their kiss over and over again with delight. He wanted her, that much was clear ... he wanted her in a way he'd never wanted a woman. Other women were just that to Rich, just people. Rich's heart was closed off when it came to allowing any intimate emotion involving women. In some cases an intimate relationship was simply a liability. Opening up and letting someone in would not be an easy task. It would take an incredible woman to not only gain access, but to penetrate Rich's heart. And, he'd even agreed to go to church with her – he'd never expected to set foot in a church again, not ever...

But he would, for Carol. The way she looked at him; those blue eyes gazing at him with such trust ...

Trust. Rich thought of how he'd led her through the crowd earlier that night, guiding her to the door of Pastis. She'd appreciated that so much, he thought with a touch of amusement. To him, it was nothing. If she only knew, Rich thought as he guided the car onto the highway. For 25 years, Rich had made a living with some of the most ruthless, most secretive, most powerful men in the country ...

Rich sighed. He'd left that life behind, for the most part. But it wasn't as simple as that ... you didn't just leave a life like that; no matter how hard you tried. It was always there, haunting his thoughts. He didn't want to lie to Carol. He didn't want to hurt her ... his life was complicated; that's why he'd never let anybody in. But, he couldn't change the past, no matter how much he wanted to.

5

Rich leaned close to the mirror, giving his face a thorough once-over to see if he'd missed a spot shaving. Carol would be arriving at the hotel in 20 minutes, and he wanted to make sure he looked presentable. He ran a palm over his cheek and felt a rough patch on his jaw line.

He dabbed some shaving gel on the spot, picked up his razor, and quickly set it down again. His hand was shaking a little. Rich took a deep breath and sat down on the edge of the tub. He was rattled, but this time his feelings went beyond a simple case of first-date jitters … he had never been comfortable with religion or prayer, and the thought of attending a church service had set him on edge. After all, churches represented love and forgiveness, morals and integrity: for most of his life, Rich had lived on the edges of these values, balanced precariously on the line between right and wrong. He hadn't been raised in the church; he'd never been a believer ... he'd never wanted to believe.

If there really was a God, he reasoned, and if there really was a heaven, then there was probably a hell, too ...

Rich shuddered. He stepped up to the sink again and carefully picked up his razor. Slowly and deliberately, he drew the blade across his face. He studied his dark eyes in the mirror, wondering if they betrayed any of his secrets – the things he'd seen, the things he'd done. At the time, those things had just seemed like a normal part of life; a part of his chosen career path. But, to someone like Carol, someone from a loving Southern home, someone who had been raised with good Christian values ...

To many people, Rich knew, his past wouldn't seem so normal.

But, Rich had agreed to go to church, and he was going to keep his word. And, since Mark had gone back to Florida to visit Melanie over the weekend, Rich had the entire day to himself. He wanted to spend it with

Carol, even if it meant going to church.

Rich turned to the closet and selected a pair of black wool trousers and a teal-colored, button-down shirt. He slipped into a pair of black Italian loafers and gave himself a final look: He had no idea what he was supposed to wear, but he guessed that he couldn't go wrong with business casual. As a final touch, he sprayed on a little cologne. Carol had mentioned that she liked the scent. Satisfied, he shrugged into his leather coat and headed downstairs to wait for Carol in the lobby.

As he rode the elevator down, Rich's thoughts turned to Carol. In all of his worry about church, he'd forgotten how excited he was to see her again. He smiled at the thought. He'd said good night to her – he checked his watch – only about eight hours ago, but it seemed like a lifetime had passed since he'd seen her and looked into her eyes.

The doors slid open, and Rich walked through the Ritz's lobby and out to the parking lot. Carol was already waiting for him, waving happily at him from her Range Rover. As Rich slid into the seat next to her, she smiled brightly at him.

"Hi, Rich – you smell wonderful," Carol said as she

started the car. "And you look very handsome, too. So, are you ready? I think you're going to enjoy Buckhead Church. Andy Stanley always gives me something good to think about, something that really applies to my life today. It's so upbeat and positive. I just love it!"

"I'm ready," said Rich. He smiled weakly. "I've been looking forward to this all morning. You look beautiful, by the way." He hesitated for a moment, and then reached over and put his hand on her knee as she pulled away from the hotel.

"Thank you, Rich," replied Carol. And, she did look beautiful: She was wearing another of her favorite Ralph Lauren skirts; an understated brown and cream wool plaid. She'd chosen a cream-colored, cashmere turtleneck that emphasized her long, graceful neck; and she wore a cropped, suede jacket in a soft, rich brown.

She chatted happily for the rest of the drive, talking about the church and last Sunday's sermon. Rich felt a knot in his stomach. As it turned out, Buckhead Church was only a five-minute drive from the Ritz-Carlton. As they got closer to their destination, Rich was surprised to see throngs of people walking toward the huge, steel-and-glass building.

Rising elegantly above the city sidewalk, Buckhead Church didn't look like any church he'd ever seen before. Rich had always thought of churches as musty old buildings with steeples and whitewashed walls; he'd imagined an old-fashioned Southern chapel filled with old-fashioned women in big, frilly hats. But Buckhead Church was sleek, modern. From the outside, it could be an art museum or an avant-garde office building. And, the people who filed past the car were from every walk of life: College kids and middle-aged couples, some black, some white, a few older people and lots of families. It was a diverse crowd; and, for the most part, they were also well-dressed.

"There it is," Carol said, pointing to the massive building as she turned into the parking lot. "Buckhead Church. It's nice, isn't it? It's really modern and contemporary."

"Yeah, it sure is," said Rich. "It's not what I expected."

Carol smiled. "Wait until you hear the service. It's so enthusiastic and practical; they talk about things that you can really use in your life. Now, my Daddy, I took him here a few months ago, and it was a little too contemporary for him. He likes the more traditional sermon. But I just think this is so inspiring. Come on, I can't wait for you to see the inside."

Rich swallowed hard and tried not to notice his hands shaking as he unbuckled his seat belt. Carol had already stepped out of the car and was waiting for him. He took a deep breath and put on his best smile, hoping that she wouldn't notice a change in his demeanor. Carol smiled again and took Rich's hand. He felt his heart speed up, and despite the cold February wind, he could feel beads of sweat forming on his brow.

Buckhead Church was even bigger up close. The building seemed to tower above them, Rich thought. He felt Carol tug his hand; she was as happy and excited as a little girl. They stepped into the building, and Rich was awestruck.

The church's entrance opened to a wide, curved hallway, three stories high and filled with sunlight. All around them, groups of people talked and laughed. There were volunteers at every doorway, mostly college students, and each one greeted Rich and Carol warmly and offered them programs for the morning's service. Everyone seemed happy and welcoming. Rich felt some of his tension slip away. He was too overwhelmed to feel uncomfortable.

"Amazing," he said, taking in the view of the vaulted ceiling. "Just amazing!"

"I knew you'd love it," Carol said, squeezing his hand. "Let's go find a seat before everyone goes in – I like to sit up close to the front where you can get a really good view." She led Rich through a set of double doors.

"Yeah, that's perfect," said Rich. Perfect, he thought. He already felt like an outsider, and he'd been secretly hoping to sit in the back where nobody would notice him. "Lead the way," he said.

The main auditorium of Buckhead Church was as vast as the rest of the building. Rich thought it looked more like the sort of place you'd go to see a rock band than a place you'd go to hear a sermon. In the center of the auditorium was a large stage, complete with two large screens and professional-looking sound and lighting equipment. As they walked to Carol's favorite seats, Rich looked up at the thousands of seats that surrounded the stage. This was not church as he remembered it, he thought. As they sat down, Rich noticed that to their right, a cameraman sat on a raised platform, checking out his equipment. He said something into the tiny headset he was wearing and nodded before turning a few knobs and peering through his lens.

This was definitely not what Rich remembered.

Carol flipped through her program, oblivious to Rich's amazement. "Oh, that's great! Jeff Henderson is the pastor today! I'm glad you'll get to hear him, Rich – he's so inspiring."

"Great," said Rich absently. He was still looking around the church in wonder.

"So, is this anything like your church in Florida, Rich?" Carol asked. "Or did you go to a more traditional church?"

"Hmm?" Rich snapped out of his daze and looked at Carol. She was smiling at him, waiting for an answer. He felt the panic come back, twisting through his stomach. He felt his palms go clammy as he searched for an appropriate response to Carol's question. He'd forgotten that he'd told her that he was a churchgoer. "Well, you know ... I went to a few churches in Sarasota, but ... I, uh – I never really found the right –"

Suddenly, the lights dimmed and Rich's words

were drowned out by the sound of an electric guitar. "It's starting," whispered Carol. She stood up to get a better view of the band. Following her lead, Rich stood, too. He breathed a sigh of relief … he hated lying to Carol, and the music had stopped him from getting tangled in another half-truth, like his car collection. He looked at Carol, but she was looking at the band, swaying gently to the music and singing along. She knew every word to the song the band was playing … and Rich could tell that she believed deeply in every note she sang. And, though she sang softly, he could tell that she had a lovely voice.

After the band finished, Jeff Henderson came out to greet the crowd. Like everything else at Buckhead Church, the energetic, middle-aged pastor wasn't what Rich had imagined. He was dressed casually in jeans and a button-down shirt, and he seemed friendly and down-to-earth. The sermon for the day, according to the program, was about leaving a legacy. Rich watched as Pastor Henderson walked to the center of the stage and smiled at the crowd.

"So, how many of you out there know the purpose of your life?" the pastor asked. He spoke in a casual, cheerful tone, as if he was just talking to a few friends instead of a crowd of thousands. Rich looked around the auditorium; every eye in the room was fixed on the stage.

"Do you know?" Pastor Henderson crossed the stage and addressed a young woman in the front row. She smiled shyly, and the pastor pointed to a middle-aged man a few rows back. "Or you? In the black sweater?" Rich was amazed at how easygoing and confident the pastor seemed, joking and laughing with his congregation. He smiled broadly and sighed theatrically.

"Well, I suppose nobody's going to say if I put them on the spot," he continued. The girl in the front row giggled. "But that's what we're going to talk about today: Why we're here, and what we're going to leave behind. Now, I believe that our life on this Earth is simply a dress rehearsal for our eternal life in heaven – but our life on Earth still matters. The things we leave behind for future generations. The things we accomplish. The good we can do in our short time here ..."

Rich watched as Carol nodded her head earnestly.

As much as he was in unfamiliar territory, Carol was obviously in her element: She had a look of calm assurance as she prayed, and she listened intently to Pastor Henderson's message. Even as a hardened nonbeliever, Rich found it hard not to be moved by this beautiful woman's obvious devotion. He looked around the room at the crowd of dedicated Christians who truly believed in God and, although Rich didn't believe in any of it himself, he felt that he understood how comforting those beliefs could be. He smiled as he looked at Carol, and his thoughts turned to his own legacy ... to a past filled with secrets; a past he guarded carefully.

A past he could never share.

✦✦✦✦✦✦

After the service was over, Carol suggested lunch at her favorite after-church eatery, Jason's Deli. It was just a short drive, she told Rich, and she had skipped breakfast this morning, something she never did. She was starving. As they made their way to the restaurant, Carol, ever the gracious host, pointed out some of the more interesting buildings and landmarks in Buckhead. Rich enjoyed the drive; it was nice to see more of the city, and he felt much more relaxed now that church was over.

Carol eased her Range Rover into a parking space. "Here we are," she said brightly. "Jason's Deli. Ooh, it's crowded! I hope we can get a table."

Rich hesitated as they walked toward the door of the restaurant. Carol was right: it was crowded. Large groups of well-dressed families gathered around tables they'd pushed together; the line at the counter stretched almost to the door. The restaurant buzzed with conversation and laughter. This was the church crowd, Rich thought as he looked around the dining room. They took their place at the end of the line. Carol passed Rich a menu.

"So, Rich, how long are you going to stay at the Ritz?" Carol asked. "I mean, it's a lovely hotel, but I'm sure you're looking forward to finding a new home here in Atlanta."

"Well, I'm not sure," Rich replied. "I can't wait to get settled, but I've been so busy that I haven't really had a chance to go out and start looking."

"Well, there's the Atlanta Country Club, of course, and there's Buckhead and Sandy Springs," Carol said. "Hey, what are you doing this afternoon, Rich? If you don't have plans, we could take a drive and I could show you a few neighborhoods."

"That would be great – I'd really appreciate that, Carol." Rich smiled and looked into Carol's blue eyes. She was so considerate; so trusting and happy …

"May I take your order?" A somewhat stressed teenager tapped a pencil against the counter and glanced at the long line he was hurrying to serve. Rich looked up and smiled sheepishly; he'd been so absorbed in his conversation with Carol that he hadn't noticed the line moving. They quickly placed their lunch orders and found a table.

Over lunch, Carol and Rich talked about their lives. Carol told Rich more about her family. Her older daughter Malinda lived in New York City and had just landed a job at MTV. Her younger daughter Caroline was in Australia on a study-abroad program for college. Carol's blue eyes lit up as she talked about her beloved girls; Rich was touched by how lovingly she talked about them. She talked about her sister, Mary Linda

Cotten, and her husband, Bennett, an orthopedic surgeon. They had two boys, Dixon and Bradford, Carol's nephews. She lovingly described her parents: her beloved father, Dr. Williams, or *Daddy*, as she called him, still lived in Macon, Georgia. Sadly, her mother had passed away in 1993.

As Rich listened to Carol talk about her family, he realized that someone like her would probably never understand his dark, godless past: as the youngest daughter of a prominent Macon pediatrician, Carol grew up in a loving, affluent home. Her family belonged to the Idle Hour Country Club in Macon, and she attended private schools. But, although they were well-off, Carol's parents demonstrated Christian values in their daily lives, instilling in their children traditional values. Carol and her siblings were raised to be obedient and respectful. Her father was always honest and hardworking. Her family members were all devout Christians, and proud to be so.

Carol's tales of growing up in the South in the 50s and 60s were fascinating to Rich: Carol told him that Daddy was forced to have two waiting rooms in his office; one for black patients and one for white patients.

The gentle, caring doctor didn't approve of segregation, but, Carol explained, it was the South, after all. That was just how things were. Carol proudly remembered that their neighbor, Judge William Bootle, was the first federal judge to allow African-American students to attend the University of Georgia in 1961.

"And what about your family, Rich? Listen to me, going on about my family, and I hardly know anything about yours," Carol said. She fixed her wide, blue eyes on him. "Are your parents in Florida?"

At the mention of his family, Rich felt like his throat was closing up; he nearly choked on his sandwich. He took a deep sip of his coffee and coughed.

"My family? Well, actually, my parents live in Canada," Rich said, trying to sound casual. At least that part was true, he thought. His parents really did live in Canada. Inside, he was struggling for the right words. "I've got a brother and a sister. I had another brother, Steven, but he died in a motorcycle accident in 1992. It was a hard time for all of us …"

"Oh, I'm so sorry to hear that, Rich. It's always hard to lose someone close to you." Carol's blue eyes showed genuine concern for Rich's loss. "Are you close to your brother and sister?"

"Well, my brother … he, um – he's in Canada, too. We don't talk much. But my sister, Lori – she loves to shop, just like you. She lives in Florida. And, my parents …" Rich paused. He was trying to step very carefully around the situation. He felt his hands go clammy as he thought of his mother and father; the arguing and screaming, his father's troubles …

"Rich, are you okay?" Carol looked worried. "Are you feeling sick?"

"I'm fine," Rich said, smiling. "I just swallowed wrong. My parents are great. My mom, she's a homemaker. And my dad's retired. He worked for Ozark Airlines when I was a kid. His health's not the best anymore, but he's doing okay, you know, for his age."

Rich felt relief wash over him. While he hadn't told Carol the whole story, he'd managed not to lie to her. He didn't want any more lies.

"They sound lovely," replied Carol.

"Yeah. They're lovely." Rich said. He took a bite of his sandwich and felt the familiar bitterness rising in the back of his throat. "So, tell me more about your family. Did you and your sister get along when you were kids?"

"Oh, yes," said Carol. "I mean, we'd fight sometimes, like all kids do, but …"

Rich smiled and leaned toward Carol, but he didn't hear the rest of her story: His mind was filled with images and memories he'd spent years trying to forget: his father's voice, yelling and cursing; his mother crying. Laying so still in his bed as a boy, hoping the fighting would stop, but being scared when the all-too-familiar blue and red flashing lights meant the police had come …

His family was a lot of things, he thought, but lovely wasn't one of them.

✦✦✦✦✦✦

After lunch, Carol drove Rich through the suburbs of Atlanta, and, as she promised, she showed Rich several affluent neighborhoods. They admired the grand, Southern-style mansions on Mt. Paran and Tuxedo Road, and then they toured Valley Road, a winding, tree-lined road that was home to many celebrities.

"Do you see that house right there, Rich? The one with the pillars?" Carol pointed to a sprawling white mansion with a beautifully landscaped lawn. It looked like something out of a movie. "That's where the Governor of Georgia resides. Also, several famous people live in this area as well. Now, we're going to drive over to West Paces Ferry – it's a beautiful area; and the houses are around $3 to $5 million – right in your price range."

"Perfect," said Rich. "And thanks, Carol. It's so nice of you to show me around. I'm having such a fantastic time. And, I hope you'll stay around for a while. After all, when I do find a house, I'll need someone with your eye for decorating to help turn it into a home!"

Carol smiled and felt herself blush. Being with Rich was so refreshing, she thought. She enjoyed being with him; he was successful and intelligent, and he listened to her. It was such a pleasant change.

Carol slowed down and stopped in front of an elegant home with a "For Sale" sign on the front edge of a wide, lush green lawn. The French manor home was finished in large, variegated brick and beautifully textured flagstone, with a true shake-shingled roof and gleaming copper downspouts. The separate guest house and pool were a classic complement to the elegant home. An ornate, wrought-iron gated fence surrounded the property. It reminded Carol of a castle. "Oh, look at this one, Rich! It's gorgeous!"

"Wow, it sure is," Rich said as he admired the stately home. "Hey, Carol, I was thinking that maybe we can do this again. I'm going to be out of town next week, but what about the Friday after next? If you're not busy, of course."

"Actually, I'm afraid I can't, Rich." Carol looked disappointed as she answered. She put the car in gear and continued down West Paces Ferry. "That Friday's my birthday, March 14, and I'm having a birthday dinner at The Lobster Bar. Several family members and friends are coming. My daughter, Malinda, and her boyfriend, Chris, are even flying in from New York to celebrate with us."

"Oh. Well, sure. I understand," said Rich. He sounded cheerful, but he secretly wondered why Carol didn't invite him to the party. Maybe she felt that it was too soon to introduce him to her family.

He was sure that she liked him, so … He shook off
the thought and smiled. Carol was an honest,
considerate person. Whatever the reason, he was sure
that it was a good one. "Well, maybe the next day.
And, happy birthday! If you didn't have plans already, I'd
offer to take you to dinner."

"That's very sweet of you, Rich," said Carol.

They spent the rest of the day looking at homes,
and later in the evening they had a leisurely dinner at
McKendrick's Steakhouse. It was obvious to both of
them that they wanted to be together; they didn't want
the day to end. They returned to Carol's house after
dinner, and sat on the couch drinking coffee and talking.

Rich took Carol's hand and kissed her. His heart
pounded. He couldn't believe what he was about to ask
her.

"Carol, can we go to your room and lay on the bed
and talk?" asked Rich.

Carol looked surprised, and for a moment Rich
worried that he'd offended her. After all, she was a
traditional, Southern woman. Perhaps he'd been too
forward. But Carol set down her coffee and looked into
his eyes. "I'd like that," she said, smiling shyly. Carol

felt safe as if she had known Rich in another life. Instinctively, she knew it was okay; something that only a woman's intuition would feel.

Without another word, she took him by the hand and led him to her bedroom.

They quietly lay down on Carol's bed. Rich put his arms around Carol, and the passion they shared drew them together. Their bodies sank into the soft, aquamarine duvet as they cradled each other. Lost in a fervent embrace, their kisses were deep and satisfying. Willingly enveloped in Rich's strong embrace, Carol forgot about the years of unhappiness she'd experienced in the bed. Rich wanted her, and his intense yearning made her feel sexy and youthful. Neither of them could remember feeling so much desire for another person…

Suddenly, Rich glanced at the clock on the bedside table. It was nearly 1:00 in the morning.

"I just remembered," said Rich as he kissed Carol again. "You picked me up this morning. I should go. I'll catch a cab so you don't have to drive so late."

"Don't be silly, Rich," said Carol. "I'd be happy to take you back to your hotel. Let me just get my shoes and I'll be ready."

After lingering for a few more kisses, Carol found her shoes and they drove to the Ritz, holding hands in the car for the entire ride. Rich made Carol promise to call him when she got home, so he'd know that she arrived safely.

That night, after she'd called Rich and said goodnight, Carol stood in her bathroom and smiled at her reflection. She'd actually lain in bed with a man, she thought. And she'd enjoyed every minute of it. She chuckled as she picked up her toothbrush, thinking of Rich's arms around her, of kissing him… she felt most wanted, attractive, and protected, as if the whole world just slipped away when she was in his arms. She loved how the scent of his cologne still lingered in the room, on her clothes and pillowcases. She'd never felt so desirable.

What a date, she thought … what a date.

6

R ich woke to the sound of pounding on his hotel room door.

"Rich! Hey, Rich! Wake up!"

It was Mark. Rich groaned and looked at the clock. It was almost 8:30. He'd had such a good time with Carol the night before that he'd forgotten Mark was getting in from Florida around midnight. He'd also forgotten about their breakfast plans.

"Rich! You in there?"

"Just a second," Rich mumbled. He got up and put on the hotel robe that was hanging on a hook in the bathroom. He unlatched the chain on the door and opened it. Mark was standing in the hallway, already dressed and ready to go. Mark's crisp linen suit was a striking contrast to Rich's terrycloth, especially on a work day. He was carrying his briefcase and he looked impatient.

"You're not ready?" asked Mark, staring at his friend's bathrobe. "Rich, we've got a lot to talk about before we leave tomorrow. What, did you have a late night last night?"

"Yeah, I guess I did. Sorry. Gimme about 20 minutes to hop in the shower and I'll be ready." Rich opened his door and motioned for Mark to come in. "Have a seat," he said. "I was out with Carol last night. We went to church. And after that, she took me to look at a few houses. We went to dinner, and – I don't know. One thing led to another, and all of a sudden, it was one in the morning." Rich felt a smile creep across his face as he said Carol's name.

"Wait a second. You went *where?*" Mark stared at his friend in disbelief.

"We went to dinner. And we looked at some houses. Carol knows all of the upscale neighborhoods." Rich said.

"No. Before that. You went to church?" Mark asked. "You haven't set foot in a church in … what? A decade? More than that?"

Rich cringed. He had a feeling that Mark wouldn't be able to let that one go. "I did it for Carol, okay? She's a very spiritual woman. I didn't want to blow it with her, so I went to church. It's not like I believe any of that stuff. You know that."

Mark didn't respond right away. He looked down at the floor for a few seconds and took a deep breath. "Look, Rich. I don't mean to be a drag or anything, but – I don't know. Do you think you might be moving a little too fast here? You just met this woman and you're going to church and you're staying out with her all night?" Mark looked at his watch. "We don't have time for this. Just get dressed and we'll go get breakfast and we can talk about the trip. I'll be waiting in the lobby."

Rich watched as Mark let himself out of the room, shutting the door a little harder than necessary. He locked the door behind his friend and turned on the shower. Mark was overreacting, Rich thought. But he did have a point about focusing on work. He couldn't let his budding romance with Carol distract him from his successful network marketing business. Especially this week: He and Mark were leaving for a business trip. He needed to have his head on straight. Rich rinsed his hair and turned off the water. He shaved and dressed quickly – he didn't want to keep Mark waiting. He grabbed his briefcase and picked up his cell phone. Checking that the door was still locked, he sat down and dialed Carol's number. He just had to speak with her again.

He felt his heart racing as the phone rang.

"Hello?"

Rich smiled at the familiar sound of Carol's graceful Southern accent.

"Hey, Carol. It's Rich. Listen, I just wanted to thank you again for yesterday. I had a wonderful time and it was so nice of you to take me out to look at houses. So, I just wanted to call and say thanks again."

"Well thank you, Rich. That's so nice of you to say." Rich could tell from the sound of Carol's voice that she was smiling.

"I'm going out of town tomorrow morning, but I'd really like to have dinner with you before I leave. Are you free tonight?" Rich asked. He hoped she didn't have plans.

"Of course," said Carol. "I'd love to have dinner

with you. I know the perfect place, too. It's called Prime – you'll love it!"

"Sounds great, Carol." Rich grinned, happy that he'd see her one more time. "I'll pick you up this time. How's 7:00?"

"Perfect. I'll see you then," said Carol.

The rest of the day was a slow procession of meetings and minutiae. Time passed slowly as Rich waited eagerly for his date with Carol. He and Mark went over files, studied maps, and checked on conference reservations for their big trip. It would be a whirlwind – six states in a week – meeting and training other network marketing professionals. Typically, Rich enjoyed these trips. He was an outgoing, social person and he loved talking to people and helping them learn the business. But this time... this time felt different. For the first time in what seemed like forever, Rich felt like he'd be leaving something behind.

✦✦✦✦✦✦

Carol stood in front of her bathroom mirror, putting on her lipstick. Rich was picking her up in an hour, and her heart raced at the thought of seeing him again. It was crazy, she knew. She stood back and admired her reflection with approval: for tonight, she'd chosen a simple, stylish black cashmere sweater and a knee-length gray skirt. She wore black tights and knee-high black suede boots. Perfect, she thought, hoping Rich would agree. She smoothed her hair and smiled at her mirror image.

She was ready.

And, she was nervous. After a day of careful deliberation and several encouraging phone conversations with her sister, Mary Linda, Carol had decided to ask Rich to the Circle for Children ball. Carol was a co-chairperson, and to her (and much of Atlanta's elite), the ball was one of the social highlights of the year. It was a glamorous event, and Carol spent much of the year helping to organize it. This year, she wanted Rich to be her date. She hoped he'd say yes. Her whole family planned to attend: Daddy, Mary Linda and Bennett; even her daughter Malinda was bringing her new boyfriend, Chris. She wanted Rich to meet her family, especially Daddy. Though she was approaching her 50th birthday, she was still a good Southern girl at heart. She desperately wanted Daddy to approve of the new man in her life.

Rich arrived on time, as always (his punctuality was something she loved about him), and they drove to Prime, talking about the homes they'd looked at and Rich's upcoming business trip. Carol felt a touch of sadness as she realized that she wouldn't see Rich for a week. She'd only known him for a few days, but it felt like much longer. She inhaled deeply, savoring the aroma of his cologne. She'd miss that scent. Was it possible to go five days without him? Rich's business was important to him, she knew – and his ambition was something she admired and respected. She turned her mind to happier thoughts.

"Rich, do you like sushi?" Carol asked as they pulled out of her driveway.

"Well, I've never really been a big fan of it," Rich said. "I've tried it several times, but honestly, the idea of eating raw fish just doesn't appeal to me. I don't know, maybe I'm just old-fashioned."

"I feel the same way," said Carol. "But both of my daughters *love* it. In fact, the restaurant we're going to, Prime, is their favorite place for sushi. Whenever they come visit, they *always* want to go to Prime. But they've got wonderful steaks and seafood, too. Oh, here's Lenox Mall – you'll want to make a left here. Prime is inside; let's use the valet service in front."

Once inside, Carol led Rich up the escalator to Prime. As they approached the restaurant, Rich slipped his hand into hers, and they walked hand-in-hand the rest of the way.

"This is a nice place," said Rich, looking appreciatively around the restaurant's interior as the hostess led them to their table. "Very modern." The dining room of Prime was dim and romantic, with soft lighting and candles on every table. The modern light fixtures and simple, elegant chairs and tables gave Prime a hip, fashionable feel, and the menu was an intriguing mix of Asian cuisine and steakhouse fare.

Carol ordered oysters on the half shell with a glass of wine. Rich opted for a salad. They ate their first course, talking and laughing until their entrees arrived. Rich's steak was thick and grilled to perfection, and Carol's salmon came with – of course – a tiny dish of ketchup on the side. As they ate, Carol noticed that her knees were shaking under the table. She took a sip of wine to calm her nerves.

"Rich? I wanted to ask you something," Carol said, hoping she didn't sound as nervous as she felt.

"Sure, Carol," said Rich. "Ask me anything."

"Would you – well, do you have a tuxedo?" Carol asked. She felt like her stomach was doing somersaults, and her heart was fluttering. She wasn't in the habit of asking a man on a date.

"A tuxedo? Sure, I've got one. It's back at the hotel," Rich said. The Toys for Tots program was a major event in Atlanta. Being a black tie fundraiser, Rich and Mark brought their tuxedos. The gala was held at the Waverly Renaissance that Rich was putting on his network marketing meeting the next day.

"Good," said Carol. She sipped her wine. "That's good, Rich, because I wanted to ask you ... if you don't have plans ... oh, my gosh, I'm so nervous!" said Carol, with a laugh. She looked down at her menu – looking into his eyes made her feel even more apprehensive. "I'm just going to ask you: Would you like to go to the Circle for Children ball with me next Saturday night? I'd love it if you'd be my escort, and my family will be there. I really want you to meet them. I know you'll just be coming back from out of town, but…"

"I would be honored," said Rich. His dark eyes met hers, and he took her hand across the table. "I would love to escort you to the ball."

Carol smiled at him and squeezed his hand gently. She looked into his warm, dark eyes and felt her heartbeat return to normal. "Thank you, Rich. This really means a lot to me. Oh, I can't wait for you to meet Daddy, Mary Linda and Bennett. Malinda and her boyfriend will be there, too. They're flying in for my birthday on Friday. They've all heard *so* much about you, and they're just *dying* to meet you," she said. "It's really a shame that Caroline won't be there. But you'll get to meet her when she comes back from Australia in August."

"I can't wait!" said Rich. "It'll give me something to look forward to this week while I'm on the road."

For the rest of dinner, Rich and Carol talked more about their families. Carol told Rich all about the summers she spent with her grandparents on Omanga Plantation in Douglasville, Georgia. They had a tennis court, a swimming pool and horses. It was her favorite place when she was a young girl. Every summer, she told

Rich, she and her grandmother, *Baba*, as they all called her, would get dressed in their very finest clothing and take a trip to see the fashion show at Rich's department store in Atlanta. Dressed in a frilly dress, lacy socks, and patent leather shoes, Carol would accompany Baba to the store's Magnolia Tea Room to see the latest styles. And, of course, every trip to Rich's meant a ride on the department store's famous miniature roller coaster, the Pink Pig.

"And what about your grandparents, Rich?" Carol asked. She dipped a stalk of asparagus in her ketchup and took a bite. "Were you close to them when you were growing up?"

"I was," said Rich. "My grandmother was a wonderful woman, a class act. Her name was Audrey, and she lived in Sarasota, Florida. That's how I eventually ended up there. You would have loved her. She was really engaging and fun to be with. She was the financial director for a children's home in Park Ridge, Illinois before she retired and moved to Sarasota. It's funny … I spent a lot of summers with her, just like you and Baba. She'd take me to her big charity events and fancy dinners; she'd take me shopping for school clothes. She really taught me a lot about how to act, like what fork to use with the appropriate dinner course, and things like that."

"That sounds nice," Carol said. "Your grandmother sounds like a very special woman. I think that my Baba and your grandmother Audrey would have liked each other."

"I think so, too," said Rich. "Hey, do you want to get some dessert? We could split the turtle cheesecake — it sounds really good."

"Sure, Rich," said Carol. "That's a great idea."

As they shared dessert, Carol asked Rich more questions about his parents. Although he cheerfully answered her questions, he didn't go into much detail about his past, and something in his eyes changed when he talked about them. *How odd*, she thought. She'd noticed the same change at Jason's Deli, too, but she'd thought maybe he was just being shy. Rich had been more than happy to talk about his grandmother, but he seemed distant when talking about his mother and father. To someone who had grown up in such a loving, close-knit family, it was difficult for Carol to understand Rich's slight change in demeanor. But on the other hand, she knew that not all families were as close as hers ...

After dinner, Rich and Carol returned to Carol's home and sipped coffee before retiring to her bedroom to hold each other and talk. They kissed passionately, clinging to each other in Carol's bed. Time slipped away as they became lost in each tender caress and deep, longing kiss. Carol kissed Rich softly twice, and touched the side of his face.

"You've got your big trip in the morning, Rich," she said. "I don't want to keep you out too late."

Rich kissed her softly and stroked her hair. "I guess you're right," he said. "I don't want to go."

"I'll be here when you come back," Carol said. "And we'll go to the ball."

They kissed one more time before Carol took Rich's hand and walked him to her door.

"I'll call you," said Rich. "I'll call you every night."

Carol nodded. He kissed her again and turned to leave. Halfway down the walkway, Rich stopped and waved at her. Carol leaned against the front door and waved back.

"I'll miss you," she said, too softly for Rich to hear.

✦✦✦✦✦✦

Rich and Mark had barely left Atlanta the first time Rich called Carol. In fact, during the seven-hour drive to Cincinnati, Rich called Carol every time they stopped for gas or food. Mark had initially been irritated with Rich. He was worried that his friend wouldn't stay focused on work. Eventually, Mark's irritation had given way to good-natured teasing. Rich was smitten. And Mark took every opportunity to take a playful jab at his friend's love-struck state.

"When's the wedding?" Mark had asked when he caught Rich hanging up his phone after they stopped for coffee on the way out of Atlanta. "I've never seen you this hung up on someone before! Seriously, can I be your best man?"

"Can it, Mark!" Rich said, giving Mark a playful punch on the arm. "Don't make me remind you how many times you called Melanie when you first met her. You were like a lost puppy if she left the room for five minutes!"

In Cincinnati, the first night of the trip, Rich had

trouble sleeping. He missed Carol. He missed seeing her blue eyes; he missed her cheerful personality. And, although he was truly honored that she'd invited him to the ball, there was a part of him that wondered why she hadn't invited him to her birthday party.

Maybe there was someone else ... Rich felt a little sick imagining Carol dating another man. No, that couldn't be it. Could it? Or, was she ashamed of him? No. If she was ashamed, she wouldn't want him to attend the ball. Rich stared at the ceiling of his hotel room. Maybe she thought that with Rich there, she wouldn't be able to concentrate on her family. There had to be a reason, Rich thought ...

A sharp whistling sound pierced his thoughts. Rich sat up and looked around the room, startled. He looked at the clock: 12:45. In the next bed, Mark stirred, but didn't wake up. Another whistle. Rich looked at the nightstand and saw that his cell phone was lit up. He fumbled for it in the darkness and flipped it open.

It was a text message from Carol: *What are you doing?*

Rich stared at the screen for a few seconds. He'd never learned how to text message. In fact, he'd always thought it was sort of silly; something that teenagers and college kids did; something for people with nothing better to do. His phone chirped again, alerting him to a second message.

I miss you, it said.

Rich smiled as he thought of Carol. He felt like he could finally go to sleep, now that he'd heard from her. He turned off the ringer on his phone and rolled over. As he drifted off to sleep, he decided that, first thing in the morning, he would teach himself how to text.

Rich woke up early the next morning. After he checked to see that Mark was still asleep, he grabbed his phone and walked quietly to the bathroom. He locked the door and opened his phone. It took him a couple of tries, but he eventually managed to send his first text message: *miss you too*, it said. He hit *Send* and smiled.

The rest of the day was busy, and Rich was glad. It was already Tuesday, he thought. Only three more days until he could see Carol again. He and Mark had rented out the hotel's conference room for a training session for new associates. They were immersed in their work, answering questions and going over sales strategies.

Rich was in his element. As the group got ready to break for lunch, Rich's phone rang. It was an unfamiliar phone number with a 229 area code that Rich didn't recognize. When he answered, he was surprised to hear a gentle, Southern voice that was nearly identical to Carol's.

"Hello, is this Rich?" the voice asked.

"Yes, this is Rich Towsley," Rich said. He moved to an empty corner of the conference room so he could hear the caller.

"Rich, it's so nice to speak with you," the voice said. "I'm Mary Linda, Carol's sister. Well, I hope I haven't caught you at a bad time. Carol said you were traveling for work, but I wanted to ask you what you were doing on Friday night. I was hoping you'd be able to come to Carol's birthday party."

Rich took a second to think about Mary Linda's invitation. It was sweet, he thought, but he didn't want to crash Carol's birthday party. "Well, Mary Linda, I appreciate the invitation, I really do. But Carol didn't invite me to her party, and I don't want to make her uncomfortable by showing up unannounced," Rich said. "I just assumed there was a reason she didn't want me to come."

Rich could hear a sigh on the other end of the phone. "That's Carol for you," said Mary Linda. "Rich, do you know why she didn't invite you to her party? The real reason she didn't ask you to go?"

Rich waited. This was it. She has a boyfriend, he thought. That had to be it …

"Rich, she didn't invite you because she didn't want you to feel obligated to buy her a gift," said Mary Linda. "My sister is very timid, and she'd just die if she thought that you felt like you had to buy her something. She's been agonizing over this all week, ever since y'all went to look at houses. I know she's too shy to ask you, so I'm inviting you. She'd be ecstatic if you came."

"I'm not sure about that," Rich said. "I don't want to intrude."

"Trust me, Rich. You won't be intruding. God told me to make this call, and Carol will be just thrilled if you're there to celebrate her big day." Rich could hear the sincerity in her voice. "Please come, Rich. And don't bring her a gift. Your being there will be a gift in itself."

Rich was silent for a moment. *That* was the reason he wasn't invited to the party? Because Carol didn't want him to buy her a gift? He couldn't believe it! That was either the worst excuse he'd ever heard, he thought, or Carol was one of the most caring, considerate women he'd ever met ...

"I'd love to go," he said. He felt a sharp tap on his shoulder and turned around to see Mark standing behind him, gesturing at the door. People were filing out of the conference room, and Mark was waiting for him so they could go to lunch. Rich gave Mark a thumbs-up and turned back to his conversation. "And, do you think it will be okay if my friend Mark comes, too? He doesn't know anybody in Atlanta, and he's not going home to see his wife this weekend. I know he'd appreciate the invitation."

"Of course," said Mary Linda. "I'd be happy to have your friend there. I'll just change the reservation for two more, and I'll see you on Friday! I just can't wait to meet you, Rich!"

"Thanks, Mary Linda. It was nice talking to you," said Rich.

Rich was stunned. He'd only known Carol for a few weeks, and he'd never met Mary Linda, but she'd taken the time to invite him to Carol's party. It was so considerate. A wide smile spread across Rich's face. For the first time, he felt like he belonged to something. He felt accepted.

He felt like he was part of a family.

✦✦✦✦✦✦

Rich and Mark arrived back in Atlanta late Friday morning and spent the afternoon resting and getting ready for Carol's birthday party.

Rich studied his reflection in the bathroom mirror as he buttoned his shirt.

"Hey Mark, you think I should wear a tie?" Rich asked.

"I dunno," said Mark. "Maybe just a nice jacket. And I think your ties are out in the car in your garment bag, aren't they?"

"I think so," Rich said. "And a few suits, too. Oh, and my tux is in there – remind me to get that later, would you? I've got that ball tomorrow and I'm going to need it."

"Sure, I'll remind you," Mark said.

"Thanks," said Rich. He sprayed some cologne

and gave himself a final once-over. He wanted to make a good impression on Carol's family. He ran a comb through his hair again. He was ready. "And Mark, what do you think – "

Rich was cut off by the sound of Mark's cell phone ringing.

"Oh, hey, Mel. What's up?" Mark said. "Yeah, Rich and I are just getting ready to – *what?* No. Oh, no. Oh, I'm so sorry. When?"

Hearing Mark's change in tone, Rich turned to look at his friend. Mark sat down on the bed quite suddenly as he talked to his wife. "Are you going right now? Okay. Well, then I'll head out later tonight. I'll see you soon."

Mark put the phone down and sat motionless on the bed. He looked pale. His eyes were red as he looked up at Rich. "It's Mel – her dad, he – " Tears streamed down Mark's face as he struggled to get the words out. "He's passed away. Remember, I told you he had cancer? We thought he had a little more time, but he just …"

With immediate sympathy Rich put his arm around his friend and clapped him on the back. "I'm so sorry," he said. "Mark, I'm so, so sorry. Do you want to go to the airport? I can drop you off before I head to Carol's party."

Mark shook his head. "I'm just going to wait until after. Melanie's going to finish out the day at work." Melanie was a fifth grade school teacher. She had been an elementary teacher for 15 years. "Her sister's on the way there, and there's nothing we can do right now, anyway. I'll just catch a late flight after dinner. Thanks, though."

"Okay," Rich said gently. "That's fine. I'll drop you off then. If it's okay with you, I'm not going to mention this to Carol. She's a very caring person, and she'll feel just terrible celebrating if she knows you've lost someone."

"Yeah, I don't want to ruin her party," Mark said. "It was so nice of her to let me tag along with you. I don't want to do anything to spoil it."

Rich and Mark didn't say much on the drive over to Carol's party. Rich drove. He was already becoming familiar with the Atlanta area, and could find his way around easily. Mark stared out the window in silence. They arrived at The Lobster Bar about an hour before Carol's party was scheduled to begin. They'd been restless in their hotel, and Rich figured it might be good to get Mark out of their room and into a more upbeat environment.

"This is nice," said Mark. Like all of Carol's favorite restaurants, the Lobster Bar was upscale and elegant. And, judging from the groups of well-dressed men and women who surrounded the bar, it was the place for Atlanta's elite to socialize and enjoy a glass of wine. Mark ordered a mixed drink and looked appreciatively at the restaurant's decor. "Very elegant."

"Uh-huh," Rich said, sipping a Coke and nodding absently. He hadn't heard a word that Mark said. He too was nervous. Although Rich had called and texted Carol several times a day during his trip, talking about how much they missed each other, what each was doing throughout the day, he never mentioned his conversation with Mary Linda. He was thrilled at the idea of seeing Carol again, but he had no idea how she would react when she saw him at the party.

"Rich?" A Southern voice came from behind him. "Are you Rich Towsley?"

Rich turned around to find an attractive blonde woman standing behind him. She smiled and reached out to hug him. "Hello, I'm Mary Linda, Carol's sister."

"Pleasure to meet you, Mary Linda," said Rich. "And this is my friend, Mark."

"Carol's not here yet, but I wanted to come up early to make sure they had enough seats," said Mary Linda. "Oh, I just hope the weather holds out. Did you hear that they're saying we could have tornadoes tonight? I prayed the whole way over here that we'd be blessed with good weather."

Rich smiled when he heard Mary Linda's charming accent. She sounded so much like her sister. And, Rich thought, Mary Linda seemed to share Carol's cheerful, bubbly personality.

"Well, I hope so, too," said Rich. "Is there anything I can do to help you get ready?"

Rich was pleased when Mary Linda put him right to work. She'd brought a tasteful banner that said "Happy Birthday Carol," and she'd made a little gift box of chocolates for everyone who was invited. Rich happily arranged the banner above their table and put the boxes at all the place settings. It felt so nice to be included.

And, Mary Linda had been right: Carol was

absolutely thrilled to see Rich. Her face lit up into her widest, happiest smile as she spotted him from across the room. She ran straight to him.

"What are you doing here?" Carol said, giggling happily. They hugged briefly and Carol smiled up at him. "This is such a wonderful surprise! And you brought Mark! That's so nice! Mary Linda, did you have something to do with this?" Carol's blue eyes were now fixed on her sister, who did her best to feign innocence.

"Maybe," said Mary Linda. She laughed and put her arm around Rich. "I called him up and told him that nothing would make my sister happier than seeing him at her birthday party."

"Well, you were right," said Carol. She turned to Rich and slapped him playfully on the arm. "And you knew about this and you didn't tell me! You're so bad, Rich!"

Carol hugged Rich tightly again and took his hand. "Come with me," she said. "There's someone I want you to meet. You too, Mark."

Carol's family was gathered around the table Mary Linda had reserved. Carol led Rich and Mark directly toward a gentleman with white hair and a bright, red bow tie. "Daddy? I'd like you to meet Rich Towsley, the man I've been telling you about, and his friend, Mark. Rich, Mark, this is my Daddy."

Rich and Mark each shook the older man's hand. At 84 years old, Dr. Williams was as sharp as he'd ever been, and his bright, intelligent eyes glinted with life. He looked at Rich and smiled. "So, you're Rich," Dr. Williams said. "Pleasure to meet you. I must say that Carol's told me a lot about you, and I'm very glad to finally meet you in person. It's nice to see Carol so happy! Anyone who can put a smile on her face is alright in my book."

"Likewise, sir," said Rich. He liked the man instantly.

"We'll be right back, Daddy," said Carol, taking Rich by the arm. "I need to introduce Rich and Mark to Malinda and Chris." Malinda and Chris were delighted to finally have the opportunity to meet Rich, the man that had been making "Mom" so happy. They also had the pleasure of meeting Rich's best friend Mark. Malinda, Carol's oldest daughter was a tall, attractive blonde woman with blue eyes just like her mother.

Malinda had graduated two years earlier from Tulane University with a degree in Marketing. Carol was obviously thrilled that at least one of her two daughters could be there to celebrate her 50th birthday.

A whirlwind of introductions followed as Carol proudly introduced Rich and Mark to her family and friends. Carol was especially happy to introduce Rich to Claire. Claire was an attractive brunette who, like Carol, looked years younger than her actual age. She had been Carol's close friend since they were seventeen. They had been especially close at Emory University, where they were sorority sisters. Claire was still like a sister to Carol, as they were exercise buddies and talked every day. She was very close to Carol's daughters, too; Rich already knew she was very much a part of Carol's life. He was glad to meet her and they liked each other immediately.

By the time they all sat down to dinner, Rich felt right at home. He was honored when Carol asked him to sit next to her at the table. Carol's Daddy sat on her other side, and Carol conversed gladly with them both. Mark was seated next to Mary Linda's husband, Bennett, and the two men were soon talking like old friends. Despite his loss, Mark seemed to be enjoying himself as he and Bennett talked about business.

After dinner, the family ordered dessert and coffee, and Mark politely excused himself to make an important call. Probably making flight reservations, Rich thought. He turned his attention back to Carol and Dr. Williams.

"Actually, I think I'll excuse myself, too, before dessert arrives," said Dr. Williams. "I need to use the men's room."

Carol's father slowly stood up, using the table for leverage. Rich looked at the crowded dining room and imagined Dr. Williams having difficulty navigating the crowd.

"I think I'll go, too," said Rich. He quickly walked to the doctor's side and led him patiently through the crowd. Dr. Williams held on to Rich's arm. It was strange, Rich thought. He hardly knew Carol's father, yet he felt compelled to watch out for him; to protect him. Rich felt honored to walk with the man.

When Rich and Dr. Williams arrived back at the table, dessert had been served and Carol was sipping her coffee and talking with Malinda and Chris. Mark was sitting at the table, looking stricken. Rich walked to his friend's side.

"Everything okay?" asked Rich in a low voice. "Did you get a flight?"

Mark shook his head. "The airport's shut down," he said. There was a trace of panic in his voice. "There's a tornado warning. They've already had two or three big ones touch down in downtown Atlanta. They're not letting any planes take off. Even private jets are grounded. I don't know what to *do*, Rich. I can't get a flight and Melanie needs me…"

"Rich? Rich, is everything okay?" Carol asked. She looked concerned. "Mark? Are you all right?"

Rich sighed. He had to tell Carol the truth. "It's Mark's father-in-law. He passed away this afternoon." Rich took Carol's hand and squeezed it. "Mark and I didn't want to tell you because we didn't want to ruin your birthday celebration."

Carol's wide, blue eyes welled with tears, and she wiped them away with a perfectly manicured hand. "Mark, I'm so sorry to hear that," she said. "If there's anything I can do, you just let me know. And, we're all going back to my house for birthday cake after this. I'd love it if you joined us."

"Thanks," Mark said, giving Carol a weak smile. "I appreciate that. I just have to figure out how I'm going to get to Tampa by tomorrow morning."

"We'll think of something," said Rich.

When dessert was over, Carol's family began drifting to their cars to meet up back at Carol's house. Rich lingered at the table and toyed with his fork, waiting for their server to come with the check. Maybe he couldn't buy Carol a birthday gift, he thought, but he could certainly pay for everyone's dinner. And, even if it wasn't Carol's birthday, paying for meals was part of a promise Rich had made to himself a long time ago: a promise that, if he ever became successful, he would always pick up the tab, whether it was a couple of four-dollar sandwiches or a lavish dinner for 200 people. And it was a promise that he'd kept.

When the server approached, Rich waved. "I'll take care of that," he said, reaching into his pocket for his wallet.

"I'm sorry, sir, but Ms. Greenbaum has already paid. She gave me her card when she arrived this evening," said the server, a clean-cut young man. "I'm just returning her card and her receipt."

Rich sighed and looked at Carol with admiration in his dark eyes. Only someone with Carol's giving, generous nature would pay for her own birthday dinner, he thought.

Carol slipped her credit card into her wallet. "Are you ready to go, Rich? I'm going to drive Daddy and Malinda and Chris back, so do you and Mark want to ride together?"

"Sure," said Rich. "We'll see you there."

Carol smiled joyously at Rich and turned to Mark. She put a delicate hand on his shoulder and looked at him, her wide, blue eyes full of compassion. "And Mark, again, I'm so sorry about your father-in-law."

"Thanks," said Mark.

On the drive back to Carol's house, Mark and Rich noticed that the sky was a strange, green color. It was humid, and the night air was eerily still: perfect tornado weather. Rich flipped on the radio and tuned it to a news broadcast. Conditions were still dangerous in Atlanta, said the announcer, and tornados had touched down as far away as Macon. Mark shifted in his seat and snapped the radio off. He looked out at the sky for the rest of the ride.

When they reached Carol's house, Mark and Rich were greeted warmly by the whole family, and everyone extended their deepest sympathies to Mark and Melanie. Mary Linda patted Mark's arm gently and told him that she would pray for him. Rich was touched. Even though he didn't believe in prayer, Rich couldn't help being moved by Mary Linda's caring, gentle nature. While Carol and her daughter Malinda went to the kitchen to cut the birthday cake, Mark stepped onto the front porch and called Melanie.

When he came back a few minutes later, he had a determined look in his eye.

"I have to get to Tampa. Tonight," Mark said. "Melanie's really upset, and she's worried about me and she's crying. I need to be with my wife."

"I understand, Mark, but how? The airports are all closed – you said so yourself," Rich said.

"I'm driving. I'll take you back to the hotel, but then I'm taking the car and I'm driving to Tampa. It's my only option," said Mark.

"But what about the weather? The radio said it was bad all the way to Macon. That's right in your path," said Rich. But he knew his words were lost on his friend. Rich could tell from Mark's tone that he was serious. Nothing – not a tornado or a flood or an earthquake – would stop Mark from going home to Melanie when she needed him.

Rich sighed. "Okay. But you have to promise you'll be careful, and that you'll turn around if it gets too dangerous. Melanie has enough to worry about right now as it is."

"Promise," said Mark.

✦✦✦✦✦✦

Mark quickly said his goodbyes to the family, thanked Carol for her hospitality and apologized for leaving so abruptly. After everyone finished their birthday cake and coffee, Carol offered to drive Rich back to his hotel.

Rich stared silently out of the window as Carol pulled the Land Rover onto the freeway.

"Rich?" Carol touched Rich's knee gently. "Are you okay?"

"Yeah, I'm fine. I'm just, well, I'm a little worried

about tomorrow," Rich said. "We had a really important network marketing meeting tomorrow afternoon, in Tampa, and Mark was supposed to take care of it. And now, with Melanie needing him with her, I just don't know what we're going to do."

It was dark in the car, but Rich could see a look of concern cross Carol's face. "Tomorrow?" she asked. "Don't you have someone else who can go?"

"I don't know," Rich said. "Normally, I'd just try to cancel it. But this is really important, and – well, I might have to go to Tampa tomorrow to take care of the meeting."

"But Rich, tomorrow night is the ball," said Carol. "I mean, I know your work is important, it's just – do you think you'd be able to make it back in time to go with me? It's so important to me, and we've been planning this for weeks."

Rich could hear the disappointment in Carol's voice, and he was instantly sorry he'd mentioned the meeting. He put a hand on her knee and gave it a reassuring squeeze.

"Carol I'll figure something out. I promise," Rich said. "I just have to get on the phone and see what I can come up with. I'll find someone to cover for me. Maybe Mark will do it. I'm not going to miss the ball."

"Oh, I'm so glad," said Carol. "It's just such an important night for me being the Co-Chairperson for the Circle for Children Ball."

Rich told Carol that he would never put business ahead of her. She was impressed that he would prioritize her over his other obligations.

"I am so honored and proud that you're sharing this event with me and my family," Carol said.

Rich touched Carol's hair gently and studied her profile. He wished she wasn't driving. He suddenly, overwhelmingly needed to put his arms around her and kiss her. "Carol, I want you to remember something," Rich said. "I will never let business get in the way of us. You'll always be the most important person to me. Always."

Carol smiled. "Rich, that's the sweetest thing I've heard in a long time," she said. "And it really means a lot to me. Thank you."

They rode the rest of the way in silence, holding hands and just enjoying each other's company. When they pulled up to the Ritz, they kissed tenderly and held each other for a moment.

"So, I guess I'll see you tomorrow evening," said Rich. He smoothed Carol's hair and kissed her forehead.

"I guess you will," said Carol. Her dazzling smile was back, and she pulled Rich closer and kissed him again. "I'll pick you up at six."

"Great," said Rich. "And happy birthday, Carol. I really had a great time tonight. Your family – well, they're great. I'm glad I had the opportunity to meet them."

They kissed again and Rich got out of the car. He stood outside the Ritz and watched as Carol drove away, then headed to the elevator.

As Rich let himself into his room, his phone rang. It was Mark.

"Hey Mark, is everything okay? You didn't get swallowed by a twister?" Rich joked. He slid his shoes off and eased back on his bed. "How's the drive going?"

"Right on schedule. I think I just missed all the really bad stuff," said Mark. "But Rich, I need to tell you something, and you're not gonna like it. I just realized …"

"Do you mean the meeting tomorrow?" Rich asked. He picked up the remote control and clicked the television on. "Look, I understand if you can't make it. Family first. We'll figure something out."

"No, it's not that," said Mark. "I'll take care of that. The funeral's not until Tuesday, and there's nothing we can really do until then. It's about your tux."

Rich froze. His tux. The ball. He sat straight up in bed and clapped a hand to his forehead.

"Oh man, you gotta be kidding me," Rich said. "Don't tell me … "

"I'm so sorry," Mark said. "I was in a hurry and I just stopped at our room to pick up a few things and I completely forgot. I've got your tux. And your suits. Didn't realize it until now. I'm sorry, Rich. I just wasn't thinking about it."

Rich sighed. "No, I understand. Look, just don't worry about it. Go home, take care of Melanie. I'll figure something out."

Rich said goodbye and set his phone down. The rollercoaster of emotions, from the melancholy of Mark's loss to the excitement of Carol's birthday party and the upcoming ball, was more than Rich was used to feeling …

The clock on the nightstand said 2:00 AM. There was nothing he could do right now, he thought. And there was no point in calling Carol and giving her something to worry about. He'd give her a call first thing in the morning and see if she knew where he could get a new tuxedo.

✦✦✦✦✦✦

The next morning, Rich called Carol and explained his tuxedo situation, apologizing a dozen times for the inconvenience. As it turned out, Carol knew of several places where Rich could find a tux, but she couldn't take him shopping. Because she was a co-chairperson at the ball, she and a few other women had to get to the Cobb Energy Center early to help prepare the ballroom for the night's festivities. She was already there, getting the items ready for the silent auction.

"I'll just call a cab," said Rich. He could hear activity in the background; women's voices talking and laughing. "You're busy. You've got enough going on today without having to solve my wardrobe problem.

Just tell me what store to go to and I'll figure something out."

"No, don't call a cab," said Carol. "I have an idea. Let me call Mary Linda and see if she can help us out. I'll call you right back."

Rich stretched back on the bed and put his hand over his forehead. He couldn't believe he'd forgotten about his tux. Just perfect. Tonight, of all nights.

Five minutes later, Rich's phone rang.

"Rich? Mary Linda's on her way. She'll be there in about ten minutes," said Carol.

"Thanks, Carol. Tell Mary Linda she's a lifesaver." Rich hung up, quickly showered and dressed and rushed downstairs.

By the time Rich got to the lobby, Mary Linda was already standing by the front desk waiting for him. She hugged him warmly.

"How's Mark doing? Did he make it to Florida okay?" Mary Linda asked as they walked to her car. "If you talk to him soon, you make sure and tell him that I'm praying for his family."

"Thanks, Mary Linda," Rich said. Much like Carol, Mary Linda seemed to be a spiritual person.

"And thanks for taking me to get a tuxedo. In all the excitement, I forgot about it, and so did Mark."

"Well, y'all had other things on your mind," said Mary Linda as she fastened her seat belt. "I'm happy to do it."

Five hours and about ten stores later, Rich and Mary Linda had found everything Rich needed for the ball: a tuxedo, a shirt, and a pair of dress shoes. As it turned out, getting a tuxedo at the last minute was an ordeal. They found a tuxedo at one store, but they'd had to search two other stores to find the right cummerbund. And, they'd had to visit three more stores to find a pair of shoes before going back to the first store to pick up Rich's altered tux. It was an exhausting day. Mary Linda had been a cheerful shopping partner, driving Rich from store to store without a word of complaint. Dragging his shopping bags and boxes out of the car, Rich thanked Mary Linda again as she dropped him back at the Ritz.

◆◆◆◆◆◆

As Rich straightened his bow tie in the mirror,

his phone rang. It was Carol, downstairs in the lobby waiting for him.

"I'll be downstairs in a second," said Rich. He quickly put on some of Carol's favorite cologne and hurried to meet her.

Rich stepped into the elevator and peered at his reflection in the polished doors. He looked like he was going to a wedding, he thought as he straightened his tie again. The new tuxedo fit him well, and he was pleased that he'd made a good impression at Carol's birthday party. He tapped his foot impatiently as the elevator crawled down. He couldn't wait to see Carol.

When the doors slid open, Rich gasped: Carol was dressed in a floor-length, body skimming turquoise evening gown that showed off her curves and her toned, tanned arms. Her honey blonde hair was curled, and it cascaded down her shoulders in soft waves, and her large, diamond earrings sparkled. He had never seen her look more beautiful.

"How do I look?" asked Carol. She flushed and spun around to give Rich the full effect.

"You look amazing," Rich said.

Carol took Rich's arm as they walked to her car, the

two perfectly matched in their formal dress.

On the way to the ball, Carol asked about Mark and told Rich again that she was sorry for Mark's loss. They talked about Carol's birthday party and the food at The Lobster Bar, but Rich really didn't hear much of what Carol said. He was too busy looking at her, taking in every inch of her elegant gown and her beautiful body.

When they arrived at the ball, Rich was awestruck by how grand an event it really was: he didn't know what to expect, but the Circle for Children ball was a truly elegant affair. The Cobb Energy Center Grand Ballroom was filled with men in tuxedos and women in elegant ball gowns, and as they walked through the room, Carol pointed out local Atlanta celebrities and politicians. It seemed that almost everyone in the room stopped to greet Carol, and she graciously introduced Rich to everyone in turn. Jeff Foxworthy was the night's honoree, and a Georgia senator was seated at the table next to Carol's family. Several local magazines, including the upscale lifestyle magazine *Jezebel*, were at the ball, taking pictures. Carol and Rich posed for the photographers, smiling happily at the camera.

As Carol stood in the front of the ballroom to be introduced as the Co-Chairperson for the ball - nobody was more proud of her than her daddy. A tear rolled down Dr. Williams' cheek as they announced the monumental effort that Carol had made in organizing the dinner, the band and the silent and live auctions. Daddy, along with Carol's friends and family were amazed at her kindness by putting others first and helping the many children that she would never meet. But that was Carol.

Carol had reserved an entire table for herself and her family, and Rich was happy to see that Malinda, her boyfriend Chris, Dr. Williams, and Mary Linda were all present. They all greeted Rich warmly, as if he was truly a member of the family. Rich danced with Carol and joked with Mary Linda about their shopping excursion. After dinner, Rich was impressed to find out that Carol had donated a beautiful diamond bracelet to the silent auction.

Wow, thought Rich. So this is what real families are like.

He danced with Carol, and her daughter, and her sister. Rich was feeling very comfortable with everyone, almost like he belonged there. And he felt intoxicated with Carol in her beautiful blue-green dress, just a few shades away from her amazing eyes.

Later that night, as Carol dropped Rich off at the Ritz, they kissed passionately in the lobby of the hotel. Although they both wanted to return to Carol's house and lay in bed together, Carol had a house full of people, and Rich didn't feel it was appropriate, since her daughter and Daddy were there.

"Thank you, Rich, I had a wonderful time tonight," said Carol.

Rich kissed her again, softly. "I had a wonderful time, too. And you really do look amazing," he said, pulling away and looking directly at her. Carol smiled immediately, like she always did when Rich looked at her.

"Rich, would you like to come to Buckhead Church with us tomorrow? Daddy and Mary Linda and Malinda are all coming, and we're going to Jason's Deli afterward. I just know that Daddy would be so happy if you came. I think he really likes you," Carol said.

"Sounds great, Carol. I'd love to," Rich said. He still

wasn't comfortable with the idea of church, but at least he knew what to expect now. And, he really liked being with her family, he thought.

They kissed goodnight one last time, and Rich watched as Carol got into her car and drove away.

✦✦✦✦✦✦

The next morning, Carol and her family woke up extra early to watch Joel Osteen on television before church. It was something that they always did when they were together, a tradition Carol loved. Malinda and Chris sat on the loveseat by the coffee table, and Daddy sat between Mary Linda and Carol.

"So, Daddy, what do you think of Rich?" asked Carol. "Do you like him?"

Dr. Williams turned to his daughter and put his hand over hers. "I like him very much," he said. "And his friend, too. I'm impressed that those two managed to keep their composure on your birthday. With everything they had going on; they still stayed to help you celebrate. That's pure class, if you ask me."

"I thought so, too," said Carol. "Rich is so

considerate of me, Daddy."

"I can see that," said Dr. Williams. "I think he's a fine man. And if you ended up marrying him that would be fine by me."

Carol flushed at the thought of marrying Rich. After all, they'd only been dating a few weeks. But she'd never felt this way about a man before ...

Carol squeezed her father's hand.

"Thanks, Daddy," she said.

7

On Monday morning Rich awoke very early. After making himself a cup of coffee in his room, he went out on the balcony to reflect on the weekend's events. Hoping that he had made a good impression on Carol's family, he realized how important to him they were becoming. Her family had made such a wonderful impression on him. What great people, he thought. They were kind, caring and loving. It was evident that they truly appreciated enjoying each other's company. Of course a comforting feeling came over Rich as he gazed at the sun rising over the horizon, and he imagined what it would be like to become an integral member of Carol's family.

Belonging, he thought. It would almost be a new lease on life. Carol's father had attributes that impressed

Rich immensely. Carol's sister Mary Linda Cotten and her husband Dr. Bennett Cotten were kind and compassionate. Carol's daughter Malinda was vibrant and positive, just like her mother.

Rich thought of Carol's family, as they were all heading back to their homes. Though he enjoyed the Buckhead church with Carol, he wasn't the type of man that would bow his head in prayer for their safe return. He closed his eyes for a moment and simply wished it.

Rich looked at the clock. It was seven in the morning. He picked up his phone and dialed Mark's number. He wanted to see how Saturday's meeting went in Tampa with the chiropractors. The Tampa meeting involved 100 chiropractors. The head of the Association was in the networking business with Rich. They were to be addressed regarding the products that Rich's company had to offer. It rang several times, and Mark sounded tired when he finally answered.

"Hey Rich," said Mark. "How'd the ball go? You find a tux in time?"

"Yeah, everything worked out fine. It was great. How about you? How's Melanie holding up?"

"As well as can be expected, I guess," said Mark.

"We're flying out for the funeral tonight. I'm just trying to take care of a few things before we go. Are you still coming down for the meeting tomorrow?"

"I'll be there," Rich said. "Speaking of meetings, how'd things go on Saturday night?"

"Great! Better than great. In fact, the owner of the company stopped in. He's going to come to the regional meeting next week, and he said to tell you he's looking forward to seeing you again."

"Wow, that's fantastic!" said Rich. "Thanks again for handling that. Carol would have been devastated if I didn't go to the ball. I really appreciate it."

"No problem," said Mark. Rich could hear a woman's voice in the background. "Yeah, Mel. I'll tell him. Okay! In a second. Hey, Rich? I gotta run, we're trying to get a few things wrapped up before we leave. And Melanie says 'hi.'"

"We need to go to dinner when I'm in town," said Rich. "The three of us. Will you guys be back on Thursday?"

"I will. Mel's staying in Alabama for a few days to help her sisters with a few things, but give me a call. We can go to lunch."

Rich said goodbye to Mark and eased back on the bed. He'd almost forgotten that he had to go back to Sarasota the next morning for business. His heart sank as he thought of spending the rest of the week without Carol. It was so strange, he thought. He'd never missed anyone like he missed her; he hated being away from her for even one day. Rich smiled as he thought of Carol's blue eyes. He picked up the phone, hoping that she didn't already have dinner plans for the evening.

✦✦✦✦✦✦

As it turned out, Carol did not have dinner plans. Rich made reservations at Morton's Steakhouse for 7:30, and Carol was picking him up 7:00. He still didn't have a car, but he was planning to drive the rental car back from Sarasota on Friday morning. For a man who was used to flying by private jet, the driving certainly seemed a waste of valuable time, but it was important to replenish the large rental car with supplies and products in order to share them. In fact, it was a necessity.

Rich looked at his watch. He'd spent most of the day getting ready for his trip, packing his bags and reviewing paperwork and making phone calls; but he still had at least an hour to kill before Carol arrived. He thought about leaving his room. How funny, he thought, he'd been at the Ritz so long that he actually thought of the room as his. Still, he didn't want to sit in the lobby for an hour.

Not accustomed to having time alone, Rich thought a stroll through the Buckhead area would be nice. Walking past the Lenox Mall on Peachtree Street, Rich knew at this point that his life had forever changed. Meeting Carol was right, he thought. He knew it. Rich had not been in a relationship with a woman for 16 years. It was his choice. As callous as it may sound, having a companion in his past life would have been an occupational hazard. A significant other would have simply been a liability. Now however, he viewed Carol as a necessity. Why had such an incredible woman been so easily dumped in his lap? Was he deserving of such a gift? In the back of his mind lingered the obvious question: did Carol feel the same way? It had only been a month. So this is what love is, he thought. Glancing at his watch it was time to get back, back to Carol.

Getting back to the Ritz, it was only five minutes before Carol had arrived. Looking at Carol was like looking into his future. Carol shared her usual smile. The outfit that she wore once again looked like it was specially created for her petite, shapely frame. Carol's blue eyes widened as she saw the new man in her life. They embraced and took a moment to feel the wrapping of their arms around each other.

"I feel like I haven't seen you in a week," Carol said, excitingly. "Are you ready for dinner?"

"Sure am," said Rich. Being a natural Southern woman, Carol handed Rich the keys to her Range Rover and said, "You drive!"

"As soon as I come back, I need to start house hunting again," said Rich. "Seriously. What do you say — do you want to help me find a house on Saturday?"

"I'd love to," said Carol, as they pulled out of the Ritz's parking lot. "We can go back to Mt. Paran. Remember that house that looked like a castle? I liked that one. And there were a few others that were nice, as well."

"You liked that one? The one with the guest house?"

"I did, Rich. I thought it was very elegant. And, it looked like it had a really big garage. I don't know if it would hold all your 11 cars, but I bet you could fit a few in there."

A lump caught in Rich's throat. He swallowed hard. *How am I ever going to break the news to her?* he thought.

They drove the rest of the way to Morton's conversing about their upcoming house hunting excursion. Rich rested a hand on Carol's knee and listened as she cheerfully described a new real estate listing she'd seen in the paper. It was easy for Rich to imagine that he and Carol were looking for a new home together. Their new home. For the second time that day, Rich's thoughts turned to marriage. He wondered what it would be like to set up a home with Carol; to live with her … to go to bed with her every night and wake up and look into those eyes every morning …

"Rich?" Carol patted his arm and laughed. "Rich, did you hear a word I just said?"

"Hmm? Oh – gosh, I was in my own little world for a second, thinking about the house. I'm sorry," Rich said. "You were saying?"

"I said, Mary Linda is a realtor," Carol said. "I'll have her pull up a list of homes in the area – it'll be a good starting point." Rich slowed the car down and turned into the Morton's entrance. They pulled up at the valet kiosk and shut off the engine. "Mary Linda will be happy to help! She just likes you so much, Rich."

Rich handed the keys to the valet and the two walked inside, hand in hand.

Rich was happy to see that Morton's wasn't crowded. On weekends, the popular steakhouse was filled to capacity. But tonight, Monday, only a few diners were scattered throughout the restaurant; Rich liked it that way. It felt much more intimate and private, almost like they had the place to themselves. They scanned their menus and a tall, neatly dressed server came to take their drink orders.

"I'll have a glass of Chardonnay, please," said Carol. "Rich? Are you having a drink?"

"Just Diet Coke for me, thanks," said Rich. He picked up his menu and began scanning its contents.

"You don't really drink, do you, Rich?" asked Carol. She looked radiant in the candlelight – her honey blonde hair fell softly around her shoulders and her diamond necklace sparkled on her slender throat. "I don't think I've ever even seen you finish a beer."

"I just never developed a taste for it," said Rich. "Sometimes I wish I did drink. I see people with a nice glass of cognac at the end of a nice meal, and I think, 'Wow, that looks good!' But in reality, I know it'd burn my throat and I'd just start coughing."

Carol laughed; her blue eyes sparkled. "Well, I think it's good that you don't drink," she said. "Now, I do like my glass of wine at dinner, but that's it. Not like some people who go out drinking for fun. I just don't understand that at all."

"I agree," said Rich. "I don't see the fun in that."

Rich watched Carol sip her wine as she looked at her menu. At least that was true, he thought. He'd had to be so careful about most of the things he told Carol, it felt good simply telling the truth about something. He almost never touched alcohol. It dulled your senses, after all. In Rich's previous line of work, you had to stay sharp. If you were slow to react, well, there were serious consequences.

"Rich?" Carol reached across the table and took his hand. Rich snapped out of the dark daydream of the serious consequences he had seen. "What are you going to order? I can't decide. It all sounds so good!"

"I think I'll have the filet as usual," said Rich. "And I'm going to have the Caesar salad to start."

"Oh, that sounds nice! I'll have the Caesar salad, too. And I think I'll order the shrimp Alexander," said Carol.

As they waited for their entrees, Rich and Carol ate their salads and talked happily about the Circle for Children ball. They laughed about Rich's tuxedo disaster. It was funny, now that it was over and the problem had been solved. Rich loved to watch Carol laugh. He loved how her blue eyes lit up; her wide smile revealing her perfect, white teeth. Carol in particular was relieved that all of her hard work was about to pay off. Carol described the live band that was going to play that evening. She explained why the "Jewel of the Nile" theme was chosen and how much it meant to her to help raise the funds for the children.

"You looked absolutely gorgeous at the ball," said Rich. "You were the most beautiful woman there."

"Thank you, Rich," said Carol. She took a sip of her wine and smiled shyly. "And you just looked so handsome in your tux!"

Rich smiled. The two of them made a handsome couple: Carol in her beautiful aqua dress and Rich in his tux. He hadn't worn a tuxedo since Mark and Melanie's wedding, years ago. And yesterday, as he straightened his cummerbund and put on his bow tie, Rich had almost felt like he was getting married. He was nervous and excited all at the same time, eager to see Carol in that knockout dress, just like a groom on his wedding day. Rich imagined what Carol would look like in a wedding dress, waiting for him with a bouquet of flowers in her hand …

Rich shook his head. It was strange. He'd only known Carol for about a month, and here he was fantasizing about their wedding. Rich chuckled softly and looked into Carol's blue eyes. *Crazy*, he thought. Things were moving so fast. But Rich had never felt like this before, about anyone.

"I wish that Caroline could have been here last weekend," Carol said, snapping Rich out of his fantasy. "I ordered the shrimp Alexander because that's her favorite dish at Morton's. I am so glad I got the Skype hooked up on the computer. The camera is nice because

I can see her when we're talking, even though she's so far away in Australia. I'm so very proud of her Rich. She had the opportunity to go to Florence, Italy or to go to Australia for a semester of college. Since she had been to Florence previously, she decided to explore another part of the world. I miss her every day. I can't wait for you two to meet."

"I can't wait, either," said Rich. "I'm sorry she had to miss out on so much."

"I'm so glad I put that silly profile on Millionaire Match," said Carol. She squeezed Rich's hand gently. "Really, Rich! I just have such a wonderful time with you. It's so nice just to get out and laugh again."

Rich stroked her small, perfectly manicured hand. He tried to respond, but no words came. He was suddenly overwhelmed with emotion. It was almost too much, sitting here with Carol, looking into her eyes and wanting her; wanting to be with her always… Rich cleared his throat and blinked, hard. He felt tears welling up, but he wasn't going to let himself cry in front of Carol. He couldn't. Rich abruptly made a big show of searching his pockets.

"Oh that figures," he said, patting his jacket pocket

again. "I'm sorry, Carol, but I need to run out and get my phone out of the car. I just remembered that I'm waiting for a really important call about the trip tomorrow. I'm really sorry. I'll be right back."

Rich didn't wait for a response. He stood up and hurried across the dining room and through the restaurant's double doors. The tears were still stinging at the corners of his eyes. Once outside, he took three deep breaths and stared out at the Atlanta skyline.

How was this petite blonde able to penetrate a hard heart that had been guarded very carefully for so many years? Somehow, she got in, got inside and stayed. *I love her,* Rich thought as he looked up at the stars. That's it. I love Carol, and I think I want to spend the rest of my life with her. Rich felt his heartbeat return to normal, and he exhaled, watching his breath in the chilly night air. After a lifetime of hardening his heart and turning his back on the idea of love and family and forgiveness, Rich Towsley had found true love.

He belonged with Carol. He just knew. He felt it in the core of his being. And he also knew that loving Carol meant he'd have to be more careful than ever. If she knew about his family, the way his real family was, not the people he told her about. Even worse, if she found out about his previous line of work, if she knew how he'd made a living only four years ago…

If he lost Carol … Rich shuddered, but it had nothing to do with the crisp night air. She wouldn't know. She couldn't, he thought. Rich would keep it that way. Rich also felt as if he had known Carol in another life. She was the only one that ever made him feel this way, a true soul mate.

Rich took one more deep breath and went inside to finish his dinner.

Concerned, Carol asked, "Is everything all right?" Carol's eyes were filled with interest as Rich returned to the table. "Rich, you're so pale! Are you feeling okay?"

Rich smiled. "Everything's fine," he said. "I've got it all taken care of."

"Did you make your call?" Carol asked.

Rich stared at her for a second, confused. "My call? Sure. It's all fine. Mark had the confirmation number for the conference room, and I needed it so I could get in there early and start setting up. For the, uh, conference." He hated getting tangled in all these lies.

Carol peered at Rich, her blue eyes searching

his face. "Rich, are you sure you're okay? You sound confused." She hadn't touched her food since he had left.

"Really, I'm fine," Rich said. "I'm sorry, Carol. I'm just sort of, well, I'm sort of nervous about the meeting tomorrow. Lots of important people are going to be there, and I don't have my wing man. Mark's going to be at the funeral tomorrow, so I guess I'm just nervous about doing it alone."

Rich hoped that he sounded convincing. The meeting tomorrow was the least of his worries, but he wasn't ready to tell Carol how he felt – not yet.

"I understand," Carol said. She gave him a warm smile and took a sip of her wine. "I imagine it's really hard to get up in front of people and talk. I'd be a nervous wreck!"

Rich took Carol's hand. "Do you want to share some dessert?" he asked. "They've got an amazing lemon soufflé here."

✦✦✦✦✦✦

It was Thursday morning and Rich was on a

mission. Mark had called earlier and wanted to hang out with his friend in Sarasota like the old days. After walking on the beach in Siesta Key, Rich seemed to be in a rush to get going.

"What's the rush?" said Mark. "We've got all day."

"I'm hungry," Rich said. "Let's go to the Crab & Fin on St. Armand's Circle in Longboat Key."

Mmmm. Nice, thought Mark. Longboat Key was the affluent area of southwest Florida. And St. Armand's Circle was loaded with fine shops and restaurants and, of course, Mark's favorite, beautiful women.

As they arrived, Mark saw an upscale men's clothing store and headed in its direction. "I actually need a new pair of sunglasses," said Mark. "Let's look in here."

Rich accompanied his friend and glanced at his watch for the third time since their arrival only ten minutes prior. After trying on what seemed to Rich almost every pair of sunglasses in the store, Mark settled on a pair and purchased them.

"What do you think?" asked Mark. "Am I movie star material, or what?"

Rich smiled and the two of them went into the restaurant. When lunch was over, Rich told Mark that there was a place he needed to run in to, and if Mark wanted to look around for a while that they could meet later. Rejecting his friend's offer, Mark insisted on staying with his buddy. Rich led the way and walked in to Alexander Jewelers, a very upscale, privately-owned, custom jewelry store.

"So, are you gonna tell me what we're doing here, or do I have to guess?" Mark asked. He eyed an emerald bracelet in the display case in front of him. "What, is it a belated birthday present for Carol or something?"

"Not exactly," said Rich.

"Seriously, Rich! What are we doing here?" Mark walked over to where his friend was standing and peered over Rich's shoulder. "Rich?"

A very well mannered man in his fifties greeted Rich and introduced himself as Alexander, the owner, and his wife, Mary. "Do you have any large yellow canary diamonds?" Rich asked the owner. Mark rolled his eyes and shook his head in disbelief as he silently moved away to look in a case some distance from where Rich was.

"Actually, we do," the owner responded. "And if you don't see anything that you like I can get you anything you need within a few days."

"May I ask exactly what you're looking for?" the man asked.

Slowly peering over his shoulder to make sure that his friend wasn't listening, Rich explained that he wanted an engagement ring. Something that was different and unique, just like Carol was to him.

After a few minutes of looking, Rich was impressed with the tasteful, custom pieces of jewelry that Alexander's offered. But he knew that this ring, like their love, would be forever. And he wanted something really special.

After careful consideration it was decided that custom canary diamonds would need to be ordered. The three stones needed to be a total weight of five and a half to six carats. In addition, Rich took the owner's suggestion of surrounding them with 56 Pavé diamonds. 18 carat prongs would be used to mount the canary diamonds on the platinum shank.

Wondering what could be taking so long, Mark asked Rich what he was doing. Just then the owner had finished calculating the total cost.

"Ninety-thousand dollars!" he exclaimed.

"Perfect," said Rich. "Perfect!!!"

Mark pulled his friend aside in disbelief. "What are you doing?" he asked.

"I am going to propose to her," Rich said.

"To who?" Mark asked.

"What do you mean, 'to who'? To Carol," Rich exclaimed, obviously a little perturbed.

"You're not joking, are you? Are you kidding me?" Lowering his voice and leaning into his friend, Mark simply asked, "Why?"

His friend's retort was also simple: "She's the one!"

"I know you're a very smart man. God knows your responsibilities as a young man (with what you used to do) were enormous. But it just seems strange to me that after being alone for 16 years with the exception of a three month relationship, after turning down all of the women who asked you out ... some that were gorgeous! And I know that Carol is gorgeous but you don't even know her! Can't you just buy a bracelet or something?"

It was evident that Mark had not the slightest idea how Rich felt.

"Have I ever been wrong in the last 26 years?" Rich asked Mark. "I love Carol and that's who I want to spend the rest of my life with!"

"I'll be outside," said Mark. He stalked out of the store and paced up and down the sidewalk until Rich finished his purchase.

♦♦♦♦♦♦

The drive back to Mark's house was awkward. Rich's attempts at conversation were met with silence. Mark refused to make eye contact, staring out the window instead. Rich finally gave up and clicked the radio on. Elvis Presley was singing about a lost letter. Rich had been a huge Elvis fan since he was a kid. Rich turned it up and hummed along with the tune.

Mark snapped the radio off. "Look. I'm sorry for acting like a kid. I really am. I know you love Carol. I get that. But have you stopped to think that maybe she doesn't feel the same way about you? Not everybody falls in love in a few weeks. I mean, $90,000? On a ring? I just don't want to see you get hurt." Agitation was obvious in his voice, even though he was trying to make amends.

"I know," said Rich. "And, honestly, yeah – I've thought about it. And you know what? I don't care. Even if Carol turns me down; even if she tells me that she doesn't love me. It doesn't matter! I know how I feel. And I want her to have the ring. That's all that matters to me."

"I think you're getting in too deep," Mark said, shaking his head. "I think this is gonna come back around and hit you when you least expect it."

Rich didn't say anything.

They drove in silence the rest of the way. Both men were relieved when Rich finally pulled the rental car into Mark's driveway. Mark unlocked the door and picked up his shopping bags, but he didn't move. He turned to Rich, making his last appeal.

"Rich. I'm not trying to rain on your parade, here," Mark said. "Just be careful. That's all I'm saying."

"Sure," Rich said. He didn't look at Mark.

✦✦✦✦✦✦

Later that night as Mark's wife lay in bed upstairs

and his two children slept in their rooms, Mark sat in his private study, door closed, and gazed into the fireplace in disbelief. As he sipped his cognac in a snifter and held his Monte Cristo cigar, Mark was dumbfounded as to why such a smart and practical man like Rich Towsley would spend $90,000 on a ring. More importantly, why would he commit himself for life to a woman he had only known for a month?

He had to do something. Mark unfortunately had the point of view that Carol was more an adversary – taking away his companion and friend of 26 years. He sat down and turned on the computer, then pulled up the Millionaire Match site.

"Let's see ... oh, there. Create a profile," Mark said, to nobody. "Sorry, Rich, old buddy – I tried to tell you! Now you're going to have to find out the hard way..."

The first field on the screen was asking for a user name.

Mark drummed his fingers on the desk for a few minutes, thinking.

Slowly, he began typing.

8

It was the front of another week, and Carol decided to indulge in one of her favorite morning activities – a walk around her country club neighborhood. She put on her tennis shoes and pulled her long, flowing hair into a ponytail.

As Carol walked in the morning sunlight, she enjoyed the picturesque homes of her neighborhood. After 25 years, her neighbors seemed like part of her family. Every turn of the streets brought back different memories of her children. After all, for most of their childhood years, this was their playground. Thinking of Rich made the walk seem easier.

Rich was so considerate, she thought as she walked past the large, beautiful homes. He always opened doors for her when they were out, and he was so easy to talk to. And he had a great sense of humor. Carol smiled. Things were going so well with Rich. Growing up, Carol's parents were warm and affectionate with each other, and Carol had always wanted that in her own relationship, but it was something that her marriage had lacked. Now, she thought, she had that feeling with Rich.

In that moment, Carol decided that with the Easter holiday approaching, she would invite Rich to spend it with her family in Macon. Her family had all liked him, and it seemed that Rich and Daddy had already formed a special bond. Yes, she'd ask Rich to accompany her to Macon for Easter. He'd be back from Florida by then, and it would be nice to spend the day with him after being apart for nearly a week. Carol decided that she would call him as soon as she returned home. Bringing Rich to Macon, especially to Daddy's house, was a monumental event. Carol had never considered any of the men she dated after her divorce as candidates for this. Macon and Daddy were sacred to her.

Carol smiled and quickened her pace. She finished her walk much faster than usual; she was eager to call Rich.

As soon as she got home, Carol picked up her

phone and started dialing Rich's number.

"Hello?"

"Hey Rich, it's Carol. I'm not interrupting anything, am I?" Carol sat down on the couch and eased out of her tennis shoes.

"Of course not," Rich said. "How are you?"

"I'm doing just fine," Carol said. She felt a nervous little knot in her stomach. She still wasn't used to asking a man to go somewhere. "I was calling because I wanted to know if you had plans for Easter."

There was a pause before Rich answered. "No. I didn't have anything special planned."

"Well, that's great," said Carol. "Because I was wondering if you'd like to go with me to see my family in Macon. We'll go to the church I grew up in as a little girl, and after the service, we'll go to the Idle Hour Country Club for Easter brunch."

"That sounds wonderful," Rich said. "Count me in. I can't wait to see your childhood home."

"Oh, I'm so glad," said Carol. "Daddy will be just thrilled when I tell him that you're coming."

Carol and Rich talked for a few minutes before hanging up. As Carol set down the phone, she smiled.

Her father would be pleased that Rich was coming, and so would Mary Linda and Bennett. It was so nice, she thought. Rich seemed to fit right in with the family, like he'd known them all for years. Family was so important to Carol; it always had been. It was refreshing to meet a man who felt the same way.

Absently, Carol ran a hand over the arm of her coral damask sofa and wondered about Rich's parents. What were Mr. and Mrs. Towsley planning to do on Easter? Did Rich ever go up to Canada to visit them on holidays? Had he told them about her? It was funny, she thought. Rich was already becoming a vital part of her family, but she hadn't even spoken to his parents or his brother and sister. In fact, Rich hardly ever mentioned his family, unless she asked about them. A look of concern crept into Carol's blue eyes. Had Rich even *told* them about his new romance, or anything about her?

Carol questioned herself for thinking such negative thoughts. She was being ridiculous. She had no reason to worry. After all, Rich's parents didn't exactly live down the street, or even a few miles away. They lived in another country. It wasn't like they could just stop by for a visit. It sometimes bothered Carol that Rich didn't seem especially close to his family. She couldn't imagine living so far away from her Daddy or Mary Linda. But on the other hand, her daughters were living far away, and she was as close as ever to both of them. Carol sighed. She was just getting a case of the jitters. Things were going so well with Rich that it was easy to wonder if things were just too good to be true …

Carol stood up and walked slowly to her desk. She needed to get her mind on something else, and she decided that she would send an email to Caroline. It was wonderful that her daughter was out experiencing the world, but Carol couldn't help feeling a touch of sadness that Caroline was missing out on so many things at home … the ball, and Carol's 50th birthday party … and, of course, getting to know Rich.

Carol sat down in front of her computer and turned it on, wondering what Caroline was planning to do for Easter. The machine hummed to life, and Carol smiled. Thinking about her daughter's adventures was already cheering her up.

Carol was surprised to find that she had a new message in her inbox. It was from someone called

Fundmanager55. Feeling curious, Carol opened the message. Fundmanager55 had seen her profile on Millionaire Match. Carol had meant to take her profile off the dating site, now that she'd met someone she felt like she could get serious about. But between the ball and her birthday party, and her whirlwind romance with Rich, she'd forgotten all about Millionaire Match. Carol made a mental note to cancel her Millionaire Match account once she read Fundmanager55's email and responded to it. Being a gracious, well-mannered Southern woman, Carol made it a point to write back to everyone who emailed her. After all, it was the considerate thing to do.

Hi there, the email began. *I'm new to online dating, but I saw your profile and I had to contact you. It looks like we've got a lot in common …*

Carol was surprised to learn that they did have many things in common. Fundmanager55 (he didn't give his real name) lived in the nearby Alpharetta area, and he had two grown children, just like Carol. He loved golf and tennis, and he belonged to a country club. He was a financial planner who'd been divorced for two years, and he had decided to give Millionaire

Match a try after a friend had encouraged him.

As she read, a smile crept across Carol's face. Whoever this man was, he certainly did share a lot of Carol's interests. And he'd been divorced, too. He understood firsthand what it was like to watch your marriage dissolve before your very eyes. Before she realized it, Carol caught herself wondering what the mysterious financial planner from Alpharetta looked like ... and then, she thought of Rich's face, his dark eyes and his kind heart. She felt a pang of guilt in the pit of her stomach – she was seeing someone now. The proper thing to do was to write back and politely explain that she was in a serious relationship.

Carol paused as she clicked the *Reply* button, her fingers poised over the keyboard. *Was* she in a serious relationship? She'd certainly been spending a lot of time with Rich, and she definitely felt a spark when she was with him. And, he'd even accepted her invitation to spend Easter in Macon. But on the other hand, she'd only known Rich for about a month. She hadn't even met his family ...

She scanned the email one more time. Fundmanager55 sounded like a nice man, and she and

Rich certainly weren't engaged. Carol was having a wonderful time with Rich, but she sometimes found herself wondering how long it would last. After all, she'd had a wonderful time with her ex-husband too, years ago. And then things had changed, and she'd been deeply hurt. She wanted to trust Rich, but Carol kept a small part of her heart guarded. It was still early in the relationship, and she wanted to protect herself from getting hurt a second time. She tapped her nails on the desk, lost in thought. Maybe it was good to keep her options open, especially since she hadn't known Rich for very long. After all, Carol thought, it's just a harmless email. Rich would never have to find out that she'd responded.

Carol began typing.

Hello there,

My name is Carol. Thank you so much for viewing my profile on Millionaire Match. I enjoyed reading your email, and we certainly do have a lot in common. I have grown children, too – two daughters. And I also enjoy tennis at my country club.

Thanks again for taking the time to email me. I look forward to hearing from you again.

Carol looked over what she wrote. It was brief and cordial, but she'd been careful not to sound too encouraging. She didn't include her phone number, and she didn't plan to contact Fundmanager55 again. She had Rich in her life, and she was enjoying her time with him. She hit *Send*.

A few minutes later, Carol was absorbed in writing a lengthy email to Caroline. She described the ball and related the story of Rich's tuxedo mishap. As soon as Caroline returned from studying in Australia, Carol wrote, the three of them – Rich, Carol, and Caroline – would have dinner at Prime.

Caroline was every bit her mother's daughter – almost a spitting image of Carol. Caroline also had glistening blonde hair, bright blue eyes, and her mother's smile. Making friends came easy to Caroline and they were bountiful. One trait that was passed down from mother to daughter was her interest in nutrition and health. Caroline was very particular in what she ate and was an avid runner. Caroline would also soon be graduating from Miami University in a year and a half.

By the time she finished writing to her daughter,

Carol had forgotten all about Fundmanager55.

✦✦✦✦✦✦

The day before Easter was clear and bright, a perfect Saturday for a drive in the upscale Atlanta suburbs. Rich picked Carol up early. He'd insisted on driving, now that he had his rental car again. As promised, Mary Linda had sent Carol a list of homes in the area that she thought might interest Rich, including the one that they had liked on Mount Paran Drive. Mary Linda had even been kind enough to make a few phone calls and set up an appointment for Rich and Carol to tour the house. Having a sister who was a real estate agent had a lot of benefits. Carol watched the scenery roll past her window and turned to Rich. He'd been unusually quiet this morning, she thought. She smiled brightly at him.

"Daddy was just thrilled that you're coming for Easter," said Carol happily. "He really likes you, Rich."

Rich smiled. "Well, good. I like him, too. He's, well, he's an amazing man. Your whole family's great, Carol. I'm lucky to be included."

Carol studied Rich's profile as he guided the car onto Mount Paran. He was smiling, but something about it seemed forced and unnatural. She couldn't read his eyes because he was wearing sunglasses. Still, she couldn't shake the feeling that something was on Rich's mind. She'd sensed it from the moment he'd picked her up. It felt like there was a distance between them; Carol felt that, although Rich was sitting next to her, he was very far away.

"Rich? Is everything all right?" Carol touched his knee gently. "Did something happen at your meeting? Is Mark okay?"

"Mark's fine," Rich said. As he mentioned his friend, his mouth formed a tight line. "I'm fine, too. I'm sorry, Carol. I think I'm just a little worn out from the trip. I didn't mean to worry you." He reached over and gave her hand a reassuring squeeze.

"I'm just glad you're okay," said Carol. She did her best to sound cheerful, but she still wasn't convinced. There was something on Rich's mind, she was sure of it.

"Is it this one?" Rich asked. He slowed down in front of an elaborate, wrought-iron gate. Beyond the gate, the winding driveway led to a stunning, brick-and-stucco house that looked like something out of a fairy tale. It even had a turret on one side. The vast, emerald-green lawn was beautifully landscaped, and the elegant home rose gracefully in the distance. At the back of the house, Carol could make out the oversized swimming pool and the guest house tucked neatly behind the four-car garage. The home looked like it had been standing for centuries, Carol pondered, not just a few months. It was like taking a step back in time. For a moment, Carol imagined that she and Rich lived in that home together, that it would be their home …

As if on cue, the enormous gate swung open, beckoning them to enter. The realtor must have seen them drive up and opened the gate, Carol speculated.

"That's it," said Carol as Rich guided the car down the gently sloping driveway. "Isn't it lovely?"

"It is," Rich said agreeably. "Now, let's see what we think of the inside."

Carol's heart pounded and she smiled. He hadn't said, "Let's see what *I* think of the house," she thought … he said "*we*." Carol suppressed a smile as she walked hand-in-hand with Rich toward the home's large front doors. As they approached, the doors swung open and the home's builder stepped out to greet them.

"You must be Rich and Carol," he said. "I'm the builder. It's so nice to meet you! Now, let's take a look at this absolutely gorgeous home." The builder stepped aside. "We'll start with the living room," he said.

As Rich and Carol stepped into the large foyer, they paused to take in the beauty of the home: In front of them, a grand staircase wound its way toward the second floor, and a crystal chandelier sparkled above their heads. The living area before them was lined with beautiful, floor-to-ceiling windows that bathed the room in natural light and afforded a breathtaking view of the pool. The foyer and living room floors were finished with creamy-white Italian marble.

"Oh, Rich! It's beautiful," said Carol. "Just beautiful."

They stood in front of the living room windows, admiring the view of the home's expansive patio.

"And you'll love the kitchen," said the builder, motioning toward the far side of the house. "Especially if you like to cook. All of the appliances are industrial quality, and there's a big island with a sink – and just wait until you see the countertops …"

Rich squeezed Carol's hand and they followed the builder into the kitchen. After that, they toured the rest of the house, from the wine cellar and the formal dining room to the master bedroom and home theater room upstairs. Every detail in the home was elegant, and no expense had been spared in its construction.

"Rich, what did you think of the master bathroom?" Carol asked. "The tile on that bathtub was – Rich? Are you okay?"

Rich had that faraway look in his eyes again, and he refused to look directly at Carol. In fact, to Carol, it almost looked like Rich was blinking back tears. To her surprise, she felt suddenly distant from Rich for hiding his feelings. She took a deep breath and exhaled slowly before she spoke.

"Rich, we're not leaving this house until you tell me what's going *on*," Carol said. Her blue eyes gazed sympathetically at Rich. "I've been asking you all day. I knew something was wrong, and you need to tell me what's going on! *Please!*"

After the builder had given such a gracious and informative tour, he asked Rich and Carol if they had any specific questions regarding the home. For the first time since the two of them had been looking at homes together, Rich didn't ask anything. Carol had asked the builder about a few things, but sensed that Rich must not have liked the home as he didn't ask anything and seemed as if he just wanted to get going. Rich thanked the builder, shaking his hand, and the three of them headed toward the front door. The builder stated that he had to shut off a few lights and lock up. Strangely, Rich asked the builder if he minded if he and Carol stayed for a while to talk about the home and go out to the back of the house to admire the garden and two acres of property that the home had to offer. The builder not only approved, but encouraged it as well.

Wow, thought Carol … *Maybe Rich did like the home after all …*

Rich squeezed Carol's hand and headed toward the lavish rear of the home. As a woman, Carol could intuitively feel that there was something weighing heavily on Rich's mind. She had felt it ever since he had hugged her earlier. Just as they sat on the stone bench in the garden area, the builder yelled down from the upstairs balcony that he was now leaving and the front gate would open up automatically as they approached

it. Rich and Carol again thanked the builder for his
time and Rich said that he would call him the next day.
This time, as Rich gazed deeply into Carol's eyes and
again squeezed both of her hands, she felt worried. She
had developed a connection with this man in such a
short period of time. Carol simply took a deep breath
and gave Rich a reassuring smile.

"You must know by now how I feel about you,
Carol," Rich said.

"Please tell me," she replied.

"From the moment I hugged you in my living room,
I could feel you. I don't mean that you just felt nice, but I
felt as if ..." he paused and took a deep breath. "As if you
were a part of me that had always been missing. You fit
in my arms perfectly, and I could feel your energy. Your
breath; your aura. I felt as if we were one."

Holding back tears, Carol said, "Go on."

"I find myself not only thinking of you constantly,"
he said. "But actually yearning for you. Your touch; your
smile. Your laughter ... The more I am around you,
the more I need ... Every home that we have looked at
together in my mind has been for us. Carol, I have never
even remotely considered any other woman I have met

in my life as anything other than an acquaintance at best. There has never been any emotion involved, or anything planned, other than what I am doing with that person in that exact moment. Somehow and in some amazing way, I seem to know, really know, with my heart and soul that I am supposed to be with you. With you and you only, forever. I love you Carol."

Numb and shaking, Carol felt like Cinderella. Could it really be this simple? This simple to have turned this man's heart ... was the journey to happiness really that easy?

Carol snapped out of her daze as she saw a tear roll down Rich's face.

"It is because I feel this way that I have to tell you what I have wanted to tell you for a while now, but I wasn't sure how you would react, so I waited. I don't know how you feel about me exactly, but I am hoping that you are my future. So I need to discuss this with you now," Rich said.

Carol's heart began pounding. Her stomach tightened, and the palms of her hands began to sweat. *Oh no*, she thought. *What were the next words about to come out of his mouth? Was he actually married? Was he in some kind of trouble? Was he sick?* Carol tried to breathe and keep her composure as she awaited his next sentence.

"About ten years ago, I dated a woman in Florida," he said. "After a brief, three-month relationship, I knew that she wasn't what I wanted. So I said goodbye and ended it. Four and a half years later, after forgetting about the relationship and the woman, she contacted me. She said that it was imperative that we meet and that we meet within a day or two. What I'm about to tell you, Carol, was just as shocking to me as it is probably going to be to you. I was divorced from Sandy, and after seven years, I dated this woman for three months and slept with her twice in the same night. About a month later, I knew that she wasn't for me and said goodbye. It turns out she got pregnant and decided to have the child. Her reason for not telling me was she knew that I didn't want to be with her, and she didn't want a man to be with her because of a child. She also realized that, having made that decision on her own, she didn't want any type of child support."

The extent of Rich's relationships was limited. He married his high school sweetheart at age 22. After six years of marriage, Rich had decided to end that union. Six years later, a brief three-month relationship ensued. Though Rich also walked away from that union, it would revisit him several years later.

Carol by now was shocked. *Why didn't Rich' just tell her this from the beginning?*

Rich continued, "After four and a half years of her mother telling her that this little boy of hers deserved a father, and that the father deserved to know he had a son, and it was unfair to not tell the man there was someone who was a part of him in the world. She finally gave in and called me. Initially, I was shocked and furious that she had kept this from me, but after really listening to her reasoning, it was understandable. I met you, Carol, and didn't want you to think that I was some guy who slept with a woman, got her pregnant and then left her. It sounded dirty, certainly not my way of doing things. It would be easy to tell anyone else, because I could care less what anyone ever thought of me. But you, Carol. You, I did care about how you felt. I waited for the right time. I know in my heart and mind that I want and hope that things do work out with us forever! He will always be a part of my life and I want you to be as well. I hope that you can understand I wanted you to see me in the right light, so to speak. I love you Carol. You really are the only woman I have ever wanted. I love you."

Carol looked at Rich and a series of emotions raced through her. She was, in a strange way, somewhat relieved. A child who lived with his mother in Florida was not threatening to their relationship. And, the thought of a small version of Rich being in this world almost made her smile. At least he wasn't married, or sick, or in trouble. Deep down though, Carol was disappointed that Rich had kept this from her. She also realized that because he shared this with her, perhaps he really did feel the way he just told her he felt.

He loves me, she thought, *he loves me*. Carol closed her eyes and smiled. Instinctively, she grabbed Rich and embraced him.

"I want to thank you for telling me, Rich," she said. "Thank you for believing in me and trusting me enough to tell me the truth."

"Can I take you to dinner tonight?" asked Rich.

As Carol stood up and said, "Absolutely," the two of them caressed for a long time, each feeling as if they had reached an important milestone in their relationship.

9

The next day was Easter Sunday and Carol woke up early. Thinking about her conversation with Rich, she realized she felt even closer to him, now that he'd told her about his son. They had enjoyed Saturday evening together, sharing a romantic dinner and going to Carol's soon afterwards. It seemed natural to find themselves kissing passionately on the bed, exploring each other's bodies and enjoying every gentle touch …

Carol chuckled happily. The thought of kissing Rich, of being in his arms, was enough to make her feel so alive, even a bit flighty. And today he was going to Macon with her, to celebrate Easter with her family. She threw back the duvet and slipped out of bed, thinking about what she wanted to wear. She wanted to look perfect today. Carol walked to the kitchen and started a pot of coffee before heading back to her wardrobe.

Carol enjoyed her coffee, then showered and carefully put on her makeup. She dressed in a pale pink Chanel tweed dress with matching jacket. It was appropriately formal for Easter at the church she had grown up attending, and the weather was supposed to be cool. A fresh color for spring, she thought, as she studied her reflection in the full-length mirror. The doorbell rang and Carol looked at the clock on her nightstand. Rich was a little early today. Smiling, she hurried to the door. She couldn't wait to see him.

Rich was standing on the front step holding two small, beautifully wrapped boxes. He looked handsome in his Ralph Lauren pinstripe suit, and Carol noticed the familiar scent of his cologne as she leaned into his embrace.

"Happy Easter," Rich said. "I have something for you. I have something for your father, too. But I want you to open yours right now!" Rich handed Carol the smaller of the two boxes.

Carol was touched. Rich was so considerate. She carefully unwrapped the paper from the little box, curious about what was inside. "This is so sweet of you, Rich! You didn't have to get me anything," she said. She lifted the box's lid and her blue eyes lit up with delight. "Oh, Rich! This is beautiful! Thank you! It's just perfect!"

Inside the box was a gleaming sterling silver bracelet. Smiling, Carol picked it up to examine it more closely. A small cross inlaid with bright yellow stones dangled from the sterling silver bracelet. "Citrine," Carol said, touching the beautiful, jeweled cross. "That's one of my favorites, Rich. I love it! I'll wear it today." Carol fastened the bracelet's delicate clasp. It looked perfect on her slender wrist.

Carol eyed Rich's other box. "What did you get for Daddy?" she asked.

Rich made a dramatic show of hiding the box behind his back. "You'll just have to wait and see," he teased. "It's a surprise."

✦✦✦✦✦✦

The drive to Macon was sunny and pleasant. Carol relaxed and enjoyed talking and laughing with Rich, especially after their difficult conversation the evening before about his son. Rich seemed more at ease now, Carol thought as she held his hand. They held hands for most of the drive.

"Rich, what are your parents doing for Easter?" Carol asked and affectionately squeezed his hand.

Rich paused. "Oh, the usual. They're probably going to church. And, after that, they'll probably have dinner with my Aunt Gail."

"That's nice," Carol twirled her new bracelet as she thought. "Do they ever come to visit you? For holidays? Or do you ever get to go up to Canada and visit them?" She watched Rich's face carefully, hoping that her questions weren't making him uncomfortable.

His expression didn't change. "They don't come here very often," Rich said. "I try to get up to see them when I can, but it's hard with my work and travel schedule."

"Are you going to call them today, to wish them a Happy Easter?" Carol asked. "I'd just love to say *hello* to them."

"Uh, yeah, sure. I'll call them, well, maybe later this afternoon," Rich said. "They'll probably be home again, by evening."

Carol smiled. "Well, when you call, I hope I can speak with them for a moment. I really want to wish them a Happy Easter. I'm looking forward to getting acquainted with your family, Rich. You're getting to spend so much time with my family, getting to know them. I realize your parents are far away, but I still want to get to talk with them a little bit, too." Carol touched his arm gently. "Do you understand what I mean?"

"I know, Carol. My parents ..." Rich took a deep breath. He hesitated, at a loss for words. "Well, they're ..."

"Yes, Rich?" Carol's eyes were fixed on him, waiting.

"They're really excited to talk to you, too." Rich took her hand. He pushed the stinging twinge of guilt to the back of his mind.

"Me too," said Carol. "I can't wait."

♦♦♦♦♦♦

Carol's view and impression of Rich was very important to him. When Carol looked at Rich she saw what the rest of the world saw – the finished product. Where Rich came from was locked away in his past and he wanted to keep it that way. Rich had severed ties with his family, a necessity for him to grow and become the man he was.

Carol wanted to do what any other excited girlfriend expected; to be able to talk with and eventually meet her future husband's family. Wishing them a Happy Easter was a normal and gracious thing to do – especially as a new addition to the family. However, Rich did not want to invite them, ever again back into his world.

They didn't talk much for the rest of the drive. Rich tried to figure out what to do about Carol talking with his parents. He hoped she would forget about the phone call he'd promised. Maybe she'd be distracted with all of the activity in Macon. But, he thought, she was interested in meeting his family, so he would have to decide how to handle the situation.

He needed a plan.

They drove up to a picturesque, white Southern mansion with stately pillars. Carol's father received them warmly, and graciously introduced Rich to his good friend and companion, Corky Holliday. Carol's sister, Mary Linda, was there, too, with her husband

Bennett and their sons. Everyone was properly dressed up for Easter, and the home was so beautifully decorated, Rich felt as if he were looking at a Southern Living magazine. Carol took Rich by the hand as she gave him the tour of the lovely home where she grew up. It was obvious where Carol had gotten her eye for interior decorating. Carol happily led Rich from room to room, pointing out a favorite piece of furniture or an especially beloved portrait as they continued along the way. Rich loved the way her blue eyes sparkled as she talked about her favorite memories of the house. She looked so happy.

The idyllic tour ended with the family in the living room, where Rich presented Carol's father with the gift-wrapped box. Mary Linda and Bennett stood by watching with approval, and Corky smiled at Rich appreciatively.

"It's just something to say *thank you for making me feel so welcome*," Rich said as he gave the package to Dr. Williams. The older man's face lit up as he tore the paper and opened the box. The gift was a beautiful, leather-bound Bible. *Dr. Howard J. Williams* was engraved in gold lettering on the bottom left corner.

Rich had purchased the Bible in Florida, at a Christian bookstore where he'd also found Carol's bracelet. Rich felt a lump form in his throat as he watched Carol's father open the gift. Rich was glad Dr. Williams was so obviously touched by the gift. Rich swallowed hard and put an arm around Carol, who was beaming at him.

"Oh my," Dr. Williams said as he lifted the book out of the box and ran a hand over the fine leather. "This is very nice, very nice indeed. Thank you very much, Rich." He opened the Bible. On the inside cover, Rich had included a handwritten note:

From one Christian man to another. Happy Easter.

Carol hugged Rich. "That was just the nicest gift," she said. "And the inscription: so beautiful! I can't tell you how much it means to me that you have such a strong faith."

Rich nodded. He smiled back at Carol, and then looked to her father as he lovingly patted the cover of the Bible. They were such a loving family; so close and caring. His own family was nothing like the happy, warm people gathered in front of him ... How could he ever let Carol know about that?

Though the handwritten note from Rich read

"from one Christian man to another" – Rich simply wanted Dr. Williams to know that Carol was with a man with like mind beliefs.

He just didn't think he could. She would never understand that side of him … He'd opened up to her about having a son, but this would be different. The boy was innocent. It wasn't his son's fault that things had happened the way they did. He had become a lovely part of Rich's life, so Rich wanted to tell Carol about finding out he had a son. But trying to explain how his family could be so hurtful, when hers was so beautiful …

She just couldn't know.

Carol's father stood and gave Rich's arm an affectionate squeeze. "Thank you, son. I'll treasure this."

"Are y'all ready?" Mary Linda said. "We need to go soon, or we won't get to sit together. Vineville is always crowded for Easter!"

"You're right, Mary Linda," said Carol. She turned to Rich. "I can't wait to show you where I went to church as a girl. Shall we go, Rich?"

"Absolutely, pretty lady," said Rich. "Would your father and Corky like to ride with us?"

✦✦✦✦✦✦

The first thing Rich noticed as they approached Vineville United Methodist Church was how different it looked from Buckhead Church. Buckhead Church was a metropolitan, modern place; Vineville was a classic church, the best of the old South. The building's traditional exterior was stone with a classic Greek pediment held up by Corinthian columns at the top of the wide front steps. Ornately carved wooden front doors were wide open for well-dressed people coming to the service. The aqua walls of the sanctuary were framed by wide, cream-colored molding; the cathedral windows of classic stained glass filled the room with light. As Mary Linda had predicted, the church was filling up fast, and Rich, Carol and the rest of the family were happy to find seats together in one of the intricately carved, dark mahogany pews. A large golden cross hung high on the wall behind the pulpit; brass and crystal chandeliers sparkled in the morning light. Rich scanned the pews in front of them, noticing that the members of Vineville Church were much older than the crowd at Buckhead.

Carol picked up a hymnal and handed one to Rich, leaning close to him. "This is a more traditional service," she said, smiling. "This is where I grew up, where I was baptized and confirmed. My family was very involved, so we were here every week. When my mother passed away in 1993, Daddy donated Bibles in memory of my mother." Carol reached out to the back of the pew in front of them, taking out a Bible to show Rich. He opened the Bible, and read the inscription, "Bible donated by Dr. Howard J. Williams, Jr., in memory of his wife, Mary Tidwell Williams." Rich nodded, touched by the generosity and care Carol's father had shown to his wife, and to their church. He used his sleeve to wipe away the beads of sweat that were forming on his forehead and upper lip. Suddenly, the organ played and the entire congregation stood to sing a hymn. They sat down again and the pastor came to the pulpit for his sermon. He was a distinguished, soft-spoken man who shepherded his flock with gentleness and kindness. He wore formal vestments: rich burgundy velvet with a large cross in the center. Rich tried to listen, but he found it hard to concentrate on the eloquent, formal delivery. These people all seemed sincere, but without the stage lighting and the band's music, Buckhead Church was a contemporary service, not the usual more formal type that most churches offer. Rich simply felt like an outsider, like someone who didn't belong here. He shifted in his seat and watched Carol and her family, wishing he could understand their sincere faith and believe as much as they did.

When the church service finally ended, the family shared Easter brunch at the Idle Hour Country Club. Rich enjoyed the afternoon, talking and laughing with Carol and her family. Mary Linda told Rich funny stories about Carol's childhood, and Dr. Williams and Corky introduced Rich to several of their friends at the country club. The unease that Rich had felt in church was gone, and, by the time lunch was over, he felt like he belonged again.

As Rich drove Carol, Dr. Williams and Corky back to the family home, Carol took Rich's hand. "Thank you so much for coming to church with us, Rich." Carol said timidly.

Dr. Williams invited everyone in for coffee. Rich

and Carol sat down together with the family in the living room. Rich had just started talking to Bennett about business, when Carol tugged on his arm.

"Rich, did you want to call your parents?" she said, her eyes wide with concern. "Oh, please call them so we can all wish them a Happy Easter!"

"Oh. Yeah, I was meaning to do that! We were having such a good time; I didn't realize what time it was." Rich said. A dark shadow came over his eyes. "Please excuse me a minute. I'll just step into the kitchen and see if I can reach them on the phone."

Carol smiled. "Oh, good, Rich! That would be just fine!" As he walked toward the kitchen, Rich heard Carol talking to Mary Linda: "Rich is calling his mother and father. They live in Canada, so …"

Rich closed the kitchen door and ran a hand through his hair. He hadn't taken the time yet to come up with his plan. He took his phone out of his pocket, opened it, and absentmindedly scrolled down his contact list. Did he have his parents' phone number? And even if he did, could he risk letting them talk to Carol? Rich had been in tighter places than this, to be sure, but he was trained to get results at any cost.

Trying to factor in Carol and her sensitive feelings was a different kind of dilemma. He saw his sister's number, but that was out of the question. He stopped scrolling on a number he hadn't called in a while...

He stared at the number, weighing his options. He could simply tell Carol that his parents weren't home; that perhaps his mother and father were still at church or dining with relatives. That might delay having to address the matter, but eventually she'd insist on speaking with them. Rich looked at his phone again. Sooner or later, he thought, it would come to this. He cleared his throat and dialed the number of a former colleague, someone he could trust in a situation like this.

"Yeah, it's Rich. I need you to do something for me." Hoping that Carol or Mary Linda wouldn't come to the kitchen unexpectedly, Rich said in a low voice, "Senti, mi devi fare qualcosa di molto importante ..."

A few minutes later, Rich came into the living room and motioned to Carol. She'd been talking with her sister, but as soon as she saw Rich, she quickly came to him, her blue eyes sparkling. She noticed that Rich was holding his phone, and she smiled warmly.

"Is your mom or dad on the phone?" She asked, reaching toward the phone.

"Well, it's my dad," said Rich. "I guess my mom is still over at Aunt Gail's house. They're probably still visiting and cleaning the kitchen after dinner, but my dad's home. And he can't wait to talk to you."

Rich felt a stab of guilt as he handed Carol the phone. She grinned at him, and he hoped she didn't notice that he didn't return her gaze. This would take care of the problem, he thought.

"Hello? Is this Mr. Towsley?" Carol asked. She paused, listening for a second. "Oh, well it's wonderful to talk to you, too!"

Rich smiled at Carol and nodded toward the door, motioning to her that he'd be in the other room. She waved at him, still listening intently to the man on the phone. As Rich eased the door shut, Carol mouthed the words "Thank you."

Later that evening, as Rich and Carol drove back to Atlanta, Carol recounted her conversation with Rich's father. "Rich, he was just so nice," she said. "I told him that he'd have to come down to Atlanta soon, with your mother. He said he'd think about it – wouldn't that be exciting?"

Rich was sick to his stomach, realizing the phone call was just the beginning of her interest in his family. "Yeah, that would be great." Looking for a way to change the subject, he said, "I really appreciated seeing all those Bibles your daddy dedicated to your mother. He must have been so sad to lose her. Was there a long illness?"

Carol turned towards Rich. "No, Rich. That was one of the hardest things about how she died. She died suddenly and unexpectedly, at such a young age. She was only 61 when she died on September 23, 1993. Rich, you would have loved her. She was such a giving, loving, and articulate person. She loved to cook. She loved simple pleasures; one of her favorite treats was a Mars Bar. I still miss her every day."

Rich gasped. "I love Mars Bars, too! They're my favorite candy bar. Did you say she died on September 23? I don't remember if I told you about my brother Steven. We were always so close, and it's still hard for me to talk about him because I miss him so much. He died on that very same day, just a year before. He was in a motorcycle accident on September 23, 1992, and he died when he was only 23."

"Oh, Rich, I'm so sorry to learn about your brother. What a coincidence that they both passed away on the same day. I always wished my mother could have known my daughters. I'm sure you wish Steven could have met your son, too. Did y'all live close at the time?"

"We were best friends growing up, but I was already in Florida when he died. I just wish I could have seen him and had a chance to say good bye," Rich said with sincere sadness in his voice.

Without a word, Carol quietly put her hand on his knee. She understood his sadness; finding the date in common and sharing how they felt drew them together in a new way. He put his hand on hers and gave it a gentle squeeze.

♦♦♦♦♦♦

That week, Rich and Carol dined at one of Atlanta's fashionable restaurants every night, ending each evening in Carol's bedroom, kissing and holding each other. They grew closer than ever.

On Thursday, Rich drove back from Atlanta to his home in Sarasota. He had a huge network marketing event on Saturday, so Friday was devoted to reviewing his paperwork and notes. Rich was hosting the event, and was also the opening speaker, so note cards with Rich's handwriting were scattered on his desk. He looked at his watch and stood up, stretching. It was nearly 10 PM and he wanted to call Carol before she went to bed.

He dialed her number and she answered on the first ring. They talked about Rich's flight and about Carol's tennis game, just enjoying the sound of each other's voice. Twenty minutes passed quickly; they said good night and hung up. Carol wanted to go to bed and Rich needed to finish getting ready for the big meeting in the morning. As he picked up his note cards, the doorbell rang.

Rich set his note cards down in a neat stack on the desk and glanced at his watch again. At this hour, it must be Mark, dropping off some materials for the meeting. Ever since their conversation after the trip to the jewelry store, something wasn't right between them. Mark said he was sorry about what he said, but Rich felt Mark had simply tried to gloss over how he felt. Most of their conversations since that day were brief and businesslike. Rich walked to the door, recognizing Mark's familiar outline in the glass.

"Hey, Mark!" Rich said as he opened the door. "Thanks for stopping by. I was just finishing going over my notes. Did you bring a few copies of …" Rich's voice trailed off as Mark thrust a few printed pages into his hands.

Rich took the pages from Mark, puzzled. "What's this?"

"I thought you should know the truth," Mark said coldly, with an odd mixture of pity and anger in his eyes. "I tried to tell you. I was just looking out for you."

Rich looked at the papers in his hand. They were printed emails. He scanned the one on top, and recognized Carol's email address. "Where did you get this?" Rich's face felt hot. "Mark?"

Mark wouldn't look at him. "It wasn't hard," he said. "I just took what I knew about her and …"

Rich stared down at the papers. He paged through them, one by one. Slowly, he began to understand. "What have you done? *Fundmanager55*? Mark! What did you think you were doing?"

"She wrote back," Mark turned away, looking

rather pale. "She never mentioned you."

Rich slammed the door behind Mark and stared at the emails. Mark used what he knew about Carol and created a profile for himself to match hers: a fake profile of a man who had everything in common with her, down to the divorce and the two kids.

How could Mark bring this to him so late at night, right before his big meeting? His mind reeled. Rich felt betrayed as he thought of Carol writing to another man. He felt angry and sad and confused.

For 16 years Rich had protected his heart from falling in love, but now his heart was breaking.

He resolutely walked back to his desk and picked up his phone. Carol was probably already asleep, but this couldn't wait. He dialed her number, his heart pounding so hard his head was throbbing.

"Hello?" Carol sounded sleepy. "Rich? What time is it? Is everything okay?" Hearing her voice made the pain worse. Rich fought back tears as he began.

"How could you do this to me, Carol? Are you still looking for someone else?" Rich struggled to keep his composure. "Mark just came and showed me your email."

"Rich, what do you mean?" Carol was fully awake, and very concerned. "What emails?"

"An email from you," Rich said. He waited for a response, but her silence was deafening.

Finally Carol responded. "I don't understand, Rich. He must be mistaken. I've never emailed Mark in my life," Carol said. "I don't even know his email address."

"Does the name *Fundmanager55* mean anything?" demanded Rich.

Carol paused to remember. "Yes, that was the name of someone from Millionaire Match," Carol said, still confused where this was going. "He wrote to me last week and I wrote him back, thanking him for his email. I meant to take my profile off the website but I had forgotten to do it. What does Mark have to do with this?"

"Why did you write him back?" Rich asked. "Were you going to go out with him?"

"I was never going out with him," said Carol. "I was just trying to be cordial. I always thank people for emailing me. It's just the appropriate thing to do."

"Mark showed me the email. He is used to being my bodyguard, so I'm sure he was trying to protect me.

How could you do this?" Rich was in tears, and Carol was incredulous. "I'm so sorry, Rich. I didn't mean to do anything to hurt you. I love you!" Now Carol was crying, too.

"I really don't have time for this right now, with the meeting tomorrow. If you love me, how could you do this? I'll be back in Atlanta on Monday, so you have some time to think about what you are doing, and what I really mean to you."

Rich didn't wait for a response, but as he hung up, he thought he could hear Carol sobbing. A part of him felt horrible that she was so upset. He hadn't meant to hurt her. But he was hurt, too. And if Mark was right, if she wasn't serious about him, he had a right to know.

Rich knew he needed to sleep, but he couldn't keep from walking down to the beach. He was devastated.

Rich wanted to believe Carol. She sounded so sincere. How could she do this to him? How could he trust her if she would do this behind his back? How long or how far he walked, he never knew. When he saw the sun beginning to rise, he went back to the house. He had a meeting to conduct, whether he was exhausted or not. His future depended on it.

✦✦✦✦✦✦

As Rich drove to the convention center, his phone rang. It was Carol. Rich let it ring two times, then three, before he finally picked up. The happiness was drained from her voice, and there was no hint of a titter. She sounded just like Rich felt: sad and tired.

"Rich? I know you probably don't want to talk, but I need to explain something to you. Why I wrote to *Fundmanager55*. Mark made that up, didn't he? That's who it was, wasn't it?" Carol was very upset, but she was trying to be reasonable about Mark's intentions. "I think Mark was trying to protect you, not to break us up. Maybe he thought I would turn out to be some gold digger, someone who just wanted to get some of your money or one of your cars. I think you should know me better than that. I want to tell you how I feel. And I want to tell you how sorry I am. In person."

"Well, I'm coming back to Atlanta on Monday. We can talk then." Rich knew how to shut out his feelings and get the job done. He sounded cold and distant, even though his heart was broken.

"I can't wait that long, Rich," Carol said. "I know you have your big meeting today and I know it's important. But I bought you a ticket for tonight. Delta Airlines. All you have to do is show up and check in. I'll pick you up from the airport. Please come home tonight, Rich. I can't go another day knowing that I've hurt you without seeing you and trying to explain."

Rich turned in to the convention center parking lot and pulled up in front of the valet. "I can do that," he said. "I'll call you when I get in."

"Oh, Rich. Thank you," Carol said. "You just call me as soon as you know when you're getting in, and I'll be there. And Rich?"

"Yeah?" Rich said, reaching for his briefcase and papers in the passenger side seat.

"I love you," Carol said.

Rich didn't say anything for a few seconds, but those words stopped him in his tracks, causing him to pause before slamming the car door. "Okay. I'll see you later."

He hung up and hurried inside, turning his focus on his big meeting.

For the rest of the day, Rich did just what he

knew how to do so well. He gave his speech and made introductions and worked the room. As promised, the president of Rich's company was there, and he made it a point to personally speak with Rich. Rich chatted with the man for a good half hour, but an instant later, he couldn't recall what they'd talked about. Like a strong magnet, his thoughts were pulled back to Carol. He wanted to trust her. He wanted to believe that she loved only him. He had to look in her eyes to know the truth.

As soon as the meeting was over, Rich quickly said goodbye, asking his colleagues to talk with those who stayed afterwards. He ducked out a side door and sped to the airport – he didn't even bother to stop at the house and pick up his things. He had what he needed in Atlanta. He sped to the terminal.

Rich impatiently pushed through security and raced down the corridor, reaching the gate just in time. He spent the flight going over the events of the past few weeks…how he had met Carol, every little thing he remembered about her. He thought about Mark, who had protected him and been his closest friend for 25 years. In his past work, he had plenty of experience recognizing scams. But this was different. His heart was involved. He cared about Carol. Did she really care for him? *Was Mark trying to protect him? What did this really prove?* He couldn't sit still or still his mind. He called Carol as soon as the plane touched down.

Carol was already waiting when Rich walked outside. She waved and smiled, but he just nodded his head. He was happy to see her, and he wanted to run to the Range Rover and throw his arms around her – but he was still so angry that it hurt. He opened the door and slid into the passenger seat.

"Did you have a good flight?" Carol asked, sounding hopeful.

"It was alright," Rich retorted, sounding unconvinced. He didn't look at her. They rode in silence, but he took her hand, and the touch was still warm between them. He looked down at their hands, and then looked out the window, but he couldn't bring himself to look at her. He tried to hold back the tears he felt welling up as he squeezed her hand. She looked over to him at a stop light, and saw the tears in his eyes.

Carol wished Rich would just tell her how he felt about what had happened, but especially about her. Would he just say good bye? Would he trust her enough to understand why she did what she did? Her mind was swirling with questions, and Rich held all the answers. As they turned onto Carol's street, the 45 minute drive had seemed like hours to Carol.

They parked in Carol's driveway and hurried into the house. Just inside the door, he turned and pulled her towards him. He looked in her eyes. "Are you telling me the truth?" He pleaded. "Yes, Rich. I never meant to hurt you. I was just trying to be charming and gracious. And I am so sorry that this happened. You have a very special friend in Mark, who wanted to protect you to do something like that, with your wealth, when other people can try to take it away from you," she rambled a bit, but didn't seem to blame Mark …

"I'll make some coffee," she said. "You've had a long day, so you must be tired."

Rich nodded and followed Carol into the living room.

Rich spent a few minutes in Carol's bathroom, freshening up. He brushed his teeth. He splashed some water on his face and studied his reflection in the mirror. He looked tired and sad. He desperately needed sleep, after walking the beach all night and working all day. But first, he knew that he had to be sure about how Carol really felt about him.

Carol was waiting for him in the living room, with two cups of fresh, hot coffee on the small table in front of her. She stood up and looked at him as he walked into the room, tears welling in her eyes, looking more like a lost little girl than a grown woman. Rich came to her and took her hands in his. She shook her head and tried to speak, but the tears she'd been holding back finally broke free and streamed down her face. Rich drew her into his arms and gently stroked her hair.

"I'm sorry," she said. "I didn't mean to hurt you. I was just trying to be courteous."

"It's okay," Rich said. "I think we both have learned from this."

Sitting down on the couch together, they felt each other's warm embrace. A few minutes passed before they began to talk. "How did your meeting go?" Carol began with a safe question. "It went very well, thank you … Carol, I was so surprised when Mark brought the emails to me. I was really starting to care about you, and to trust you."

Carol looked up at Rich, and haltingly explained

how things had happened. She told him that she saw the email, and realized that they had only been dating a month, so she couldn't really say how serious it was, even though she hoped it would be. Rich told her he hoped it would be important to her, because it was important to him.

Even though they were both exhausted, they continued to talk. They shared their broken feelings, and then were able to express the strong attraction that first drew them each to the other. In the way that only lovers can, they shared forgiveness and delighted in the hope for a new day tomorrow.

"I love you," Carol said.

Rich looked into Carol's deep, blue eyes as she said those words, and he knew she meant it. "I know, Carol. I love you, too."

10

Rich was busy with networking that week in Atlanta, but his birthday was coming soon. He began to think about how he wanted to celebrate. He wanted Carol to be part of his plans. He picked up his phone to call her. "How about dinner at Prime tonight? I feel like a quiet evening with you, sharing some good food, and I want to ask you to do something special and fun with me. Say about eight?"

"I would like that very much, Rich. I'll be ready." Carol replied.

The day passed quickly for both of them, and Carol carefully dressed for dinner in a floral pencil straight skirt with a solid floral appliqué tee shirt, and a featherweight cashmere sweater tied around her shoulders in case there was a slight chill in the air.

As the valet parked the car, Rich and Carol talked
on the escalator going up to Prime. They were seated
in the same special place they had been before, and
enjoyed a delicious meal in a pristine atmosphere.
Rich waited until dessert was served to ask Carol the
question he had considered all day. "My birthday is in
just a few days, on April 10th. I decided I really want
to celebrate with you. Why don't we get away and be
together? I would like to take you to Las Vegas for my
birthday."

Carol was so excited, she immediately agreed to go.
"That would be wonderful, Rich! And I hope you have
a very happy birthday this year. I'd be honored to share
it with you."

"Let's make this trip just the two of us. We can say
that we're going away to celebrate my birthday. I won't
take Mark with me, as I usually would do. That way,
we can really be alone." For the past 25 years, Mark had
gone everywhere with Rich, so Carol had no idea how
big this statement really was for Rich.

"That would be fun, Rich. I agree, we need to
be alone. I don't even want to tell Sherry where we're
going. She's been asking so many questions about our

relationship lately, that I think I'll just tell her you're going to surprise me with the location. That way no one will bother us. We can be alone and enjoy some time to rest together," Carol smiled. She felt so comfortable with him, even though she'd only known him a month. She acknowledged to herself that, to her surprise, she didn't think she would feel embarrassed to stay in the same room with him. She just wanted to be with him.

"I saw Trent Carlini, an Elvis impersonator, on television once, and I've always wanted to see him in person. He's playing at the Sahara Hotel. We can shop and see the sights in the daytime, and I have a couple of special places in mind for dinner. Sound like fun, pretty lady?" Rich was almost surprised to feel so excited.

"It sounds wonderful, Rich!" Carol beamed.

After dessert, they went back to Carol's to talk as they had become accustomed to doing. After drinking coffee together in the living room, they retreated to the comfort of Carol's bed. Carol was so glad that Rich had come back, and that he truly forgave her. His arms around her felt especially strong and secure that evening.

Time flew by. Suddenly realizing the time, they

said a sweet farewell and Rich quickly drove away from Carol's house. It was three in the morning.

This time of night is full of dark silence, thought Rich. Everyone was sleeping peacefully. But only two blocks from Carol's house, Rich saw that everyone had not enjoyed a pleasant night's sleep.

On the far side of the road in front of him, Rich saw what had been a very large, four by two foot square, solid cement mailbox pillar. Two pieces of cement, each a foot square, had been forced from the smashed mailbox and thrown forty feet away. Twenty feet further down the road, Rich saw what had hit the mailbox. Instinctively, Rich stopped and got out of his car to examine the wreck.

Impact with the mailbox was so hard that both airbags on the BMW had been deployed. The airbags were covered with so much blood that it had run down and dripped from the bottom of the car door. Someone had been in an accident, crawled out of the car, and Rich was concerned the driver was laying in a ditch somewhere. He wondered if the driver was dead.

Professional habits took over. Rich took his shirt, covering his hand with it to reach under the car door and pull it open. He wanted to make sure the driver hadn't been thrown into the back of the car. Blood was spattered and smeared on the front seat, but the back was relatively undisturbed.

He started back to his car to get a flashlight, but soon realized the rental car he was driving would not have his flashlight in the glove compartment. He turned to continue trying to see if the driver had fallen close by. He got as far as the wooded area next to the house directly across the street from the car, but still didn't see anyone. "Hello? Hello? Hello?" Rich softly called. No one answered. Everyone in the house was asleep, so he tried not to disturb them.

The night was dark and still. Without a flashlight, he would have to get help. Sliding back into his driver's seat, he drove out of the Atlanta Country Club towards Johnson's Ferry Road. Seeing a police car coming towards him, Rich flashed his lights. The police car slowed and stopped across from his car in the road. Both car windows rolled down, and Rich stated, "There is a single car accident over there. There's blood all over the inside and outside. I don't know if they wandered somewhere, or where they went."

"Could you please show us?" the police officer asked. "Absolutely," replied Rich. He came around and headed back to the scene of the accident.

At the accident, Rich showed them what he had observed. The police officer began to question Rich very closely. "How did you know to use your shirt to do that? How did you know to look in the back like that? And then you followed the blood and you went to the left and the right? And it doesn't seem to bother you." Rich injected, "No, not at all."

The police officer continued, "Most people would be afraid to do that." Rich said flatly, "Well, not me."

Rich went over that way and the police officer asked him if he had seen anybody. Rich repeated that he had seen no one; he just found the remnants of evidence in the path the driver took in walking away from the car. "That's pretty good police work," the officer told Rich. Rich just laughed, but continued, "Did you see that the entire car is still on? The engine's off, but everything else is still on. That shows that the vehicle stopped suddenly. Most likely the water hose is torn out and the radiator is gone. But the electrical system is still on. The reason I looked inside to make sure no one was in there: that's how the fire starts. But I didn't touch it. I left it on."

Finally, the police officer's partner ran the tag on the car. It led to a neighbor who lived just down the street. They walked down toward the house.

The police officer rang the bell and woke up the people at the address given for the car's license. A man answered the door, and admitted that he had been driving the car. Rich noticed a young man had come down the steps behind his father. The teenager had fresh cuts and blood on his mangled face. The officer asked about the injuries, and the father insisted that his son had been in the passenger seat. This made no sense to Rich. Looking at the police officer's face, Rich knew the officer didn't buy this story either, but he seemed willing to let it go. Rich shook his head as he walked away.

Rich didn't notice the next door neighbor had also come outside to take pictures of the accident scene. Rich was too busy watching the officer talking to the man as he took the blame for his son. It seemed they all knew the real story, but no one objected to the cover up.

It was 5:15 AM by the time Rich curved the circle

of the roundabout at the street leading away from Carol's house. The sun came up as Rich finally lay down to sleep.

✦✦✦✦✦✦

Then next morning, Carol went out for her customary walk around the neighborhood. She loved to see the beautiful houses, and enjoy the seasonal flowers in bloom. Several neighbors were standing around talking about an accident that had happened the night before. They even had taken pictures, and especially pointed out a man unknown to any of them who stopped to help. The man was driving a Toyota Prius. This was the same kind of car provided for Rich by his business. Carol's heart sank as she looked more closely at the man they were all talking about, because he had been so brave to check it all out and call the police. The man was Rich! Mortified that the neighbors would figure out that this man had been at her home until 3 AM, Carol didn't say anything about recognizing Rich in the pictures.

✦✦✦✦✦✦

That evening Rich picked Carol up for dinner, and as usual, Mark came along. As they were driving out of the neighborhood, Rich saw one of the neighbors and stopped to talk about the results of the accident, telling Carol about what had happened as he talked with the neighbor.

As they continued toward the restaurant, Carol said, "Rich, I feel like I should tell you that I'm just really embarrassed. I saw that neighbor this morning, and they showed me the pictures of the accident. I saw you in them, but I didn't say I knew you. I was glad to hear you had helped, but I didn't want them to know you had been at my house so late at night!"

"I surely didn't mean to embarrass you, Carol. I knew it was important to stop, in case someone had been injured and was lying on the ground needing help. Don't worry so much about the time. It's really none of their business anyway!"

Carol began to think about this, because she had always cared what people thought of her and what she did. Unable to hold back any longer, Mark interrupted her thoughts. "Rich, it may not matter what they think, but you need to be more careful. You don't just wander around in the dark, especially when I'm not there. That was not very smart."

Rich bristled at this remark. "Carol's neighborhood is just fine, Mark. Relax. I know what I'm doing."

As they ate dinner together, everyone tried to ignore the tension they still felt. Rich was glad he had decided not to take Mark on the trip to Las Vegas with Carol. Carol was trying to make small talk, and said, "Rich, I'm so excited about your birthday. I wish I knew where we were going!"

Rich's heart sank as Mark turned to him with a look of betrayal in his eyes. "Where are you going? I need to make arrangements!" Mark demanded.

Rich tried to smile as he replied, "Mark, Carol and I are going away for a couple of days. Nothing big, nothing to worry about. Just the two of us."

"What happens if something goes down while you're there?" Mark was livid.

"I'm no wimp!" Rich persisted. "I can take care of myself!"

"No, that's not the point! Why take her? Why

don't we all go?" Mark was really hot.

"No. I want to be with her only. I want to get away with her." Rich ended the conversation with a smile. Mark would just have to understand that he would not stand in the way of his relationship with Carol.

Rich wanted everything to be perfect for his trip with Carol. The seats on Delta Airlines and the reservations at the Bellagio were simply the best. Carol was impressed that he would make first class accommodations, and even more excited about their trip.

On Monday, Carol went for her morning walk, and Rich began to think about the trip. Rich realized that Carol would expect his mother to call him to wish him a happy birthday. Carol would wonder what kind of mother he had, and he didn't want Carol to think he had an uncaring mother. He and his mother didn't even speak to each other, but he just couldn't bring himself to explain his family situation. After some deliberation, he decided on a plan.

He thought of an older woman, Harriet, who was about his mother's age; he had known her and her husband for twelve years. When he met them they were in their fifties and he was in his thirties. He made them more money than they had ever made before in his network marketing business. He had actually shared the last eight Christmases with them, so they were like his family.

He called Harriet. "I need to talk with you about something that's going to sound strange." He said he was coming to Florida and would explain what he was doing then. She said, "I'll do anything for you, Rich. We wouldn't have a roof over our heads without you."

Rich got right to the point. "I know this is unusual, but trust me. I've never been dishonest with you. I need a favor but I'm going to have to tell you why after."

"Anything!" Harriet replied.

"I met somebody." Rich said simply.

"You met somebody?" Harriet queried.

"Yeah!" Rich smiled.

"As in a woman?" Harriet was surprised.

"No, a guy named Lars! *Yes*, a woman! We're leaving today to go to Vegas. You know what my parents are like, but Carol doesn't. I don't want to have to explain to her. Would you call me on my birthday, like you're my mother?" Rich gently asked.

"What's the harm in that? Yes, Rich. I'll call." Harriet agreed.

"Her name is Carol." Rich loved saying her name.

"Tell me more about her." Harriet was definitely interested in any woman that would turn Rich's head.

Rich went on to tell her about Carol, about their relationship and about Carol's family. Rich explained that Carol had already talked with a man he said was his father but he had made the excuse that his mother was still at Aunt Gail's. Harriet said, "Hang on. I have to get a piece of paper to write all that down."

Rich was proud to have someone, even if it wasn't really his mother. She was sort of like a mother to him, in a weird way. Carol's family was wonderful and he didn't have anyone like that. This was someone who did know him, who knew what kind of person he was. It was easy to justify. He wanted Carol to hear about someone who loved him.

As Rich hung up the phone, he started to feel something he had never even worried about before... guilt. He felt pressure, but he thought that if Carol talked to someone about him, and it made her happy, then everything would be okay.

✦✦✦✦✦

They flew out of Hartsfield-Jackson Airport on Tuesday morning, because Rich's birthday was on Thursday. They were both excited to be going away together. They boarded the aircraft and took their adjoining seats in first class. Carol put her two women's magazines in the seat pocket in front of her, as Rich put his USA Today and Wall Street Journal on the seat next to him.

Caring for Carol as he did, Rich instinctively double-checked to make sure that Carol's seatbelt was buckled and snug.

About thirty minutes into the flight, Carol glanced over to Rich, who was reading his paper. She was suddenly struck by the reality of their situation. *I am actually flying two thousand miles away with a man I have known for only two months. Obviously, we'll be sharing a hotel room and bed. I'll be letting him see what I look like first thing in the morning!*

Leaning toward Rich, her nervousness strangely melted into comfort. Something in Carol told her that it was okay, as she was reassured and realized she trusted Rich. She gently took his hand and placed it over her hands as she rested their hands on her stomach and slowly dozed off. Rich looked over to see her sleeping peacefully and he smiled. They were together. The four hours flew by and they were in Las Vegas.

The room at the Bellagio was delicious, all colored in chocolate and cream. The walls looked as if they had been dipped in chocolate, and the bed linens were finely woven cream.

Carol enjoyed shopping for gifts for her girls, as Rich took in all of the city's glamour. Rich didn't mind all of the shopping because he was with Carol. They enjoyed dinner at the Picasso, an elegant French restaurant inside the Bellagio. Rich and Carol discovered that neither of them enjoyed gambling, so they just had fun seeing all the fabulous sights that lit up Las Vegas nights.

Returning to their room at the Bellagio, Rich thought they seemed more like a couple returning home, as they had done for years, rather than two people who had only known each other for a few weeks. In Rich's eyes, Carol was already his wife. Making love slowly over a long period of time, they simply fell asleep holding each other tightly.

Waking up early the next morning, Carol was wrapped not only in a soft blanket, but also in Rich's strong arms. Carol wished she could turn the clock back to enjoy this warm and safe place, to spend a few more hours feeling so special.

Being an early riser, Carol was soon anxious to start her day with Rich. Feeling his warm breath on the back of her neck as he slept made it hard for her to move, but nature was calling… Rich awoke shortly after Carol had left his side.

After breakfast and a short workout in the Bellagio fitness center, Rich and Carol dressed for the day. "Are you sure that you don't mind shopping with me today? We could go and do something else if you would prefer…" Carol offered. "I'd love to take you shopping, Carol!" Rich was surprised to be happy with shopping.

Three hours later, Carol was pleasantly surprised that Rich seemed so at ease. His patience as she shopped certainly earned him some brownie points that day.

The second evening, they saw the Cirque du

Soliel production, KÀ™. Carol was amazed at the international cast of world-class acrobats and characters performing in, on, and above the stage. It was truly a breathtaking experience, set in a magnificent theatre reminiscent of a European opera house.

The whole day was like a dream come true for Carol. No one else was around, just the two of them. They had dinner and went to a show and spent time together.

Rich woke up on the morning of his 44th birthday excited he was sharing this day with Carol. He knew he wanted to be with her, and not just for this trip. He felt bad when Carol said, "Don't get me wrong, I love being with you, but in front of God, this isn't right."

In Carol's eyes there was only one way to do things in front of God – the right way – Carol knew from her Christian upbringing that a man and a woman's union should be taken in proper steps, including saving the sharing of a bed when a couple became husband and wife. But with Rich she couldn't resist.

Rich thought, *who cares about that?* He didn't understand how Carol thought about this at all. Not knowing what to say, he said, "I'm so glad you love being with me, because I love being with you, too. How about some breakfast?"

At breakfast, Harriet called to wish him a happy birthday, posing as his mother. Rich smiled as he handed the phone to Carol, "This is my mom, Carol. Her name is Linda. She wants to say hello to you." The two women chatted for a few minutes.

Carol thought she sounded lovely. "I can't wait to meet you!" said Carol. "Please come to Atlanta and be our guest so that I can get to know you." Harriet said, "That would be very special. I'll talk with Rich about that. I would love for you to come to Canada, as well, so I could show you where Rich grew up. Now, promise me that you're not getting married out there in Las Vegas. Don't get married without family to share this joy with you."

"Oh, don't worry. We're just celebrating his birthday, Mrs. Towsley. We wouldn't think of getting married without our families being with us to help us celebrate!"

Carol was so happy. She finally had gotten to talk with Rich's father a few days before, and now with she had talked with his mother. She felt like she was beginning to develop a relationship with the people who were closest to Rich, and she felt deeply satisfied.

But she wanted more. She wanted to meet them in person, to see them face to face. Phone calls were fine, but some things you didn't experience about a person unless you could look them in the eyes. She also knew that Rich had a brother and a sister, so Carol really wanted to talk with them as soon as she could.

Rich's phone continued to ring, until he finally put it on silent. He told Carol about good friends who called, and a man he said was his brother. So many people were calling to wish him a happy birthday! Dozens of friends and acquaintances from all over the country, Canada, and Europe left messages, but most of them weren't in English. He listened to the calls later, so he wouldn't have to explain them to Carol.

On the evening of Rich's birthday, they saw Trent Carlini, the Elvis impersonator. Rich had the best time, because he had been an Elvis fan all his life, and Rich thought Carlini was the best Elvis impersonator. Carol laughed and sang along, and Rich enjoyed how her Southern accent blended with the King's. Best of all, Rich thought, he shared the whole day, his birthday, with Carol. That night they shared real passion, love, incredible feelings. They couldn't get enough of each other.

✦ ✦ ✦ ✦ ✦ ✦

The trip was over all too soon, and they were back on the plane to Atlanta on Friday.

They sat in two large club chairs. Rich reached over to put his hand on her leg. Carol put her hand over his, and she was soon asleep. Rich looked over at her, and studied her beautiful, relaxed face. An odd feeling came over him, like she was his soul mate, his wife.

He wondered, *what if this could work? What if I just sweep the crap of my life under the rug so it would work? I could imagine her being 70 and falling asleep next to me on a plane, going places together for the next 20 years.*

He was so confused, so perplexed. He could never imagine doing this to her, hiding so much from her. But he couldn't imagine her finding out the other side of his life. He resolved that she would never know. He made the decision looking at her sleeping that I hope (he wished he could pray) by fate or that weird thing called life that I'm looking at her when she's in her seventies and she'd have been my wife for 20 years.

Rich thought about the tremendous time in Vegas with Carol. This is the first time he felt guilty about concealing who he really was or at least who he had been. Rich thought about Carol's father. What a kind and loving man he was! He was such a spiritual person, a sincere Christian who adored his family. Even though Rich didn't understand why Carol worried about what God might think, Rich really wanted Dr. Williams to think he was a good Christian man.

Rich's thoughts were interrupted as the pilot announced they were landing.

✦✦✦✦✦✦

Carol called Sherry as soon as the plane touched down. "We're coming back from Las Vegas!" Sherry interrupted, "Las Vegas? I can't believe it!" Carol continued, "I can't talk now, but Rich and I would like to take you to dinner at Prime on Saturday evening. Can you come?" Sherry agreed to come.

Rich drove Carol back to her home from the

airport that evening, and the wonderful trip was over.

Carol invited Rich into her home for coffee, and they sat on the sofa in her living room to savor the moment. They began to talk about their growing relationship.

Rich had always seen such a sweet, loving Carol, but that night as they sat on the couch, Carol firmly held his arm. She said, "Are you embarrassed by me? Are you ashamed of me because I'm southern? If you're not, if you do think about me the way I think you do, I would think you would want your family to meet me. I want to meet them. I've only had one little conversation with your mother. If we're going to be together, I want to see them. I want a definite time we're going to meet them. I know my mother, if she was alive, would be devastated if I was serious about someone before she had met them."

Rich changed the subject, but he knew he was in trouble. Carol wasn't going to let it go. He would have to introduce Carol to someone in his family if he wanted their relationship to continue to grow. They talked about the fun they had shared in Vegas, and enjoyed being together.

Rich said good night, kissed Carol good bye, and headed back to his place in Buckhead. It wasn't a good night for Rich, however, because he spent most of the night agonizing over what he would do. He wanted Carol to be his wife, but he was sure she just couldn't handle knowing about his past. There was so much she didn't know.

Rich was born on April 10, 1964 in Hamilton, Ontario, Canada, at Henderson Hospital, to Donald and Linda Towsley. Linda gave birth one month before her seventeenth birthday. Donald was almost twenty. Within two years, Rich's sister Lori Ann was born and the family moved to a rough neighborhood on the south side of Chicago. Donald, having just a tenth grade education, had eagerly accepted a job as a cleaner with Ozark Airlines.

While Rich knew that Carol had spent her summers riding horses and playing on her grandparents' acreage, Rich's experience had been so different. If he was lucky, on hot summer days, teenagers would take the side cover off fire hydrant across the street from his apartment. Rich and the other young children would find a spot in the water that spewed from the hydrant and be carried down the street by its force. It became a poor man's water park.

The neighborhood was a place where immigrants hoped to survive and get a start in the US from subsistence jobs. When Rich went to kindergarten, he stood out as the only white boy, and the only one from Canada. His classmates were black or Latino, so they were connected with those communities. He didn't fit in either group, and he learned to survive by fighting. Later, he learned Jiu Jitsu and Kempo karate so he could win more fights.

Carol had enjoyed loving parents, and a father who was a doctor and provided a good life for his family. Her mother had invested her days giving her girls a proper upbringing. How could Rich explain to Carol that his memories of his parents were hearing his father beating his mother as Rich lay in bed in the next room; the screaming they directed at him, his sister, and their two younger brothers; and the ways he found to escape? Not once had he heard his parents speak of loving each other or their children.

As he grew older, Rich would escape home in the summertime by sneaking on the subway and into

Wrigley Field, the home of the Chicago Cubs. He couldn't be there legitimately, because he never had the money for a ticket, but he learned to love baseball and he could forget his life for a few hours. Carol wouldn't understand that he often stole what he wanted, or that he tried to find a safe place in the homes of his friends from school.

Years of dirtball fights at local construction sites helped him make friends, and also developed his pitching ability. He was asked to join a little league baseball team as the pitcher, and Rich loved playing baseball. The only thing he hated about baseball was seeing his friends looking good in uniforms their mothers had washed. He made excuses for his dirty uniform to cover up his mother's neglect.

Carol had taken him to the home where she had grown up. A recurring nightmare Rich had never shared with anyone was the day his family's building was condemned. His family and all his neighbors were forced out, and Rich watched as a bulldozer leveled the building that had been his home. He had no childhood home to share with Carol.

His parents moved back to Hamilton, Ontario,

where he had been born. He was twelve, and Canada felt like a foreign country since he had grown up in Chicago. School was hard, because they used the metric system, many words were spelled differently, and French class was mandatory. Worst of all, there was no baseball. He did make friends with Mike Mansfield, and this relationship would influence his life for the next thirty years...but Rich knew he couldn't begin to go there with Carol.

Rich was sure that Carol was just too sheltered, too genteel, too much of a good Christian for her to understand what his life really had been. He decided she just didn't need to know, because that was all in the past. He had taken care of himself very well, and he had treated her well, just like a good Christian. If he told her now, he was sure she'd be gone. Maybe he could tell her the truth after they had been married...maybe later, but not now. For now, she would have to meet a better family than the one into which he had been born.

✦✦✦✦✦✦

On Saturday evening, Carol had asked Sherry to join her and Rich for dinner. They decided to take

Sherry to Prime, as it had become one of their favorite restaurants.

As the host seated them, Sherry noticed a new ring on Rich's hand. It was gold, diamond studded, and a substantial size. Most significant to Sherry was that Rich was wearing it on his left hand. Sherry probed, "Rich, what a beautiful new ring! You guys didn't get married in Vegas, did you?"

Rich looked directly at Sherry and simply said, "No." Rich looked at Carol, and she smiled, but Rich was sure Sherry didn't believe him. Carol's agreement with his statement didn't convince Sherry either. They didn't say anything more about the ring, but the rest of the meal, they could tell that Sherry was irritated.

Thirty minutes after Rich and Carol dropped Sherry off at her home, she called Carol. She thought Rich was gone, and she demanded the truth. "You did get married, didn't you? I know you did! Tell me right now!" Carol slowly replied, "No, Sherry. We went to Las Vegas together to celebrate Rich's birthday. He had seen Trent Carlini, an Elvis impersonator, on television, and he wanted to see the show in person. We went to the Sahara Hotel for the Elvis show and had a wonderful time. He didn't want to tell me where we were going because he wanted it to be a surprise. It was just a lovely three days together."

Sherry had been a very dear friend to Carol, but she had become jealous that Rich had come into Carol's life. Sherry's husband had passed away a year before, and she had latched on to Carol to fill the emptiness. Carol was spending too much time with Rich, and taking a trip with him was more than Sherry could stand.

To Carol's surprise, Sherry insisted, "Carol, this is moving much too fast. I can't be friends with you if you are set on seeing Rich this way. I just know he will hurt you, and you'll be glad I forced you to back off."

Carol loved Sherry, but she couldn't put Sherry before Rich, because she knew that she loved Rich. This arrogant assertion by Sherry forced Carol to make a choice. "I don't know what's going on in your life, Sherry. I don't know if you're unhappy with me, or if I've done something wrong. If I've hurt your feelings, I'm so sorry."

"I don't like Rich. I don't think he's right for you. If you continue to see him and have made that choice to be with him, then that's it with our friendship."

"Sherry, I can't do that. I'm sad that you would make me make that decision. I would never do that to you. If there was someone important in your life, I would want you to be happy, to find romance. We have a totally different relationship than what I have with Rich. You are my very dear friend and I would hope that you would want me to have a wonderful romantic relationship, too."

Carol hung up her phone, sad that it would come to this. Carol would not talk with Sherry again. Carol knew that she loved Rich, and he was much too important to her to let Sherry get in the way.

11

Carol finished her daily walk, showered, and dressed. She needed to call Mary Linda and Daddy to tell them about the trip. Everything had gone so well, and she wanted to share her happiness with them. *How do I tell them that I feel like Cinderella?* she thought. Just like Cinderella, Carol knew that she didn't ever want the clock to strike midnight. She wanted her dance with Rich to go on forever … *Do I actually tell my family that my search is over, and my handsome prince is finally here?* Carol hesitated for a moment, thinking about how her daddy may respond.

The phone rang twice before Mary Linda answered. "Hello, Mary Linda. This is Carol!"

"Well, hello, Miss Jet-setter!" Mary Linda joked.

"Are you back safe and sound?"

"Yes, I'm back home safely, but honestly, I wish I was still in Las Vegas," Carol replied.

Laughing, Mary Linda agreed all that glamour and glitz and so many fine shows and restaurants made it hard to forget Las Vegas. Carol wasn't thinking about all that…she was thinking of being with Rich. She closed her eyes and she could still feel Rich's arms holding her tightly. She could smell his cologne and almost hear him breathing on the back of her neck. She had goose bumps just thinking about it! Carol opened her eyes, and her heart sunk as the spell was broken. For the first time since meeting Rich, Carol felt herself missing him, wanting him near.

"Is this a good time to talk?" Carol asked.

"Absolutely! I have a few minutes before lunch that we can visit. Bennett and I went to see Bradford at Auburn this weekend, and Bradford asked how you were doing." Mary Linda was glad to talk with Carol. They usually spoke at least every other day, and Carol hadn't spoken with her last week while she was away with Rich.

"Please tell my sweet nephew, Bradford, that I

couldn't be better! Rich took me to Las Vegas last week to celebrate his birthday with him. We had such a great time! We stayed at the Bellagio, and saw two shows. I think you would have loved the Cirque du Solilel, Mary Linda. The artistry is amazing. You've seen them before, haven't you?"

Mary Linda remembered, "Yes, Carol, Bennett and I saw Cirque du Soliel a couple of years ago in Atlanta. I love the colorful costumes, and the acrobatics are astounding!"

"This show was called *KÀ*™, and the MGM Hotel had a special stage where the performers even used a special elevated center circle, doing intricate acrobatics as the stage rose and turned. It was amazing!" Carol recalled.

"That does sound incredible, Carol! Did you and Rich have anything special to eat while you were in Las Vegas?"

"Yes, Rich took me to two fabulous restaurants …"

The conversation lasted over an hour, as Carol described the room at the Bellagio, and they talked about the Elvis impersonator. Carol and Mary Linda had been close growing up as sisters, and had been best friends since they were in junior high, so they shared almost everything going on in their lives with each other.

After a salad for lunch, Carol called Daddy. She happily talked about all the things they had enjoyed, especially how patient Rich was while shopping with her. "Daddy, Rich is such a gentleman, and so affectionate. He reminds me of you! And I spoke with his mother on his birthday!"

Daddy liked Rich, so he was happy that Carol had been able to celebrate Rich's birthday with him. Daddy added, "Carol, I'm so happy you were able to speak to Rich's mother on the phone. I'm sure she is as nice as he is. That is a special day for her, too."

"I'm really glad you like Rich. I want someone who can share his family with me, as I have shared my family with Rich." Carol was touched by her daddy's gentleness. "Thanks, Daddy. I'll talk to you soon." *He's a fine man,* she thought as she lay down her phone. *I'm glad Rich likes Daddy. I hope Rich's father likes me, too.*

About that time, Rich called. "Hi Carol! I'm sorry I'm going to be so busy this evening, catching up on work from last week. I won't be able to have dinner with you tonight, but I'd like for you to spend the day with me tomorrow. I want you to join me at a meeting where I can introduce you to some of the people working with me."

"I'd love to be with you tomorrow, Rich. I'm tired after the trip last week, so I'll be just fine having a quiet evening tonight. What kind of meeting did you have in mind for tomorrow? I want to pick out something appropriate to wear," Carol explained.

"We'll be going to Bill Shaw's house, Carol. He was Ted Turner's top employee. He's been with Ted for over thirty years, and he is in my network marketing business. There will be a number of professional networkers there, and several prominent local business people. Business casual is what you will want to wear. I'll plan to pick you up in the late afternoon." Rich sounded excited.

He had never taken a woman he personally cared for to a meeting with him. This would be a kind of test, both for him, and for Carol. He always had several streams of income, and people involved in one stream didn't know about the others. Rich liked to keep it that way. No one needed to know about what he did, or how much money he made. If Carol was going to be in his life, this would have to work differently.

She had gently questioned him about the expensive house he wanted to buy in Atlanta, especially because she still thought he had eleven cars and a house on the beach in Florida. Wealthy Atlantans often had beach houses, so Rich had made this excuse and Carol had accepted it. She didn't really understand network marketing, and this was one stream he could let her see. She would meet the type of people involved, and understand how lucrative it was.

Rich would wait to see if this would be like so many other people he had gotten to know too well. When people knew how much money he might have, they were eager to hang on, to enjoy what he could do and let him spend money on them. He didn't need for people to know he had money, because he kept his business to himself. He didn't need to impress people, or to draw attention to his wealth, or himself for that matter.

But letting Carol in was different, Rich thought as he drove to pick her up for the meeting. When Mark realized Carol was going with them, Mark said, "What, are you crazy? Bringing her to this? What's going to happen if you break it off?" Mark kept talking about what might transpire if it didn't work out between Rich and Carol. Rich said, "I don't think of Carol that way. I'm going to be with her forever." Mark was silent, and seemed unconvinced.

Rich was undaunted. He could show her this business, because all these people saw him as a successful networker. He had helped many of them make substantial sums of money in legitimate multi-level marketing businesses. These were real business associates and friends.

As Carol walked into the chic country club home with Rich, she felt all eyes turn to them. Rich was the center of everyone's attention as he offered her his arm and she circled the room with him for the whirlwind of introductions. Her grace and elegance were at home in this setting, as she took her seat at the front of the crowd to watch her man in action. Rich was confident and professional, and proud to share this aspect of his work with her.

Even as he began his presentation, he pushed back the fear that began to grow in his mind and heart. *Carol was different*, he realized. She could see this side of him, this professional businessman. But the other side of him, this he feared her ever coming to know. If Rich could have it his way, she never would.

✦✦✦✦✦✦

Rich and Carol really enjoyed the day together, and talked about the people Carol had met over coffee that evening. "Rich, I really liked getting acquainted with your business associates. Thank you for making me part of your life. I particularly enjoyed meeting Bill and Sheri Shaw. Their Southern hospitality certainly shined. I can tell that they both adore you." Carol said.

"Thank you! I am very proud to be with you, Carol. You're such a beautiful lady, I feel lucky to have you by my side." Rich smiled nervously. He had a reason to be nervous, as Carol brought up *that* subject again.

"Rich, I asked you a question that was very hard for me to ask the other night, and you didn't really give me an answer. Is there a reason you're not letting me meet your family?" Carol's eyes met Rich's, but he immediately turned away.

He knew what he had to do, and turned back to look at her. "Carol, let's arrange for our families to meet. I can call my parents, my brother, and my sister, and ask them if they could come to Atlanta for a weekend to meet you and your family. I know Caroline couldn't be here, but maybe Malinda could come."

"Rich that would make me so happy! I've wanted to meet your parents, and to show them just how much we care for each other. My family could stay at my house, and we could reserve rooms for your family at the Ritz Carlton. I'm sure they would enjoy staying together and having some time to visit." Carol was elated.

Rich tried to be excited, and he was glad that Carol was so happy. Inside, however, Rich was wrestling with such mixed feelings. Carol had already spoken on the phone with a woman who was not his real mother, and a man who was not his real father. Meeting them in person would be much more complicated. He had started down this path of a substitute family, and now he would have to get this family to show up for the weekend. He looked over at Carol, who was so beautiful and beaming with joy. He would just have to make this happen. He loved Carol too much to let her down.

✦✦✦✦✦✦

That weekend, Rich went to Florida to create the substitute family for the weekend meeting. He personally sat down with two women who could pose as his mother and sister. While he was in Florida, where Carol couldn't overhear, he would also call and arrange for a substitute father, brother, and brother-in-law. He had already introduced Carol to his mother and father over the phone, so these two roles would remain the same. The sister and brother-in-law, and the brother would have to be arranged. If he could get these five to show up, along with Mark and Melanie, that would be a respectable family.

Rich was surprised at the churning in his stomach. After all, he had spent 25 years in an occupation keeping his real identity secret. He had accomplished numerous jobs with great skill. His performance had been perfect, and he had never been caught. He was good at what he did. Why would this be any different?

He was playing a role, and the others would, too. Carol just couldn't find out. That was the real issue. He wanted Carol to trust him, and he was creating a fake family so she would trust him more. But what else could he do?

Rich lamented how this kept getting deeper and deeper! He was used to pressure, but serious stuff, real life and death, rather than just some lady wanting to meet his family. He would lie next to her and think; *I didn't do this on purpose. I just wanted to love her and be with her.* But Carol had told him how much her father and her family liked him. She only wanted to make the same impression on his family. That only made it worse.

++++++

Rich began to make his arrangements. He contacted Harriet and Kim, and they agreed to meet for lunch with him. He could relax a little, visit with them, and then talk about what he needed for them to do for him.

First he talked with Harriet, a tall, attractive woman with dark hair. She was in her sixties, and she had pretended to be Rich's mother when she spoke on the phone with Carol. Rich was nervous, because he knew Harriet had some strong beliefs. She and her husband always prayed before dinner at Christmas or Thanksgiving when Rich had dined with them. Rich didn't close his eyes, but he just looked down at the table and waited for them to finish. Still, he wondered how Harriet would respond to his explanation.

Rich reminded Harriet, "You're like a real mother to me, since I've spent so much time at your home in the past 12 years. And, haven't I been like a good son, providing for you with our network marketing business? How could I ever introduce Carol to my mother, when I haven't seen her in eighteen years? You know how I left home at sixteen by selling my motorcycle and buying a one-way ticket from Canada to Sarasota, to live with my grandmother and get away from my parents. If my grandmother were still alive, I'd have some kind of family to show Carol. But she's been gone now for years. I miss her every day, but I wouldn't think of pretending that my parents ever took care of me the way she did. I just need for you to say you're my mom. Just this once, for me, so Carol knows I have a family who loves me."

Harriet answered, "Rich, I'll agree to do this for you on one condition. You know I'm a Christian, and I would never push my beliefs on you. But I want you to understand that I don't like this deception. Do you really, truly love her? And are you going to marry her?"

Rich replied sincerely, "Yes, yes I am!"

"Okay, what are you going to do if something happens to you and she has to call your parents?" Harriet was deeply concerned.

"I just won't give her the number, I guess." Rich changed the subject. "I'll pay for you to come up to Atlanta. I'll buy first class tickets, put you up at the Ritz, and pay for your time there."

"If you do that, I'm not coming. I don't like the sound of paying me to do you a favor. You did so many favors for me and my husband, so that we'd make money in network marketing with you."

"That's different, that's networking." Rich countered.

"You've made us more money than I thought I'd see in a lifetime, and all in just four years. You don't need to pay us for this. It's not about the money. We want you to do the right thing. Are you really sure you're going to marry her?" Harriet repeated.

"Yes, I am going to marry her. And, trust me, this is the right thing. I've put a lot of thought into this, and I'm going to do this – with you or without you." Rich was adamant. Reluctantly, Harriet looked down at her food, thinking carefully. She turned to look at Rich. "Rich, I'm only doing this for you because I truly think you are in love with Carol and you will make each other happy."

Rich explained some of the details Harriet would have to keep in mind if she was going to pose as Rich's mother. Rich would buy a ticket to Atlanta for Harriet to fly in from Sarasota, Florida. She would have to pretend to be Linda Towsley from Hamilton, Ontario, Canada, and remember she was the person Carol had already met on the phone.

Rich explained that Carol had already talked with a man posing as his father, too. "Rich, I can't pretend to be someone else's wife. That would be wrong. You'll have to find another way to do this without my husband."

Rich quickly adapted his plan. "Harriet, let's just

say that my father is coming, but at the last moment, he won't be able to get there. Carol will be disappointed, but she'll understand that something came up at the last minute. Then you won't have to deal with that. Okay?"

Harriet agreed.

Now Rich turned to Kim, a thirty-two year old dear friend, who with her husband had made substantial money with Rich in network marketing. She was unenthusiastic, but she let Rich persuade her to do it. She agreed to pose as Lori, Rich's sister. Rich explained that his sister was from Florida, just like Kim was, so this part would be easier for Kim to play.

Harriet and Kim had known each other for about five years, since both had been involved with Rich in his network marketing business. At least they knew each other, and would enjoy being together in this. They finalized the other details. Rich would pick Harriet and Kim up at the airport on Thursday, and they would stay for the weekend at the Ritz Carlton in Buckhead. Rich just hoped the other people would come, so that he would have a good turn out for this event. He certainly didn't want to have to do this again!

Rich thanked them sincerely for what they were doing for him, and for Carol. They chatted for a few minutes, but the tension in the room made conversation difficult. Rich was glad when Harriet said she had to leave for her hair appointment. He said good bye, and headed off to his next stop. At least he got what he came to ask them for.

As he drove away, he was relieved that Harriet and Kim had agreed to his plan. He didn't understand why it felt as if there was something heavy lodged in the pit of his stomach. He had done jobs before that included so much more risk, but he had never felt sick doing it. He was a professional, and he did his job.

Rich told himself this was no different. He had been well trained in his network marketing, and in his other line of work. He was confident he would pull this off. *It was just another job,* he told himself. He would perform perfectly, and everything would be fine. Carol would know that he had people who loved him, too… Carol. What would she think of him if she ever found out? He wanted to be with her. He wanted her to like him, and he had never cared what anyone thought before Carol. He wasn't used to feeling guilty about what he did.

◆◆◆◆◆◆

Rich made phone calls to others who would be coming for the weekend. Kim needed a convincing person to play her husband, so Rich decided to ask Mike Heckerman. Mike really was his brother-in-law, albeit a former brother-in-law. He had been married to Rich's sister, but they had been divorced. Rich really liked Mike, and they had remained friends after the divorce. Rich's sister had ruined two more marriages after divorcing Mike. Now she was married to a psychiatrist, and Rich ironically thought when his sister married this man it would work. She finally had someone who could deal with her emotional state.

Rich talked with Mike, who had moved away from Florida and lived in Seattle, Washington. He would have to fly to Atlanta very early on Friday, because he would pretend to be coming from Florida. Mike agreed, but he reminded Rich, "You know I'm not a doctor, Rich. Don't expect me to be knowledgeable in that line of work. I'm just a salesman. If you're okay with that, then I'll be glad to help out. It will be nice to see you again, and I'll enjoy meeting Carol."

Perhaps one day – maybe a year or so after they marry – Rich could tell Carol the truth. He thought after a year he would have demonstrated his love and sincerity toward her, but she would have had the opportunity to experience his passion for her.

Next Rich called Pat Ellis, an old friend who agreed to pose as Rich's brother. Pat would be flying in from Orlando, to stay at the Ritz Carlton with the others. Pat didn't see any problem with the part he would play. "Glad to help out, Rich. Carol must be some woman for you to bring her into your life. But I'm sure you've thought about all the issues. Good for you!" Pat was set.

Rich called Landon, a long time friend from Ohio who would pose as Uncle Alan. This was an easier call, because Landon worked with Rich sometimes and was used to concealing his true identity. Rich made the same arrangements with Landon to fly into Atlanta, and explained that he would pretend to have come from Miami, since that was where Uncle Alan lived.

Finally, Rich called Mark, and invited Mark and

Melanie to come. Rich agreed to buy their tickets, and to have a room for them at the Ritz. Mark said he would have to see what Melanie thought before he could commit to coming. He thought they might have plans that weekend. Rich flatly told Mark that this was part of the job, and he expected Mark and Melanie to be there. Mark didn't really respond, but Rich was used to Mark being where ever Rich needed him to be. He would be there.

Rich had the actors he needed for all the parts. He made some notes about how to keep this fake family looking real. Harriet was from Florida, but his real mother was from Canada. His brother-in-law, Mike, was flying in from Seattle, but Mike had to pretend to be the current husband of his sister, who lived in Florida. The woman playing his sister would be coming from Florida, the correct location of his real sister, but Mike and Kim would have to pretend to be married, when they had never met.

The extras, his fake brother and uncle, as well as Mark and Melanie, would help him keep it all together. Pat Ellis was actually from Florida, and Landon had spent many summer vacation weeks in

Florida. Rich would count on them to fill in some of the conversations and help him keep Carol's family away from too many personal questions that would expose the play. Carol already knew Mark, and Mark knew all these people, so Mark would be essential for helping him keep all this together. He thought Carol and Melanie would like each other, so they could talk more easily. Melanie and Mark would just have to remember all the roles the others were playing.

All this would be very difficult to maintain over three days. How would he keep it all straight? Rich felt he was going to be sick.

◆◆◆◆◆◆

With all the arrangements made for his created family to come for the weekend, Rich packed to head back to Atlanta. Rich thought about Carol, about the weekend, and about everyone coming to see them. He decided he would ask Carol to marry him that weekend. He had the ring. All the people who were important to Carol would be there. He could surprise her and still have everyone there for her. As long as his substitute family performed as if they were real, it would be perfect. He would like to have these friends there when he asked Carol to marry him, to share his real joy.

This idea even made the whole thing seem more justified to Rich. To his surprise, he wished he could pray for all this to work out. He never prayed, but Carol and her family made it seem like this was a natural thing to do. They were respectful, but they seemed to talk to God as if he was a real person who could actually hear and help them. Maybe it would make him feel better, but he couldn't bring himself to try praying. He would just have to wish for this one.

He finished packing, and decided to make a very important purchase before his trip. He had pretended to have eleven cars in his Millionaire Match profile, and this was a natural thing for him to want, because he loved fine cars. Carol had noticed the Mercedes 500SL several times as they were in traffic, and she had commented about how beautiful it was. Rich had taken her to the dealership in Atlanta, so that she could drive one, but the sticker price scared her, so she just admired the floor model.

Rich decided he would buy Carol a Mercedes 500SL for a wedding present. He drove to South Tamiami Trail, stopping at Mercedes-Benz of Sarasota. The salesman arranged for delivery that afternoon to Rich's home of a white Mercedes 500SL with blue interior. Rich was pleased with the purchase, and more excited than ever about his plan to engage Carol.

◆◆◆◆◆◆

With the new Mercedes 500SL safe in his garage, Rich headed back to Atlanta. As he drove, he went over all the plans in his mind, wishing them to go smoothly. The date was set for May third. He had made plane reservations and dinner plans for everyone. His mother and father, his uncle, his sister and brother-in-law, and his brother would all fly into Atlanta. He would pick them up at the airport without Carol, because she couldn't see where the flights were coming from. He would be sure to remove all the airline luggage tags, because they might show the flight originations. Carol would be busy with her family, he reasoned, so she didn't need to accompany him.

By the time all the plane tickets had been purchased and the Ritz Carlton hotel rooms paid for, Rich had spent more than ten thousand dollars. He knew he loved Carol enough to make all this expense worthwhile, but he hoped everyone would pull off the charade.

He would have to make sure that Carol's daddy, sister, brother-in-law, and her two nephews all came. Hopefully, Malinda could get off work, and fly in Friday evening or Saturday morning, after his family had already arrived. That way they wouldn't be at the airport at the same time. Caroline was still abroad, so she wouldn't be able to be there for the engagement, even if it was at another time.

Rich made a mental note to check all the arrangements for her family, so that he would know if he could engage Carol on Saturday evening. He wanted to call Dr. Williams to ask for Carol's hand before the weekend. He wanted to make it perfect for Carol. After all, she was perfect for him, he thought.

◆◆◆◆◆◆

Over the past few weeks, Carol's sister, Mary Linda, had been travelling back and forth from Albany, Georgia, to Atlanta to help Rich find a house. Rich and Carol had settled on the house on West Paces Ferry with the grand gated entrance. Before going to Las Vegas, Rich put an offer on the house, and Mary Linda began the process of inspections.

Over the weekend that Rich was in Florida, Mary Linda learned that someone else had previously put in an offer that was accepted by the seller, so the house was no longer available. Rich and Carol decided that they would all go look at houses together on the weekend that both families would be together. This would be a fun activity for everyone.

✦✦✦✦✦✦

It was Wednesday morning, the day before everything started. Rich had lain awake most of the night, worrying about each detail of his plan, hoping it would all come off as he hoped. He didn't want to wake Carol, so he silently slipped out of bed.

He tiptoed into the luxurious bathroom, closed

the door, and turned on the shower. The day was just dawning, and the room was mostly dark. Rich walked into the marble shower room, leaving the lights off. He was tired, so tired. The warm water was soothing, and seemed to wash away some of his worries.

He loved Carol. He wasn't really sure how he had come to this point. But here he was. He had a fake family coming to meet Carol, so that she would feel she knew him well enough to accept his marriage proposal. After they had been married for a year or two, he would slowly reveal what he had done. He was doing all this for love, so why did he feel so guilty?

His deep thoughts and the dark shower were suddenly flooded with light. Carol flipped on the light, coming in to use the bathroom. She was surprised to realize Rich was standing in the dark shower. "Rich! I'm sorry, I didn't know you were in here. Why are you standing there in the dark?"

"I didn't even think about the light. I know where everything is, and I think I'm coming down with a cold. I hope it's not the flu. I just don't feel very well. The light is bright on my eyes, but the warm water feels good right now." *It was a little lie, and did no harm,* Rich thought.

♦♦♦♦♦♦

Later that morning, when Carol went out for tennis, Rich called Dr. Williams. "Good morning, sir. I am looking forward to seeing you this weekend. How are you today?"

"Why, Rich, how good to hear from you! I am feeling well today. We have a lovely weekend planned, don't we?" Dr. Williams was smiling.

"The reason I'm calling, Dr. Williams, is that I have a special plan for this weekend. I need your consent to make it happen. I would like to ask your permission to marry your daughter. I love her more than I can say, and I want to make her happy for the rest of her life." Rich held his breath.

"I would be privileged to give you my approval to ask for Carol's hand. I think she really cares for you, Rich. I hope you will be as happy as Carol's mother and I were. I only wish she could have been here to share this joy with us." There was a wistful joy mixed with sadness in Dr. Williams' voice.

"Thank you, sir. I hope we will be so happy, like

you said." Rich could almost breathe now. "I'll look
forward to seeing you on Friday, then."

Rich also called Malinda, and quickly told her his
plans to engage Carol. Carol would be back from her
walk soon, so he couldn't talk long. Malinda seemed
happy for her mother, but offered her regrets for the
weekend. Sadly, she wouldn't be able to get away from
work to come.

◆◆◆◆◆◆

Wednesday afternoon was very busy. Carol was
preparing for Rich's parents to come, and she insisted
on having his parents stay in her home on Thursday
night. They could have dinner out, but Carol wanted
Rich's parents to feel like family and stay with them that
evening.

Rich had unexpected business that called him
away. The destination that evening was Tampa, Florida
– a brief meeting for two hours and a quick turnaround
would complete the required transaction. He sat out
by the pool, consulting with the guys. There was some
serious stuff going on and Rich would have to take care

of it. He told Carol that one of his guys had a problem, so he would be gone for three to four hours that evening. Carol understood how sometimes work calls a man away unexpectedly. What she didn't know was that he was getting on a private jet to fly 500 miles away.

During the hour return flight to Atlanta, Rich contemplated if he could ever tell Carol. *How could a loving woman like Carol even remotely understand?* He didn't want to hide anything from her, but deep down Rich knew it was essential not to let her know about his private business. He had guarded it in the past with perfection. And once again he concluded that the mere chance of losing her due to her not understanding was a risk that was not worth taking. He wanted her, needed her in his life forever.

12

The big weekend was just days away. Rich and Carol reviewed all the plans, so that everything would flow smoothly during both families' visit. Carol felt very relaxed; surprisingly, she had the confidence that Rich would be there to help with all of the arrangements.

Though Carol was comforted with the presence of Rich, she was still a girl at heart. Excited to meet Rich's family was an understatement. Carol meticulously planned everything. She made arrangements for the entire pool area and driveway to be pressure washed. She ordered not only new plants and flowers in the pool area, but fresh, cut flowers to place through out the home were to be delivered on Thursday a few hours prior to Rich's parents' arrival. Next came the food:

Carol was careful in making sure she got the items for breakfast, lunch, or snacks that Rich's family enjoyed.

Though Rich was impressed watching Carol scurry around, the guilt began to compound. *Here was this angel*, he thought, *going out of her way to both make a good impression on his parents and to utilize her skill set as a perfect hostess.* The guilt grew because deep down, Rich knew that the weekend's plans were not going to live up to what they were perceived to be. Getting engaged was an absolute – it was who would be celebrating that was the issue. Feeling like a complete lowlife for the first time in his life, Rich escaped to the bathroom and jumped in the shower. He couldn't believe he was going through with this. All of these people were coming in. How would he be keeping up with it all?

Thursday, May first had finally arrived; Harriet's flight would be arriving at 11:30 am. "Well, your parents will be here in about four and a half hours!" Carol exclaimed. Of course, Rich knew that only his pretend mother, "Linda" would be arriving. Harriet, as she was known to the rest of the world, would be flying first class that morning enroute to Atlanta from

Sarasota, Florida, not Toronto, Ontario, Canada, as everyone thought. Rich was going to have to come up with a valid reason for his father's non-arrival for the festivities – and he had a very short time to do it.

Carol noticed that Rich seemed to get ready relatively fast and was heading out to get his parents two hours earlier than needed. "I have a few stops to make prior to getting my mom and dad," Rich said. "Okay…be careful! I can't wait to meet everyone!" Carol said with a smile.

Driving with no particular place to be, Rich had to think what to tell Carol regarding his dad. He hated going through with the lies that lay ahead this coming weekend, but the reward of spending his life with the woman of his dreams made it certainly worthwhile.

After stopping in the early morning to get a coffee and contemplate the Dilemma Number One, Rich decided what he would do. He called Carol and told her that his mother had left a message on his phone earlier in the morning simply stating that his dad had been feeling under the weather from an ear infection that was too painful to fly so he would catch a later flight the following day. His mother, however, was under no circumstances missing out on the opportunity to finally meet Carol. Though disappointed with Rich's father's absence, Carol graciously understood and was happy to have Linda (Rich's mother) still arriving.

"Since your mother was kind enough to insist on coming without Donald, I would feel awful sending her to the Ritz to stay in a strange city all alone" Carol said. "I insist that she stay here with us – at least until your father arrives on Friday." Rich quickly agreed, somewhat relieved that Carol was still upbeat after getting the news.

"This will give your mother and I time to get to know each other," Carol exclaimed. "Perfect!" said Rich. As Rich hung up the phone, he thought about explaining this to Harriet in a manner that would seem justifiable. He knew deep down that the more personal time that Harriet and Carol spent together increased the chance for disaster … Carol was smart … He hoped Harriet would be up to the task.

When Harriet's flight arrived, Rich picked her up and greeted her with a big hug. "Thanks again, 'Mom!'" They both smiled as Harriet rolled her eyes. During the drive back to Carol's Rich reviewed the weekend plans and events one more time, including informing Harriet of her accommodation change for the evening.

"Try not to talk too much about my childhood. Keep the conversation about the present and future if you can," said Rich.

"Don't worry, Rich, I'll be just fine, but I'll try not to say anything too definite about anything else. You lived in Canada, and went to school there. But I don't know how to speak French. Will Carol expect me to do that?" Harriet was getting nervous.

Rich was already nervous, but he tried not to show it. "Just tell her that being from Ontario you were not required to learn French as a student. Then, change the subject. Talk about shopping, things you like to wear, stuff like that. Carol loves to shop, so she'll have fun showing you her favorite boutiques. And we'll both have to remember that your name is *Linda*."

Carol was nervously and anxiously waiting for Rich and his mother to arrive, repeatedly glancing in the mirror to make sure her lipstick and hair were perfect.

Carol was ready to graciously receive her guest. Colorful fresh flowers filled a vase in each room. She had purchased English muffins, cereal, fruit, and orange juice because this is what Rich said he remembered his mother liked for breakfast. Carol wanted to make a good first impression on the woman she hoped would become her mother-in-law. Carol appeared poised and elegant on the rich velvet sofa as she waited for her guest to arrive.

Rich knocked on the front door, and then opened it for Harriet. "Carol, we're here!" Rich called to Carol, but she was already walking to meet them in the foyer. "Carol, I'd like to introduce you to my mother." Rich wanted to smile, but Carol didn't notice him as she turned to Harriet. "Linda! How nice to meet you! I have enjoyed talking with you on the phone, and Rich has told me so much about you. I really appreciate how far you have travelled to be with us this weekend."

Harriet smiled nervously. "Carol, I'm glad to meet you, too. Rich has told me how beautiful you are, and I have to agree with him! And your home is just incredible!"

"I'll bring in your bag, mother," said Rich as he turned toward the car. "Carol wants you to spend the night here in the guest room, since Dad wasn't able to come. Speaking of Dad, will he be okay by himself tonight?"

"Your father came down with an ear infection, but
he has a new prescription for it. Flying in that condition
would be too painful, but with the medicine tonight
he should be able to come tomorrow with your sister
and her husband," Harriet tried to sound sincerely
concerned.

After showing Harriet her room, Carol gave her
the grand tour of the home. Harriet was obviously
impressed. Carol described the bistro where they would
be dining and soon after the three of them drove to the
restaurant.

They were seated at a table and the server asked
if they would like a drink before dinner. Harriet was
hungry and tired, still nervous, and feeling the stress
of posing as Rich's mother. She ordered vodka on the
rocks, forgetting that Rich had told her his mother
didn't drink. Carol ordered a glass of white wine so that
Rich's mother wouldn't be drinking alone. Rich asked
for his usual, a Diet Coke.

They enjoyed their drinks, had an appetizer, and
continued to talk. Everything seemed to be going
smoothly, but when the server came to take their orders

for dinner, Harriet added, "Oh, would you please bring me another drink." Rich was mortified. "Mom, you don't drink! I can't believe you're ordering another vodka!"

"Oh, Rich, I've changed. After you children grew up, I loosened up a little. I take yoga, and I have a drink in the evening to relax. I'll have another vodka on the rocks, since this is a special occasion." Since Rich wasn't drinking, she looked to Carol, as if to ask if Carol would have another glass of wine when she had her vodka. Carol said, "Well Linda's having another, so I'll have another glass of wine." Carol smiled at Rich, and he nervously smiled as he asked for a refill on his Diet Coke and gave the server his dinner order.

Harriet had shown genuine interest in Carol; she wanted to get to know the woman whom Rich was so infatuated with; that he was willing to go through with such an elaborate plan in order to spend his life with her.

When the food finally showed up, Carol and Harriet commented on how delicious everything looked. Indeed the meal may have been delicious, but Rich certainly didn't taste it. He quickly gulped it down as he carefully monitored the conversation. Just like a tiger waiting to pounce on its prey, Rich was ready to intervene at the slightest sign of trouble during the conversation. Carol seemed happy, slowly taking in her new future mother-in-law's features, mannerism and views. Harriet, making mostly small talk, got through the meal's conversation with relative ease, certainly thanks to the two drinks she had consumed during dinner.

Carol insisted on having coffee at her house, which would give her and Rich's mother a chance to talk in a quieter environment. Reluctantly Rich agreed, and the three of them drove back to Carol's.

While Carol was making the coffee in the kitchen, Rich suggested that perhaps immediately following the coffee Harriet should act exhausted from the flight and head to bed a little early, minimizing the time that could expose any issue. "Linda, how do you take your coffee?" Carol asked. "Just a touch of cream," Harriet said.

During coffee, Harriet again complimented Carol on her taste in clothing, jewelry, and decorating. Her comments were sincere, since Harriet was truly impressed with Carol's lavish taste and style. Quickly finishing her coffee, Harriet yawned. "Linda, you look tired," Carol commented. "You've had a big day traveling."

"I have," said Harriet. "As a matter of fact, I think I am going to go change and go to bed, if you two don't mind." Relief entered Rich's body as he smiled and agreed.

Rich offered to show his mother her room. Carol and Harriet hugged and said their good nights. Rich showed Harriet her room. When the coast was clear he looked at Harriet and said, "What's with the two drinks?? I told Carol you didn't drink!" He said as he slightly smiled.

"I'm sorry Rich, I was feeling a bit overwhelmed, and it calmed me. You were right, though, she is just a doll. I can easily see why you have chosen her as the one. I wish she really was my daughter-in-law." Harriet said with a big smile.

Rich thanked Harriet and hugged her as he left the room and closed the door behind him. *Whew!! One day down and two more to go*, he thought.

That night Rich held Carol even tighter than usual. "My mother really, really likes you, Carol. She now understands why I feel the way I do about

you." "Really?" said Carol. "Yes, Carol, *really*." Rich
reassured her. As they started to drift off to sleep Carol
mentioned that she hoped that Donald, Rich's father
felt better and that she was excited to meet him, along
with everyone else.

A tear rolled down Rich's face. As he discreetly
wiped it away, he told Carol that everyone was looking
forward to meeting her, as well. After Carol had fallen
asleep, Rich tried in his mind, one more time, to
consider telling Carol the truth. She deserved it. But he
knew that there was a slight chance that Carol would
tell him goodbye if she found out. This was a chance
that was simply not worth risking. Though Rich felt
like a rope used in a tug of war, with both sides pulling
at him and his stomach in knots, as long as his lady
felt happy and safe, the end justified the means. Falling
asleep Rich thought to himself one more time, *one day
down, two to go.*

♦♦♦♦♦♦

Friday morning seemed to come quickly. Rich
showered and dressed right away then joined Carol in

the kitchen for coffee. Fortunately, Harriet, *AKA Linda*, was still in her room, so Rich could relax, not worry about Harriet slipping and saying the wrong thing. "I just love your mother," said Carol. "Thank you. I'm glad!" Rich said.

Rich had to pick up his brother- and sister-in-law today, along with his sister and brother-in-law, and of course, good old Dad!!!

Carol had suggested taking Rich's mother to the Lenox Mall shopping, then to lunch, as Rich made the two different trips to the airport to retrieve the rest of his family. After Harriet awoke and the three of them ate breakfast, Rich pulled Harriet to the side and said, "Whatever I call about today regarding people missing flights and changing plans, just act disappointed and go with the flow, as they say."

"How are you going to explain only Mike, your brother-in-law, coming in?" Harriet asked. "I'm sure I'll think of something," said Rich.

Leaving Carol and Harriet alone all day didn't help Rich's stomach in the least, but he had no choice. He had been in much tighter situations in the past. Rich kissed Carol and Harriet good bye and headed out to the airport for pick-up number one, his brother, Scott, and father, and sister-in-law.

Rich knew that there was simply only one legitimate excuse for his first three siblings not to arrive in Atlanta: missing their flight and not being able to get out of Toronto that day or the next as all flights on Air Canada had been booked. Rich had told Carol in the past that his younger brother Scott was not very reliable and had to be told several times in most cases to do something.

Driving, Rich felt sad. Not having a decent loving family had never really been an issue with him. Since a young boy he had learned to accept the fact that his family was what he was dealt in life. However, Rich wished that he had loving siblings to let Carol and her family meet and get to know, like most normal people.

Looking at his watch, it had been two hours already. Rich called Carol to tell her of his brother's incompetence. He had arrived for an international flight with his wife and Rich's father only thirty minutes prior to the departure time. Rich had to act furious.

Carol and Harriet were shopping and Carol was very understanding. "Perhaps they will get on the next flight to Atlanta," said Carol. "It will work out. Dinner isn't until seven, so everything should be just fine." "Thanks," said Rich. Harriet asked what was happening so Carol passed her the phone. Rich explained the scenario to Harriet who acted disgusted and somewhat embarrassed that her son, Scott, would be so irresponsible.

Hanging up the phone, Harriet apologized to Carol for her family's foolish error. As Carol and Harriet sat in the tea room at Neiman Marcus, Harriet once again apologized for Scott's indiscretion. Carol was disheartened they would be unable to share the family weekend, but she was glad to be with her future mother-in-law. Carol smiled and assured Harriet that she understood. She couldn't wait to take Harriet to some of her favorite boutiques.

Mike would be arriving from Seattle, Washington in the next few hours. Of course, everyone was to think that he was a psychiatrist who was arriving from Sarasota, Florida. At least he was on his plane and making the festivities. One last task lay ahead: explaining why Kim, who was playing Lori, Rich's sister, wouldn't be coming. *This it getting ridiculous*, Rich thought.

Rich waited until 90 minutes prior to Mike's arrival to call Carol. Ninety minutes is the time it would take a flight that was really coming from Sarasota, Florida. Rich called Carol and told her that Mike had called him from the airport and was boarding the flight. Lori had to remain home, as their sixteen-year-old son, Mark, was still sick and throwing up with a fever. Like any loving mother she was afraid to leave her son. Lori urged Mike to go ahead and she would catch a plane tomorrow when Mark felt better. But Mike was coming.

Carol was disappointed at this odd turn of events, but she thought it was all just a bad coincidence. Carol wondered about it for a few minutes, but in the excitement of her own family coming, she had other things to occupy her attention.

"Oh, great news!" Carol said to Rich, "Mary Linda called earlier, and Bennett didn't have to go on his trip! He will be here, and so will Mike. They can talk about their work, so I'm sure they'll get along just fine!" Carol was so excited, but Rich wanted to scream.

Bennett was a doctor, and Rich's brother-in-law

was supposed to be a doctor. How could Rich keep them apart, so that Bennett wouldn't know the ruse? Mike would be nervous about sitting by Bennett because Mike was supposed to be a psychiatrist and Bennett was a real orthopedic surgeon. If Bennett asked Mike any questions, Mike wouldn't know how to answer without giving away his fake identity.

Rich didn't tell his brother-in-law that Carol's brother was now going to be there. After Rich picked him up at the airport and had put the bags in his car, he spilled the bad news.

"I was talking with Carol just now, and she mentioned that her brother-in-law Bennett was not going to be away at the conference, so he's coming for the weekend. Bennett is an orthopedic surgeon, and you are posing as my current brother-in-law, who is a psychiatrist. That means you are both doctors, like her daddy. Carol's father is retired, so he probably won't talk about your professional work, but you will have to pretend to be a psychiatrist. At least Bennett is a surgeon, not a psychiatrist."

"How in the hell am I supposed to do that?" Mike demanded. "I don't know the first thing about medicine.

He'll recognize I'm a fraud right away!"

Rich tried to sound more confident than he felt. "If you're a psychiatrist, you can just talk about how different it is working to heal people's minds instead of their bodies. I'll try to make sure you don't sit by him. Perhaps you can sit by Harriet, Carol, or me so you won't have to worry."

Mike was less than satisfied. "This isn't going to be easy, Rich. I'll do the best I can."

✦✦✦✦✦✦

By the time Rich took Mike to the Ritz Carlton, and he checked into his room, they had a few minutes to catch up before dinner. It was the most relaxed Rich had felt all day. Carol had dropped Harriet back at the hotel so she could freshen up before dinner. Rich called Flemings Steakhouse to change the reservation to nine persons, now that Carol knew who would actually be there.

When Harriet was dressed for dinner, Rich, Mike and Harriet left the Ritz and made the short drive to Flemings. Rich didn't talk much, because he needed to think about his plan. *Where should everyone sit?* He needed to keep Bennett, the orthopedic surgeon, Carol's brother-in-law, away from Mike, so Mike didn't have to talk about medicine all evening. Bennett and Mary Linda would sit on one end of the table. He would seat Carol's father next, and Carol would sit by him so they could talk. He would sit by Carol, naturally, and Harriet would sit by him, since she was posing as his mother. Mike would sit on the other side of Harriet. Rich put himself in the middle, to try to keep control of the conversation.

When Rich came to the table that had been reserved, Carol and her family were already seated. Rich was relieved that they sat together, so he simply put his fake family next to him on the other side.

The first thing Bennett said was directed to Mike. "Say, I understand you're a psychiatrist. I'm an orthopedic surgeon. I'll look forward to talking with you tomorrow when we go to look at houses!" Mike smiled, "That will be great!" Rich tried not to panic. He would look forward to it too, with terror.

Dinner was delicious, and everyone seemed to have a pleasant evening. Rich talked easily, and kept them entertained with stories so there was not a lull in the conversation. Harriet remembered not to order more than one drink. As soon as dessert was finished, Rich encouraged everyone to turn in early, so that Carol's father would have enough rest for the next day.

◆◆◆◆◆◆

Carol and Rich dressed on Saturday morning, and went to the Ritz to pick up Harriet and Mike. Mary Linda and Bennett would drive with Dr. Williams, and they would all meet at the OK Café for lunch. The OK Café was a classic diner located on West Paces Ferry in Buckhead, so everyone had fun reminiscing about different diners where they had eaten in the past.

When they were seated, Rich explained, "Mike sends his regrets for the afternoon. He had some paperwork that he had to do, finishing patient files on his computer to email by the end of the day. He's going to miss some fun, but he'll be there for dinner tonight!" Bennett was let down by the change, but he understood a physician's busy schedule. Rich was glad he had averted disaster. Six hours to chat would surely expose Mike as a fraud. The paperwork Mike did was homework on his assignment, trying to bone up on psychiatric terms before their conversations at dinner that evening.

Rich and Carol had decided to look at a couple of houses that afternoon, so they all enjoyed talking about the afternoon's activities. Rich enjoyed chicken fried steak, and Carol chided him for choosing this instead of the Southern style vegetables she was enjoying. *Calories are the least of my worries right now*, Rich thought. He just winked at Carol. She laughed, and they all enjoyed lunch together.

Rich arranged to meet them at the first house after he picked up Mark and Melanie at the airport. He pulled onto Interstate 75, and called Mark as he drove to the airport to pick them up. Mark answered the phone, and informed Rich that he was still in Florida. Mark said flatly, "I just decided I couldn't, or wouldn't come. I will not be part of this relationship with Carol that you seem to be set on."

Rich angrily retorted, "I'll bet you never even told Melanie about the weekend! If you never intended to come, the least you could have done was to tell me before I bought the tickets and all! You're no friend of mine anymore!" Rich angrily slammed the phone down on the seat and clamped his jaws together hard enough that he broke one of his back bottom molars. Pain shot through his jaw. He could hardly see to drive. Shocked that such a close friend of 25 years would let him down on such an important time in his life, Rich was baffled.

Rich turned around, but didn't go straight to the first house. He had to get a hold of his anger before he could explain to Carol that Mark and Melanie weren't coming. He took her aside to tell her and he was surprised to find Carol didn't mind. "Rich, Mark never seemed comfortable with us being together. I never blamed him for what he did on Millionaire Match, because I thought he was trying to protect you as his close friend. But I just don't think he wants us to be together. It will be okay," Carol took his arm and patted it reassuringly.

The second house was on West Paces Ferry, and it was as fine as its classic Atlanta address. Everyone commented on the stucco façade, with the circular drive and covered entry, but they found the marbled foyer simply breathtaking. Rich thought the two-story library, completely covered with mahogany shelves accessed using the rolling ladder, was the most impressive room.

Rich really loved this house the best. Carol thought it was too large for just the two of them, but she insisted she would be happy if Rich wanted it. Rich told Mary Linda that they needed to put in an offer on the house the first thing on Monday.

••••••

The big evening finally arrived. Everyone dressed for dinner, and Rich and Carol made sure everyone arrived at Morton's Steakhouse for their reservation. Rich's Uncle Alan was the only one still missing, so Rich stepped out to call him. After waiting an appropriate length of time, he came back and explained to Carol what transpired.

"Uncle Landon and his wife flew in on his private jet and stayed at the Crown Plaza near the Perimeter Mall, which was close to the restaurant where I had previously told them we would be dining. Initially I had invited them to Ray's on the River instead of Morton's Steakhouse for the dinner on Saturday evening. When

I decided to come to Morton's, I forgot to tell Uncle Landon the change of plans. I feel absolutely terrible, Carol. He must have spent $10,000 on jet fuel, not to mention the cost of his pilots, to be a part of this very special occasion. Then not to be included after all of his time and effort! When I finally got a hold of him, they had ordered dinner, after waiting until an hour past 6:00. Landon said not to worry; he would love to meet you in the near future." Uncle Landon and his wife were devastated that they missed the festivities and the opportunity to meet you, Carol and your family."

Rich's uncle was a complete fabrication, and this story almost pushed Rich over the edge. He made an excuse about his tooth hurting and bolted for the restroom. His tooth was killing him. He stood in front of the mirror staring at himself. He felt like garbage, and was having a heck of a time keeping up with all the lies. He's making up stories about why so many didn't show up, and the excuses are wearing thin.

He tried to justify the lies ... I'm going to buy her a house. I bought her a car. I bought her a $90,000 engagement ring. I really do love her. Maybe if we just rush the wedding, I can tell her the truth afterwards.

Then maybe she'll decide she has to stay, since we're married and all. Rich realized he was sweating and anxiously tried to wipe his brow with a paper towel.

He had somehow managed to make the weekend work. Mike and Harriet had done their jobs perfectly. Mike, who actually was Rich's brother-in-law, had divorced Rich's sister over 12 years earlier, but he and Rich remained very close over the last 23 years. He knew a lot about Rich's likes and dislikes, so he was able to play his role a little easier.

The moment of truth had arrived. Taking one last look in the mirror and a deep breath to follow, it was time to ask Carol, in front of her family and Rich's two cohorts, to marry him. Rich knew that, unlike some of the weekend's events, this was at least pure, honest, and real. Walking back to the table Rich had walked behind Mary Linda, Carol's sister, whom he had asked to hold the ring in its box in her purse. Rich carefully motioned for it and put it in his left hand.

Walking over to Carol, who was engaged in conversation, all of his anxiety from the weekend seemed to suddenly vanish. All eyes from the table fixated on Carol as Rich knelt in front of Carol. Taking her left hand with his right, he told Carol that she would make him the happiest man on the planet if she would give him the honor of marrying him and being by his side as his partner for life.

"Carol, will you marry me?" Carol's eyes instantly filled with tears of joy. Without hesitation, Carol glanced over to her father, who was smiling and who also had a tear of joy. She squeezed Rich's hand and said, "Yes!"

The entire table and restaurant broke out in applause and cheers. The ring was nothing short of stunning. Three canary diamonds, totaling five and three quarters carats, surrounded by 56 pavé diamonds sitting on a platinum base. The three canary diamonds were held in place with 18 carat gold prongs. It was breathtaking.

The rest of the evening was full of handshakes, hugs, and many pictures taken by Dr. Williams, Carol's father, and by Harriet (Linda to everyone else). Dr. Williams asked Mike and Harriet for their addresses in order to send them copies of the pictures that he had taken of the memorable event. Rich intervened, and gave Dr. Williams an address in Canada that was an old address where he lived many years earlier. Mike followed suite and gave a Sarasota address that he and Rich's sister had lived at years earlier when they were still married. Dr. Williams knew that this way Rich's other family members who missed their flights would have a picture of this memorable occasion.

That night Carol went to bed, not in a bed, but on Cloud Nine. Lying next to her, Rich fell asleep holding his fiancée. Together, they now felt like one.

13

As daybreak came on May 4, the Sunday morning after their engagement, Carol awoke held in Rich's strong arms. Feeling his arms around her seemed pleasantly normal, but she thought about how yesterday had changed her life. *Was it all a dream?* She yawned and stretched, and the brilliant ring, a 5.75 carat canary diamond, surrounded by 56 pavé diamonds gleaming from her left hand assured her that this was not a dream. The fairytale had come true. A tear of joy rolled down her cheek as reality set in ... she really was engaged. Carol Greenbaum would soon become Mrs. Richard Towsley.

A little overwhelmed, Carol quietly slipped out of bed and walked into the kitchen to make coffee.

Waiting for the coffee to brew, Carol looked around her home of 25 years. Starting this new chapter in her life would mean letting go of the past, especially the sad memories that lingered there. She had enjoyed many happy moments in this grand home, but so many sad memories seemed to dominate her thoughts of this place.

"Hello, my fiancée!" These bright words broke into her reverie, and Carol turned around to see Rich coming toward her. He was her man, the man she would soon marry.

Rich grabbed Carol's hand and led her to the bedroom. The coffeemaker beeped to tell them that their coffee was ready, but they didn't hear it. They were too busy drinking in the love they passionately gave to each other.

Carol felt her reservations had disappeared. She felt different making love to Rich, because she was marrying him. She belonged to him, and had a ring on her finger to mark this commitment. In her eyes, they were one.

✦✦✦✦✦✦

Carol would soon begin the monumental task of planning her wedding, but she wanted to share her joy with her daughters and friends first. She began making calls, excitedly telling those closest to her the life-changing news. The first she wanted to inform were her two daughters. Malinda lived in New York, and she would actually be coming in the following Sunday with her close friend and roommate to visit Carol for Mother's Day. Then she wanted to tell Caroline, who was still in Australia on a college exchange program. Both daughters were a little surprised, as they knew that their mother and Rich had only been dating for three months.

In addition, the divorce between the girls' parents had seemed to not quite settle in the girls' minds. "Why rush things?" Malinda asked her mother. "I had not even had an opportunity to meet him yet, Mom," Caroline stated. The concern in her daughters' voices was very evident.

"I understand," Carol said. "I know that Malinda has only met him once, Caroline and I think that when you meet him, you will love him."

"Well, we'll see Mom," said Malinda.

Next, Carol called her sister Mary Linda, and asked her to be her matron of honor. Mary Linda was thrilled! She jumped for joy in her own kitchen at the idea of being her sister's matron of honor. Next Carol called one of her very good friends, Claire James. Claire had known Carol for over 26 years as she was in college with Carol's older sister, Mary Linda. Claire was ecstatic. She congratulated Carol as tears of joy rolled down Carol's cheeks.

Finally, Carol called Rich's mother, Harriet, aka Linda, and his sister, Kim, aka Lori. Though Harriet was present for the engagement and was aware of the joyous news, Carol wanted her to join all of the girls who would be in the wedding party to shop for dresses. Kim, who was unable to attend the special weekend's events, was honored that Carol wanted to include her in the wedding party. And both women readily accepted. Rich had given Harriet a cell phone that had a 416 area code – this way it would appear that Harriet actually lived in Ontario, Canada instead of Sarasota, Florida.

As Sunday evening approached, Carol began

her wedding task list. Though there was much to do, Carol was in her element. Planning large scale events was her forte. Rich had been privileged to see the end result of her talent in March when he had attended the Circle for Children event that Carol had assisted in planning.

Monday morning, Rich had awakened early, had breakfast with his bride-to-be, and told Carol that he would be back prior to lunch. A half hour later, Rich pulled into the parking lot of Tassles and strode quickly into the fine jewelry store. He remembered Carol telling him that Judith Ripka was one of her favorite jewelry designers. Knowing that he would have to be gone for a few days on business, Rich felt compelled to give his bride another token of his affection.

His network marketing business was growing daily, but it was the other business that was calling him away. Carol had no knowledge of this private world where Rich was a professional, but it was as lucrative as it was dangerous. Maybe if he gave Carol a gift made possible by this work, he could feel justified in leaving, instead of feeling guilty for hiding what he was doing. He spotted the perfect gift for Carol. Judith Ripka had set yellow sapphires and diamonds in an 18 carat, large yellow gold cross necklace. *Like my fiancée, it's perfect!* Rich thought as he had it wrapped for Carol.

◆◆◆◆◆◆

Having lived in Atlanta since her college days, Carol knew where she wanted her wedding and reception to be held. The Fox Theatre, a historic landmark in the heart of Atlanta, had become distinguished in Southern tradition for hosting some of Atlanta's finest weddings. Carol enthusiastically explained to Rich how beautiful their wedding would be at the Fox Theatre.

Being from Florida, Rich initially thought that a theater was an unusual place to have a wedding, but he was eager to please her, so he agreed to go there with her in order to secure a date.

Rich told Carol that she could choose the date she would become his wife. Though Rich was an intelligent man, like most men he had absolutely no idea of the intricacy and advance planning required for a wedding. He would soon begin to understand.

Later that evening at dinner Carol was in awe as Rich surprised her with her necklace. Holding back tears of joy, Carol hugged Rich tightly, thanking him for her incredible gift. "I'll wear it to church every Sunday!" Carol said. That evening, Carol wore her necklace to bed as her fiancé held her tightly. She was happy.

With Rich gone early the next morning, Carol began making plans. Looking diligently at the calendar, she decided that six months was ample time for wedding preparations, especially in the late fall. A date of Saturday, November 22, 2008, was chosen. Carol first began to write out her guest list, as this would be an ongoing project for at least three months.

The historic Fox Theatre was indeed where she wanted to marry the man of her dreams. Carol was elated to find that the date she had chosen to get married was available at the Fox Theatre. She made an appointment for her and Rich to take a tour of the grand facility the following week.

Catering her wedding was next on the agenda.

Being an Atlanta socialite, Carol knew that Affairs to Remember had done a remarkable job in catering some rather lavish events that she had attended in the past. Affairs to Remember had a long and distinguished track record of some of Atlanta's best weddings, so naturally in Carol's mind, there was simply no other choice. An appointment was made also for the following week as she wanted to include Rich in the process.

David Lavoy was a very highly recommended, upscale florist that had two decades of experience. Like Carol, his creativity was well known. David listened to his clients' requests and thought of every intimate detail. Again, an appointment was made.

Claire, Carol's close friend of 26 years, wanted to give the bridesmaids' luncheon for Carol. After discussing the event, Carol and Claire had settled on the Swan Coach House in Atlanta. The elegant, historic home was a museum, and the coach house had been converted into a tastefully decorated tea room. Carol was thrilled with this choice.

When considering the guest list and accommodations, the Four Seasons Hotel was near the Fox Theatre and had all of the amenities that the guests would require. Carol briefly spoke to one of the event coordinators and also set an appointment to look at the facility for lodging and the rehearsal dinner.

Finally, during her preliminary plans, Carol made a list of three places to shop for the ultimate wedding dress and bridesmaids' attire. Simply put, the next six months of Carol's life were going to be busy.

◆◆◆◆◆◆

Getting back from his "business trip", Rich couldn't wait to take Carol to dinner and catch up on the events of the last couple of days. Rich wanted to spend every moment with his fiancée that his schedule allowed. Knowing that he would have to fly to Florida for the day the following week, during dinner Rich asked Carol if she would like to accompany him for that day. He was meeting with the CEO of a network marketing company. He emphasized that this was not a really important meeting, but having her company would be wonderful.

"Where will we be going in Florida?" Carol asked. "We'll be flying into West Palm Beach and then take a limo into Palm Beach Gardens," Rich said as he took a sip of his Diet Coke.

"Palm Beach!" Carol blurted out, losing her naturally gracious demeanor. Rich was certainly surprised at her response. "Yes, Carol, Palm Beach Gardens is the location of the company where I'm going to meet the CEO."

"Oh … I see … Okay." Carol regained her composure, but not her normal smile. "You'll like Palm Beach, Carol, it's …" Looking at Carol as he spoke, the irony hit him. Carol knew Palm Beach all too well. Her ex-husband and his family resided in Palm Beach. She and her ex-husband had even owned a second home there and both had been members of the Palm Beach Country Club. Her new life with Rich was just beginning. Returning to Palm Beach would bring up some painful memories.

Carol looked with a kind of resolve into Rich's eyes as she quietly said, "That's fine, Rich. I still want to be with you, no matter where it is."

Rich's heart sank as he chided himself for not

thinking of how hurtful it might be for Carol to go to Palm Beach. The last thing he ever wanted to give to Carol was even one second of pain.

Carol seemed to read his thoughts. Reaching across the table to touch Rich's hand, she said, "You are part of me forever, and I would go anywhere in the world with you." Rich's heart leaped and he grasped her hand tightly. "I love you, Carol, and I want you to be with me always."

✦✦✦✦✦✦

The next day Carol was happy to see that Kim, aka *Lori*, had left a message on the phone that she was very much looking forward to flying up to Atlanta from Florida to meet Carol and go shopping for the bridal dresses.

Carol also had heard from her oldest daughter, Malinda. She confirmed that she would be arriving from New York City with her roommate Nadia to come home to be with Carol and Rich for Mother's Day. "I can't wait to show Malinda my ring!" Carol exclaimed. "I only wish that Caroline wasn't so far away in Australia. I would love to have seen her on Mother's Day, as well."

"That's wonderful, Carol! And don't worry for a minute about plans for Sunday dinner on Mother's Day. I'll make all the arrangements, so it will be a real treat for you," Rich offered. Carol appreciated Rich's willingness to take charge of making plans. She wanted a man who would be capable of leading their relationship, who took the initiative to take care of her. She loved Rich for being a different sort of man, a man she could be proud to call her husband.

14

Carol's normally quiet grand home was about to be turned upside down this week. It was Monday already and over eight appointments were already set for the week. Rich's sister, Kim, would be coming in on Thursday of the next week for dress shopping and Harriet, Rich's mother, would be arriving the day before, on Wednesday. Friday evening, Carol's older daughter, Malinda, would be coming in for Mother's Day with her New York roommate, Nadia.

First stop of the week's journey was at the Fox Theatre with Rich. Carol excitedly yelled to Rich, "We had better get going!" as she grabbed her purse. "We have to be at the Fox in an hour!"

Smiling that Carol was so happy, Rich grabbed his keys and they headed out.

Arriving at the Fox Theatre, the number of "undesirable-type" people that wandered the streets of downtown Atlanta surprised Rich. Though the Fox was a historical landmark, the location, like some downtown metropolitan areas, was a little on the rough side.

Rich had learned to be very aware of his environment – it was instilled in him since his early teens and an absolute necessity for his "other" line of work.

After parking the car in a small lot adjacent to the Fox Theatre, Rich got out to get a ticket to pay for the parking while Carol was on her cell phone telling one of her friends the exciting news from the prior weekend.

Rich immediately saw an African American man about 6'2" rapidly approaching the vehicle. Like a protective mother, Rich quickly put himself between the man who was obviously interested in asking Carol for money. "Beat it!" Rich blurted out – startling the intruder – stopping, the man looked at Rich then mumbled to himself and continued to move toward the vehicle and Carol.

"Get lost!" Rich said in a loud, unfriendly tone. Little did this man know who he was dealing with and when it came to Rich, nor did he remotely understand his skill set. Carol was the very last person on this earth to bother when it came to Rich.

As the man took an aggressive step toward Rich, it was over as fast as it began. The man's 6'2" frame fell to the concrete parking lot very fast and hard. Staggering and trying to get up, Rich picked up the man and threw him onto a parked vehicle four feet away. Standing over the bleeding and dazed man, Rich told him of the inevitable demise that awaited him if he came near the vehicle again. The vehicle was not of interest to Rich – it was what was inside the vehicle ... Carol.

Oblivious to what had just happened, Carol exited the vehicle and apologized for keeping Rich waiting. Smiling, Rich said, "No problem!" as he clicked the remote control to lock the vehicle. He hugged his wife-to-be and walked with her to the Fox Theatre.

Walking into the Fox Theatre, it was evident that entertainment history had left its mark here. There were picture of various entertainers, shows, plays, and events from decades past.

Meeting the event coordinator at the Fox Theatre, Carol and Rich proceeded with the tour.

The coordinator and Carol discussed the time and preparations Carol wanted. During the hour meeting Rich let his fiancée talk and listen to suggestions from the event planner. His fiancée being happy was all that mattered to Rich. Carol noticed that when they got to the main ballroom where the wedding would be held, Rich frowned. Not having the creative eye that Carol had, Rich simply saw a large, dark room, not what he had in mind for his sacred ceremony. Carol pulled him aside, saying "Trust me! I can make this into something very special." Knowing what Carol had done with her home, he smiled and said, "I trust you."

Leaving a deposit at the Fox, they returned to their vehicle. Checking off Task One on their list, they high-fived each other and headed to their two o'clock meeting. Affairs to Remember was considered by many to be the elite caterer in the Atlanta area. With their vast inventory and multiple options for various themes, they were highly sought after by Atlanta's elite.

Carol and Rich were greeted by the receptionist and offered refreshments. Not really being in his element, Rich once again handed the reins over to Carol regarding style to quantity. This particular meeting was very long and involved. More than ever, Rich now appreciated Carol's eye for detail for such a large event. The representative and Carol finally finished two hours later, and the proposal would be emailed to Carol in three to four business days.

With the day's business settled, Rich and Carol went to dinner at Houston's off West Paces Ferry Road, just down the street from the grand mansions they had looked at two weeks earlier. Getting back to the house, the two of them took advantage of the quiet time together talking about their future as a married couple. Tomorrow the fun would continue with various meetings for the November 22 festivities.

Getting up and following her usual routine, Carol ran out the door to attend her Body Pump class that she loved so. Carol attended the hour class every Monday, Wednesday, and Friday at the Gold's Gym close to her home.

Rich had taken the time to make some business phone calls prior to going with Carol to solidify the plans.

Their first meeting was with the florist Carol had chosen for the wedding, David Lavoy. Mr. Lavoy was as much an icon in the floral world as was the Fox Theatre itself. Carol and Rich were greeted by a gracious man who was an assistant to Mr. Lavoy.

When David entered the office, he and Carol hit it off right away. Rich was not as enthusiastic about floral arrangements and linens. Rich had to excuse himself to take an important business call, but first he let David know that whatever Carol wanted was what she was to be given.

After a twenty minute call, Rich came back in to take part in the decision process. "What do you think of these?" Carol asked. Smiling, Rich answered, "They're beautiful, just like you!" "Perfect answer!" Mr. Lavoy responded, as they all laughed.

Suddenly Rich's phone rang again, but this time the call said "Private." Rich immediately apologized for having to go outside again. This call was from his "other" life and demanded his utmost attention.

When it came to doing this secret part of his life, nothing could interfere ... not even Carol.

Thirty minutes into Rich's call, Carol looked outside. What could be so important to keep him talking this long, when he knew that they were in the middle of picking out flowers for their special day? Another ten minutes had passed before Rich was able to hang up and come back in. Rich whispered to Carol, "I'm so sorry, Baby! Of all the days …" "Who was that?" Carol asked very concerned, almost worried. "Oh, it was a very, very important business call that I had forgotten all about! It was actually a conference call and they were all depending on me to be included. So, what did I miss?"

Shrugging her shoulders, Carol briefed Rich on what she and David had decided as preliminary choices. Two hours had gone by relatively quickly. Again, a proposal was to be put in the mail for Rich and Carol to review.

Next came a meeting at the Four Seasons Hotel to discuss accommodations for their wedding party and guests. A tour of various sized suites had been arranged for Rich and Carol along with discussions on food – parking and gifts to be placed in their wedding party's rooms. It was decided that parking and food would also be bestowed upon the guests and friends.

Carol liked what the Four Seasons had to offer – a nod of reassurance from Rich – she decided this was where everyone would stay. Once again, a proposal would be drawn up and at least this one would be faxed. In two days, they had gotten the majority of the legwork done. Carol was focused and on a mission. Rich appreciated her efficiency in dealing with wedding plans with such speed.

Leaving the hotel, Carol noticed that her man was slightly limping. "Are you okay, Rich?" she asked. "I'm fine, thanks. My left foot just hurts a bit." Rich had broken his foot while living in aspen, Colorado four years prior.

After lunch, Rich kissed his bride-to-be and asked if she had needed him for anything else. He had wanted to go to a few automobile dealerships – particularly he was interested in a couple years old Porsche Carrera. "I don't have tennis today," Carol said. "Would you mind if I went with you? We could talk about the cake for the wedding and about getting everyone here for the big event." "Sure – if you wouldn't be bored. I know that cars aren't your thing," Rich said. Like Rich, Carol wanted to know all of her spouse, including his interests, and she was actually looking forward to going.

Carol smiled when she listened to Rich talk to the

different salesmen. She was impressed that he knew as much about the Porsches as the salesmen, and in some cases, even more.

Leaving the last dealership, Rich's foot seemed to have worsened. Rich had a titanium small rod in his foot for six weeks back in 2004 and besides the broken bone he had torn tendons in his foot as well.

His foot had been bothering him for the last two months and seemed to progressively be getting worse. Carol, being a loving partner, was concerned.

That evening after dinner, Rich wanted to go back to the dealership to look at one particular Porsche. Carol had never seen Rich so enthused about anything like this before; it was nice to see him want something for himself.

About 9:00 PM, Rich had returned excitedly talking about the 2001 forest green Porsche Carrera. He also was getting concerned about his foot; it was really starting to bother him. Carol looked at Rich's foot. It was swollen and she knew that it needed to have something done to it. "You know, Rich, my brother-in-law Bennett that you met is an orthopedic surgeon. We could take a ride down to Albany, Georgia, if you would like. He's an excellent doctor and he would be glad to take care of you." Rich replied, "That's very nice of you ... Let's see how my foot is in the morning."

Making love to Rich that night, Carol was genuinely concerned about Rich's foot. She hated the idea of him being in pain. She would make the call to Bennett in the morning to ask him if he had time to see Rich.

The next morning Carol paged Bennett on his cell phone. Bennett told Carol that he had time to work Rich in his busy schedule that day and that he really liked Rich the few times he had met him. He would be honored to look at Rich's foot. Carol thanked him and said that they would be down to Albany at 1 pm. In the meantime, Carol called her father, Dr. Williams, to see if he would like to be picked up and go along for the ride, since they would be driving right by the Idle Hour Country Club where he lived. Carol's daddy was thrilled to spend time with Carol and his future son-in-law.

Rich jumped out of the shower, grabbed a coffee and asked Carol if she liked the Porsche they had looked at yesterday. "I really loved the tan interior, and the fact that it's a convertible was great! If I was to buy that today, I would like it to be our car," Rich said. "Think of it as our first major purchase." Carol smiled – that was the second time that Rich had referred to something as "theirs." First the home purchase and now the vehicle - it made Carol feel secure; it made her feel good.

Carol told Rich that Bennett wanted to take a look at his foot and that it would mean a lot to her if he included Bennett in his diagnosis. Always wanting to please his fiancée, Rich agreed. Carol wanted to include Bennett because he also treated her father; she wanted to keep things in the family.

Rich asked if they needed to visit anyone regarding the wedding. If not, he wanted to purchase the Porsche they had looked at, as most likely it would not last long, with its low miles and unique color. He said he could get back by 11 am so that they could head down to Macon and pick up Dr. Williams and then proceed to Albany, Georgia.

Malinda and her friend Nadia would be arriving the next evening from New York for Mother's Day, so Carol was off to the fresh market to gather the necessities the weekend would require. Rich had a friend pick him up to drive him to the dealership to purchase the Porsche.

After consummating the deal for the Porsche, Rich wanted to get Carol something special for Mother's Day. He had already made reservations for Mother's Day at the Ritz Carlton in Buckhead.

Driving the new Porsche, Rich pulled into Bellisimo Jewelers, a designer jewelry store, and purchased Carol a beautiful bracelet. Weighing over 70 carats total, each of the 15 emerald-cut semi-precious citrine stones were identical, finely set in an 18 carat gold Florentine setting. He had the salesperson wrap the special gift in a pastel floral paper, tied with a pink organza ribbon. He couldn't wait to give it to his fiancée on Sunday for Mother's Day.

15

Carol put the last item in the dishwasher and started to walk out of the kitchen when she heard the roaring of an engine pull into the long driveway of her home. He bought it – she thought. There was Rich in a beautiful, shining Porsche Carrera convertible. It was a deep green color with a bright tan interior. Carol walked out of the side door through the garage feeling the vibration of the powerful engine even more.

Rich quickly got out of the driver's seat and motioned for Carol to sit inside. Carol kept thinking how gorgeous the car was as she sat inside it and felt it vibrate. Hopping in the passenger seat, Rich said, "Let's go take her out for a spin!" smiling at Carol.

It was then that Carol realized that the

Porsche was a "stick" as she referred to it, a standard transmission was something that she had not ever tried driving. "I'm so sorry," said Rich, "I didn't even think as to whether or not you could drive a manual transmission. No worries! I will teach you. Let's switch seats and let me take you for a spin in our new weekend cruiser!" he said excitedly. Carol loved the fact that Rich had referred to the Porsche as "our" weekend cruiser. Carol got into the passenger seat and buckled herself in. As they drove through the Atlanta Country Club, Carol couldn't believe how many men and women who were out walking, running, bicycling, or gardening would stare at the vehicle. It was simply stunning. Carol liked the wind blowing through her long, blonde hair and tried to pay attention when Rich would push in the clutch with his left foot and work the stick. It was foreign to her, but learning to drive it with Rich would be fun. Getting back Rich pulled his Mercedes out of Carol's garage and put the Porsche in its place. The two of them left for Albany with one quick stop to pick up Daddy in Macon, Georgia in order for Bennett to look at Rich's injured foot. Daddy was thrilled to see his obviously happy daughter and

Rich when they pulled into his home to pick him up.

"Thank you for including me! I certainly appreciate it," he said. "You're so welcome, Daddy," Carol replied. "I know that Bennett is looking forward to seeing Rich and to attempt to fix his foot."

"He sure took care of me!" Dr. Williams stated.

The three of them made it to Albany Georgia right on time. Rich filled out some brief paperwork and went into the exam room so that Bennett could check Rich's foot.

To Carol and Rich's surprise, Carol's sister Mary Linda and their two boys were already there. After the typical warm greeting that loved ones share, some small talk was made and then Bennett entered. "Oh, I forgot to tell you two that Mary Linda and the boys thought they would stop by to see you , since you were right here, just down the street from where Bennett and Mary Linda live," Bennett explained.

Rich liked Bennett, very much. The three or four previous encounters with Bennett were very pleasant and Rich found him interesting. In addition, Rich had respect for Bennett. He had made his own way through medical school – the hard way.

Bennett's father had passed away when Bennett was young and Bennett took responsibility to care for his brother David who had special needs. Yet Bennett broke through those obstacles and became not only a physician, but an orthopedic surgeon.

After looking at Rich's foot, Bennett decided that a very powerful and painful shot into the top and bottom of his foot should take care of the ailment. Assuming that everyone except Carol would be leaving the exam room, Rich waited for the nurse to come in with the necessary items. Entering the room, the nurse smiled, saying hello to everyone as she put on her latex gloves to perform the procedure. "I need to warn you," the nurse said to Rich, "there are hundreds of nerve endings on the bottom of your foot. To be honest, this shot has been known to make grown men cry, quite literally." Rich was surprised to find Carol's entire family, minus Bennett, still in the room waiting in anticipation to watch the procedure. *Aren't they going to leave?* Rich thought to himself. *A little privacy would be nice.* Rich realized that Carol's family were close, but this seemed ridiculous to him.

Carol's family viewed this as being supportive.

They were there to help, in their minds. Carol patted Rich on the shoulder and said, "Let's hope this makes it better." She barely finished her words as the nurse stuck a three-inch needle into the lower arch of Rich's foot. Pain was simply an understatement! *More like being electrocuted* were the words Rich would have chosen.

He clinched his fists and made a type of low growling noise. He kept his foot perfectly still as previously instructed, but wanted someone in the room to hit him in the head with a sledgehammer! The nurse hadn't exaggerated by any means. Taking a deep breath and regaining his composure, Rich was happy that the worst was over. The second much smaller shot on the top of Rich's foot was a cake walk compared to the first one.

Bennett returned to look at Rich's foot one more time and gave it the green light to put his sock and shoe back on. Bennett warned Rich that inside the shot was a numbing agent. This agent would wear off in four to six hours and there would be significant discomfort for two or three days. Rich shook Bennett's hand and thanked him. Asking Bennett where he was to pay for the procedure, Bennett said, "Don't worry about it! It's on the house." Surprised and grateful, Rich hugged Bennett and thanked him again.

After dropping off Carol's Daddy, driving back to Atlanta, Rich made the comment to Carol that it was a little embarrassing making the noises that he made while getting the shot in the front of her family; and he was surprised that they stayed in the exam room. Carol explained that they were a medical family and that since he was now part of the family, there wasn't anything to feel funny about at all. *Part of the family!* He thought. He felt special.

Friday had arrived and Carol drove to Hartsfield-Jackson International Airport to pick up her daughter Malinda and her roommate Nadia. Mother's Day would be fun with at least one daughter in town. With Caroline being in Australia, the distance prevented her from coming home and getting back in time to return to school.

Rich had made reservations for dinner that evening at Malinda's favorite restaurant, the Lobster Bar. Carol had graciously invited Rich to her home for cocktails and hors d'oeuvres to properly be introduced to Malinda's roommate Nadia. Driving to Carol's home, Rich reflected on how Mother's Day was just another day for him. He had never viewed Mother's Day as a special day in the way most people had.

Rich's telephone began to ring. It was Harriet, the closest one in the world he had viewed as a mother. "Hello, this is Rich."

"Rich, it is Harriet! I just received the beautiful lavender roses you sent me for Mother's Day! They are absolutely gorgeous! As always, you are so generous and thoughtful," Harriet said.

"Well, you are certainly deserving of it. You have been very generous and thoughtful throughout the years to me. You have always been like a mother to me, so I wanted to honor you today," Rich warmly explained. "What are your plans for Mother's Day weekend?"

"My husband is taking me out to dinner on Sunday, along with my children. What are your plans?" Harriet said.

Rich answered, "I am on my way to pick up Carol, her daughter Malinda, and Malinda's roommate Nadia. I am taking everyone to dinner at the Lobster

Bar."

"That sounds so nice." Harriet said, "Again, thank you for my beautiful flowers. Please give Carol my best!"

"I will ... and I will call you on Mother's Day in front of Carol," Rich reminded her.

"I will look forward to talking to you on Sunday. Bye-bye!" Harriet said.

"Bye!" Rich said as he ended the call.

Rich entered Carol's kitchen and greeted Malinda. "Hi Malinda, How are you? It's so good to see you again! You look great!" Malinda said, "Thank you. It is very nice to see you again. I want to introduce you to my dear friend and roommate Nadia. Nadia, this is Rich, my mom's fiancé." "Hi Rich! It's so nice to finally meet you. I have heard many nice things about you," Nadia said.

"Hi Rich," said Carol. "I see you have met Nadia and Malinda. Can I offer you a Diet Coke?" "Yes, please," said Rich.

After a light conversation, it was time to head out for dinner. The Lobster Bar was a well-known eating establishment featuring fresh seafood that was located in Buckhead. The dinner was delicious! After dinner, Carol invited everyone back to her home to have dessert and coffee. Rich was concerned about staying over at Carol's house while Malinda was home visiting. "Don't be silly," Carol said, "You are my fiancé, soon to be my husband. By the way, Malinda and Nadia thought that my engagement ring was absolutely incredible and amazing!" "That's great," Rich said, "Just like you, Carol."

Saturday the girls went shopping all day. Carol told the girls how happy she was with Rich and that she couldn't wait for Caroline to meet him. *Perhaps we could visit Caroline on her birthday,* Carol thought, *I wonder if Rich has ever been to Australia?*

"Where are we eating tonight, Mom?" Malinda asked. "Rich made reservations at Aria for 7:30 tonight," Carol replied. "Wow!" Malinda said, "Nadia you will love it there! Aria is widely regarded as one of Atlanta's finest modern restaurants. They specialize in American and French cuisine, and they have the most delicious cream of celery soup."

Prior to leaving to house for dinner, Rich motioned for Malinda to come over to him while

Carol was still putting on her make up in the powder room. He handed her a box and asked her to hide it in her purse. "it's your mother's Mother's Day gift…I'm going to give it to her after dinner tonight," he said. "Oh, that's so nice of you!" Malinda said, "She's going to be so happy. I can't wait to see what it is, and the look on my mom's face when she opens it!" "Well, your mother is an incredible woman," he said, "She deserves it." Malinda smiled. "Yes, she is, Rich. Yes, she is!"

The four of them enjoyed the three-course meal and intimate atmosphere of Aria's. Nadia commented to Malinda how delicious the food tasted and how prompt and courteous the service was. "Good choice, Ms. Greenbaum," Nadia said.

Rich gave Malinda a nod, and she pulled the beautifully wrapped box out of her purse. "Well, I certainly know that you're the best fiancé in the world! And from what the girls tell me, you're the greatest mother in the world. So this is for you! Happy Mother's Day! You can open it one night early if you like." Malinda and Nadia watched as Rich handed Carol her gift.

When Carol opened the box she looked at her

bracelet, closed her eyes and sat silent for a moment. Without a word, she hugged Rich tightly. Malinda and Nadia had tears come to their eyes. *Pure romance*, thought Malinda. Carol finally took the bracelet out of the box and admired its size and unique design.

Sliding the beautiful 18 carat gold bracelet with so many emerald-cut citrine stones on Carol's delicate wrist, Rich thought it looked exquisite. "Thank you, thank you so much!" Carol said. "Malinda, did you know about this? What a wonderful surprise! You three have made it a memorable evening. I can't wait to wear my bracelet tomorrow!"

Carol always enjoyed Andy Stanley, pastor of the Buckhead Church; he delivered a heartfelt and inspirational message about how special mothers are, and how important a good mother is for a child. Wearing her new bracelet, and feeling the love of the man at her side, this Mother's Day message was especially precious to Carol.

Rich took Carol and the girls to the Ritz Carlton in Buckhead for their Mother's Day brunch. The large buffet was incredible. The pink and cream ballroom was a beautiful setting for a luxurious meal: caviar and several seafood selections, waffles and an omelet station, several unusual salads, and a full dessert display. Each mother was greeted with a red rose, and Carol felt like royalty as she was escorted to their table.

There was so much to enjoy; too soon it was time to get Malinda and Nadia back home to pack for their trip. The flight to New York departed at 8 pm. Carol always hated it when one of her daughters had to leave. Although they were adults, in her eyes they were still her precious babies.

✦✦✦✦✦✦

The girls arrived at the airport as planned. The weekend seemed sweet and satisfying, but always too short. "I can't believe we're back here at the airport!" Rich laughed. "It was Tuesday morning and the two of them were flying to Palm Beach for the day. Carol admired the fact that Rich wanted her to attend one of his business meetings with a CEO of a network marketing company. In her previous marriage, she was never asked to be included in anything that was business-oriented. At 7:00 AM, already the Atlanta airport was buzzing with passengers.

Rich and Carol sat in first class, the only way Rich flew if he was not flying by private jet. As they landed in Palm Beach that feeling had come over Carol again – the uncomforting reminder of the Palm Beach Country Club and the memories that she had tried to forget.

During the meeting with the CEO, Carol was impressed at the respect the man showed toward Rich and the amount of information Rich knew about the industry he was in as a whole. He really was, as the CEO said, "At the top of his game." Carol was impressed at how knowledgeable Rich was regarding his craft – Carol also was aware at how impressed the CEO of the Network Marketing company was with Rich's obvious experience and success in the industry.

Carol seemed somewhat relieved as they lifted off from the Palm Beach International runway on their way back to Atlanta.

Atlanta was her home, the place where she had the courage to change things and reinvent her life. Besides, it was where they were going to create new memories together.

Kim, aka Lori, would be coming in from Florida to join Carol, Mary Linda, Claire, and Harriet, aka Linda, for wedding dress shopping on Thursday.

Getting back home and checking messages, Malinda had left a message telling Carol how much fun she and Nadia had over the weekend and that Rich seemed to be exactly what Carol needed.

Thursday afternoon, Rich finished his last meeting that had been scheduled for the day and went to the airport to pick up his pretend sister, Kim. So far all of the deceit with which he had paved the way to impress his love had gone as he had planned. He tried not to think about it as a series of lies, but more like an obstacle course that needed to be navigated in order to make his bride-to-be feel like part of his family and thus feel closer to him.

Picking up Kim, Rich hugged her and thanked her for coming. Since they had known each other for nine years, they knew one another well enough to speak frankly to each other. Kim told Rich that after talking to Carol on the phone that she really liked Carol and felt special being part of their celebration.

She also didn't like the lying, but she rationalized it by knowing in her heart she was helping two kindred souls come together.

On the drive back to pick up Carol for dinner, Rich briefed Kim on what had transpired since the engagement, including the reaction by everyone when Kim and the rest of Rich's family (with the exception of Mike and Harriet) couldn't make it. Once more, Rich reminded Kim of their supposed childhood adventures and family history.

Carol opened the front door and greeted Kim as if she were her own long-lost sister. Carol commented on how beautiful Kim was, with her long, flowing brown hair, and full brown eyes and lips. "I am so happy to finally meet you!" Carol exclaimed. "Aw … you're so sweet!" Kim said. "'Y'all please come in," Carol said. Kim would be staying at the Ritz Carlton in Buckhead, so Rich left her bag in his Mercedes.

Carol gave Kim a tour of her home, stopping to look at the various pictures and giving a brief explanation of each. Carol had a knack for making people feel welcome and at ease. Her Southern charm and soft mannerisms made Kim feel welcome. After bonding, the girls teased Rich: one for knowing his past, and the other for being his future.

The three went to a very upscale Italian restaurant in Buckhead called Pricci. The girls enjoyed a nice glass of wine while Rich had his usual, a Diet Coke. Kim explained to Carol how excited she was to take part in the dress shopping for the wedding. She also was looking forward to meeting Mary Linda, Claire, and Bennett.

After a delicious meal and coffee, Carol and Rich took Kim to her hotel. Carol grabbed Rich's hand and excitedly said to Rich, "I love your sister! She is so beautiful and nice. Just like you!" Rich thanked Carol and held her hand tightly during the ride home.

That night in bed, Carol felt even closer to Rich. "I know that your sister and I are going to become great friends," Carol said. "I hope she feels the same about me." "I know she does," Rich said. "I can see the way she looks when talking to you." Holding each other tightly…they slept.

✦✦✦✦✦

Mary Linda and Bennett arrived at Carol's home at 11:00 as planned. Rich's mother, Harriet, was supposed to arrive to participate in the dress shopping around 3:00 at the airport. The call came at 11:30 sharp. "Linda" as she was known, called to say that Donald's ear had gotten worse, to include fever and she was afraid to leave him. "Your family has had more ailments in the last week than any I have ever known!" Bennett said jokingly. "It's unbelievable!" Rich agreed.

The ladies were to all meet at the Saks Fifth Avenue bridal department at the Phipps Plaza mall in Buckhead at noon. Kim could simply walk across the street from the Ritz Carlton and Claire lived with her husband Dennis in a beautiful high rise only a quarter mile away. Carol and her sister Mary Linda drove to Phipps, which gave them a chance to visit further. "Well, are you nervous?" Mary Linda asked. "Actually, I'm not! I'm more excited than anything," Carol said.

Rich and Bennett enjoyed a guys' shopping day, first going to the golf pro shop and then to lunch at a sports bar. As they got to know each other better, Rich and Bennett relaxed and enjoyed each other's company. Rich was beginning to feel part of the family, and he liked the feeling.

The girls all met with anticipation. A very nice woman who was the representative sat with Carol and talked about her ideas for what style wedding dress she had in mind. Though it was a lengthy process, Carol enjoyed every minute of it. Carol tried on a half dozen dresses, searching for what seemed an eternity to find the right fit. Kim went to the back to look for another dress for Carol to try, and the representative brought the one Kim selected to the dressing room.

When Carol walked out of the dressing room with this dress on, they knew the search was over. Everyone, including Carol, stared at the magnificent dress. It looked as if it had been designed to fit Carol. With a bodice of antique ivory silk lace intricately sewn with seed pearls and princess seaming, it fit smoothly from her bust to her hips, then flared down to the floor in a full ball gown supported by a tulle petticoat.

With Carol's dress chosen, the search for complementary bridesmaid's gowns began. After searching carefully for a style that could be altered and would pleasingly accentuate each woman's figure, they found just the style. A golden champagne color was chosen to coordinate with the colors of the wedding venue. It was a beautiful silk fabric, and everyone was pleased.

The girls went to Twist for lunch, an eclectic fusion style cuisine in the same shopping area, where they celebrated their success. Carol and Mary Linda said goodbye to Claire and drove Kim back to the Ritz Carlton so she could freshen up before dinner.

Dinner at the Blue Ridge Grill was fun. Talking and laughing together, they shared childhood memories, remembered old friends, and pondered how they had ended up where they were in life. Rich and Kim were careful about what they said, but joined in the spirit of reminiscing, and they all had a great time. *Being part of Carol's family would be nice*, Rich thought. He started to envision holidays together with them … *but only them, not anyone from his family.* After all, his real family was right where Rich wanted them … very far away … There was another group of people who were especially close to Rich … people who were part of his private world … Rich knew he would have to keep them away from Carol, too.

✦✦✦✦✦✦

Saturday included shopping and some sight seeing for Kim, then dinner at what was not only Malinda's favorite restaurant, but also becoming Rich's, as well: the Lobster Bar. Before Rich knew it, the evening was over. Kim had performed her role to perfection, much to Rich's relief. Taking Kim to the airport on Sunday, Rich let out a sigh of relief. Like his other world, once again perfection.

Carol had decided that she missed her younger daughter Caroline too much. She wanted to go to Australia for Caroline's birthday on June 5th. Caroline wouldn't be home for another three months and to Carol, it was unbearable.

As Rich and Carol were strolling through the mall, Carol had decided to ask Rich if he would accompany her to Australia. She desperately wanted Rich to meet Caroline and her birthday would be the perfect opportunity.

Being typical Rich, he readily agreed. Carol was so happy. She thanked God for the man in her life and wanted him to stay there forever. Her family adored him and her friends had given approval a few months earlier.

Carol decided that since she was in Neiman Marcus, she would look for a gift for Caroline. "I also would like to get her something for her birthday," Rich said. "That is so sweet of you!" Carol said, "Are you sure?" "Absolutely!" said Rich.

Carol entered the boutique in Neiman Marcus that was dedicated to Chanel. Carol had selected something that she knew Caroline would like: a pair of diamond encrusted Chanel backward C earrings. Rich chose a beautiful necklace that had the Chanel insignia hanging from it. "Would Caroline like this?" Rich asked. "Oh my, yes she would, Rich! That would be so thoughtful! The question is, are you sure?" Rich laughed as he asked the salesperson to please gift wrap this special birthday present.

Out of the corner of his eye, Rich saw Carol admiring a Chanel diamond bow-shaped bangle bracelet. He noticed the gleam in her eye and turned away so she didn't see him looking.

♦♦♦♦♦♦

The following evening, Rich was in the mood for Italian food, so they found themselves together, as usual, and at Pricci's. They toasted the past weekend's successful shopping, especially finding Carol's perfect wedding dress. As they talked about going to Australia together, the waiter brought out a covered basket. Carol assumed it was the delicious, hot Italian bread Pricci's usually served, but Rich pushed the basket toward Carol and said, "After you, my dear." As Carol opened the napkin, she froze. Staring up at her instead of bread was the Chanel diamond encrusted bow-shaped bracelet from Neiman Marcus! "How did you know? This is incredible! How did you get it here?" Carol was shocked. Tears formed in her eyes as she took out the magnificent piece of jewelry.

The waiter walked by smiling and said, "Wow!"

Carol actually arose from her seat and simply walked over to her fiancé and kissed him. Softly, in his ear, she whispered, "I love you so much! God has answered my prayers. It's not the gifts, Rich, it's the thoughtfulness and kindness you have shown me during our relationship. You are truly my soulmate."

Those words were priceless to Rich.

After a romantic evening, the valet brought the Mercedes around and the two of them started driving home. Carol thanked Rich again for the beautiful surprise.

"Speaking of surprises," Rich said…He reached behind his seat and handed Carol a small black box.

"What's this?" Carol asked. "You're already in my good graces for the rest of your life, after tonight's present!"

"Open it and see," Rich said. Inside the box was a ring that matched the Chanel bracelet he had given her earlier. "This is one of the most memorable nights I have ever had! I still don't know how you knew I loved the bracelet, but the ring now has me baffled!" Carol exclaimed.

"Well, the important thing is that you enjoy it. I always want you, my baby, to be healthy and happy. Always! I love you, Carol."

16

The following morning Carol called her daughter Caroline to tell of the exciting news. "Caroline," said Carol, "How are you?"

"I'm fine, Mom!" Caroline said. "Well, Caroline, I know your birthday is less than two weeks away – you know that I've missed you terribly – so after talking with Rich, how would you like Rich and me to fly to Australia on June 4 so that we can be there to celebrate your birthday on June 5?"

"Mom, don't tease me like that! Are you being serious?" Caroline asked.

"Absolutely I am! I want to see you for your 22nd birthday, so I will be there and Rich cannot wait to meet you!"

Caroline was ecstatic. "Thank you, Mom. Thank

you so much! What an incredible birthday gift! You being here will be awesome!"

"Would you like to get seven to ten friends together and we can go out to your favorite restaurant to celebrate your special day? Mom's treat!" Carol asked.

"Mom, you're the best! That will be fantastic. Rich is okay with coming all of the way here?" Caroline asked.

"Of course!" said Carol, "He is looking forward to the trip, but more importantly having the opportunity to meet you."

"Please tell Rich thank you for me, Mom," Caroline requested.

"I will," Carol said. "Decide where you would like to go for dinner on your birthday and invite whomever you like. I will make our flight arrangements," Carol said. "Let's talk tomorrow or the next day and I will give you the particulars on our flight arrangements."

"Mom, I am so happy! Thank you again!"

"You're welcome, sweet thing!" Carol said. "Night, night!"

Though it was morning in Atlanta, the time difference made it late evening in Australia. Carol was just as excited as Caroline was. She missed her daughter very much and couldn't wait for her to meet Rich.

Later that day Carol stopped by a travel agency not too far from her home and decided that she wanted to treat Rich to the Australian trip. First class to Los Angeles, then on to Australia was not cheap! Two first class, round trip tickets were expensive, not to mention a week's stay at a five star hotel. However, this was her sweet and loving fiancé, so expense was not an issue. After coordinating flights and the hotel, Carol couldn't wait to show Rich the tickets and hotel that she chose for their trip.

Later that night after a home-cooked meal at Carol's, Rich suggested that they go for a sunset drive in "their" Porsche with the top down. "Let's go to Buckhead and get a coffee, then drive around town a little," Rich said. "That would be great!" Carol said. "Since we will be driving with the top down, let me grab a hat to all of this blonde hair underneath." While in the bedroom putting on her hat, Carol grabbed the itinerary for their Australian trip to show Rich a little later during coffee.

The two of them barreled down the highway,

enjoying the warm May weather and holding hands in between the gear shifting like an old married couple. Arriving at the coffee shop, they ordered and decided to sit inside near the fireplace to enjoy the ambiance.

"You're positive that you want to go to Australia with me?" Carol asked. "Don't be silly!" Rich said. "Of course! I already booked the time off for June 4 through the 14. I am looking forward to going, actually." "Good," said Carol with a big smile, as she pulled out the itinerary. "I went to the travel agency today and paid for our tickets and hotel. Before you say anything, I want you to know how much I appreciate all of the wonderful dinners and beautiful jewelry and gifts you have given me. This I my way of saying 'Thank you.'" Rich was taken back by the thoughtful gesture. "I don't know what to say," said Rich. "A beautiful blonde wants to take me to Australia for ten days and stay with me in a five star hotel. I feel like I have just won big from a game show!" They both laughed and Rich thanked Carol sincerely, squeezing her hand. He told her how beautiful she was on the inside as well as the outside.

Rich decided to put the convertible top up on the drive home so they could listen to some music as they drove back to the Atlanta Country Club.

✦✦✦✦✦✦

The next morning, Rich was up early. Out of the norm, he awoke before Carol, put on his shorts, t-shirt, and running shoes and with his cell phone headed out the door. He had left a note for Carol that he was walking and would be back in an hour or so. Calling on his cell phone, the man on the other end answered in a different language. Rich spoke the language fluently, and talked to the man in great detail for forty-five minutes. It was set. Rich would be in New York the following day for a three-day stay.

It wouldn't be easy explaining to Carol why he would need to be in New York … Long Island in particular. Before walking up Carol's driveway, Rich decided that the only logical place he could say that he was going would be to Florida for business. Of course he would also see his son, Jack, while he was in Sarasota.

"There you are!" Carol said. "I am proud of you for walking this morning. What made you decide to walk?"

"Well, I wanted to enjoy the early morning air. In the afternoon I usually have too much going on and it's typically too hot."

"That was smart," Carol said.

After eating breakfast and showering, Rich told Carol, as he was getting dressed, that unfortunately business called and he needed to get down to Tampa as soon as possible. Rich knew that he would be in Florida at least two or three days to take care of the matter at hand.

"I understand," said Carol. "Do whatever you need to do. I will be right here waiting for you when you return." Guilt ran through Rich's veins. Carol was so accommodating. He truly hated being untruthful with Carol but he could never reveal this other side of him… certainly not now, anyway.

Carol suggested that she would be shopping for the Australia vacation while Rich was away. "If you need anything for the trip, just make a list and I will be more than happy to pick it up for you. When you get back from Florida, we will only have two days before we go to Australia." "Thanks!" Rich said. "I will write down a few things."

◆◆◆◆◆◆

Back at the airport again, Rich boarded his first class seat bound for Kennedy Airport in New York. Though he hated to leave Carol for three days, his other line of work was not only a priority, but a way of life.

Carol texted "I miss you" to Rich prior to his take-off, followed by "Enjoy Florida, and your son!" He texted back "I love you" again, feeling guilty.

New York went as planned. The periodic calls to Carol were masked by how the Florida weather was and that Jack, Rich's son, was doing well. Rich told Carol that he would try to stay busy with Jack during the down times from business to take his mind off of missing her. Carol was excited. Rich would be landing and coming home within a couple hours. As always, she wanted to look her best for her fiancé's arrival. They would be going out to dinner at the Blue Ridge Grill to play catch-up.

Dinner was delicious. Carol seemed her happiest when she was with Rich. With him, she knew that she could just be herself, talk about anything that came to mind and because Rich always put her first she felt special. Getting back to Carol's, the two held each other and enjoyed Carol's home-brewed coffee. "I can't wait until the day after tomorrow," Carol said. "I'm not looking forward to the 22 hour flight, but I am looking so forward to seeing and being with Caroline! I'm so happy that you two will finally meet."

"Me, too!" Rich said. "And thank you for picking up those things for me."

"You're welcome, sir!" Carol said, smiling.

"Since tomorrow is Sunday, after Buckhead Church, I still need to grab just a few more things from CVS. Perhaps we can get something casual and simple for dinner," Carol suggested.

"Perfect!" Rich said. Grabbing Carol's hand, he led her to the bedroom. After all, they hadn't been together in three days.

✦✦✦✦✦✦

After attending the eleven o'clock service at Buckhead Church, Rich and Carol went to the Tavern in Phipps Plaza for lunch. Jason, their usual waiter, brought them "the usual." The two of them had a lot of running around to do prior to tomorrow's adventure. Getting home, they both put on comfortable clothes and went to the stores to find what they needed, things Caroline couldn't get in Australia.

Returning, the two finished all of their packing. Being a typical couple, Carol had three suitcases and Rich had just one. Dinner time had approached and neither one of them wanted to get dressed up again. *Casual was definitely the theme of the evening*, they thought. Carol suggested that the Flying Biscuit on West Paces Ferry would be perfect. They could get breakfast, lunch, or dinner from the Flying Biscuit menu. Very casual.

During dinner, Carol's sister had tried to call Carol's cell phone several times. "I wonder why she keeps calling?" Carol said as she switched her cell phone to vibrate. "I'm trying to enjoy my dinner!" She exclaimed.

When dinner was over, Rich routinely grabbed the check to pay. Reaching for his wallet for money, he realized that in rushing out the door he forgot to bring his money. "Oh, no!" Rich exclaimed.

"What's wrong?" Carol asked.

"You're not going to believe this! I left my money at home! Damn!" Rich blurted out.

"I didn't even bring my purse," Carol said worriedly.

"No problem. Let me just tell the manager," Rich said. "I feel so stupid. We'll look back and laugh at this, trust me!"

The manager laughed as Rich told him he would be back in less than an hour to pay for the meal. "Take your time, sir," the manager said.

Carol, now relieved, exited the Flying Biscuit quickly, as Rich followed. "Unbelievable!" Rich said, laughing. "When we get home, I can run back up here alone." "Sorry about this," Carol laughed. "Next time let's make sure you have your wallet!"

Rich left the parking lot a little faster than usual, wanting to get back to pay for their meal. "No don't get pulled over!" Carol said. "You don't have your license!"

"I won't!" Rich said.

Not even 45 seconds into the drive home, Carol's sister Mary Linda called again. This time Carol answered. "Hi, Mary Linda!" Carol said.

"Carol!" Mary Linda said frantically, "Where are

you?"

"I'm just driving home from dinner," Carol said.

"Is Rich sitting next to you?" Mary Linda still sounded frantic.

"Yes," Carol was concerned at her tone.

"Okay, hang up the phone and call me as soon as you get home. Call me when you can get alone in the house. Make sure you call me the second you walk in. Okay?"

"Fine," Carol hesitated as she hung up. "I wonder what that's all about," Carol said to Rich.

"Who knows?" Rich said. Pulling in the driveway, Rich went into the bedroom to retrieve his wallet. "Let me just use the restroom before I drive all the way back there," Rich said.

Once again, Carol's phone rang. It was Mary Linda again. "Let me see what she wants," Carol said.

After about three minutes, Rich exited the restroom. Carol was standing in the middle of the kitchen, as white as a ghost. "What's wrong?" asked Rich. Carol started to tremble. As Rich approached to ask again, this time she backed up, almost as if she was afraid of him. "Carol, what's wrong?" Rich asked.

Tears filled Carol's eyes as she asked Rich "Are you a con man?"

"What?" Rich said. "What are you talking about?"

"My sister said that she found out that you're a con man. She said that you are not who you say that you are, and that the people who came here were not your real mother and sister!" Now crying, Carol asked, "Rich, why would she say that? Please tell me that she is wrong. Please! I trusted you and love you!" She said.

Rich's heart sank. *How did they find out about his pretend family?* He thought. "Carol, I love you, and I don't know what you're talking about."

Suddenly the phone started ringing again. It was her sister. "Please tell me she's wrong! Why is she saying this? Was that your mother and sister? I feel sick. Talk to me, Rich, please! What's going on? Is Rich your real name?"

"Don't be ridiculous!" Rich said.

The constant ringing of the phone was driving Carol crazy. She answered it. This time her sister was yelling to get Rich out of the house. "He's dangerous! And he carries a gun!" Mary Linda said.

Crying, Carol handed Rich the phone. "Here, you

talk to her and ask her why she is saying this."

"I'm going to call the police!!!" Mary Linda was yelling.

Rich hung up the phone. This time Rich grabbed Carol's shoulders. "Listen to me and listen carefully! I love you! Calm down and we can talk about my family."

"What do you mean 'talk about my family'?" Carol cried. "I was going to marry you! We're leaving for Australia in the morning!"

Rich knew his world was caving in fast. "Listen to me. Let me go pay the bill at the restaurant before they close. I'll come back and explain Trust me!!" Going quickly into the bedroom, Rich grabbed his passport and the cash that he was taking to Australia. As Carol continued to cry and question him, Rich grabbed the Porsche keys and said he would be right back.

The phone rang again and Carol picked it up. Mary Linda and Bennett were asking Carol if Rich had left yet. Rich heard Carol ask Mary Linda why they called the police.

Rich fired up the Porsche and told Carol he would return after he paid the bill at the Flying Biscuit.

Sweat was pouring from Rich's forehead and his

heart was racing. *Did his entire future just collapse in front of him?* After a lifetime of guarding his closest secrets without a single flaw ... *how could this have leaked out so easily? Carol,* he thought. His heart ached at the thought of her thinking that Rich had deceived her. Rich suddenly forgot about the unpaid bill at the restaurant. *What was going through Carol's mind?* He thought, *Why did Mary Linda say that I carried a gun? Why would she call the police?* She didn't know his other world. How did she know of his fake mother and sister? Rich got on I-75 North and just started driving.

Carol was on the phone now with her nephew Bradford. Bradford was as disappointed as everyone else. He truly liked Rich. Bradford was extremely fond of Carol and Rich had met the criteria to get Bradford's approval to be with his Aunt Carol. He thought how nice it was going to be with his fun and new "Uncle Rich" – that dream appeared to be shattered now.

Suddenly there was knock on the door. *It's Rich!* Carol thought. But when she opened the door, it was a police officer. *She did it!* Mary Linda had actually called the police. The officer explained that they received a call about a very dangerous man at this address, and relatives were worried because he carried a gun.

Not knowing what to do, Carol explained to
the officer what her sister had told her. The officer
decided to run Rich's name through the system as a
precaution. Unlike what Mary Linda had said, Rich
was not wanted, nor did he have any criminal history
whatsoever. His address showed up in Florida where he
said he was from.

Relieved somewhat, Carol thanked the officer and
said she was fine. Bradford had still remained on the
phone with Carol. He told Carol that his mother and
father were sending a friend down to stay with her, an
old gentleman who was a private investigator, just to be
with Carol as a precaution.

The compilation of feelings inside of Carol simply
left her in a daze, she was scared, traumatized, and
found herself shaking almost uncontrollably. The
thought of keeping her composure to tell Caroline that
she couldn't fly to Australia was overshadowed by the
sadness and hurt that Caroline would experience with
the heartbreaking news.

Carol found herself in a living nightmare. She was
due to take off for Australia in 12 hours with her fiancé,

who was now apparently not who he said he was. *Oh my goodness,* thought Carol. *What about poor Caroline?* She was expecting Rich and Carol to arrive soon.

Carol felt nauseous and confused. She was shaking. *Where is Rich?* She thought. I have to try to call him. Carol called, but Rich didn't answer. She left a message. "Where are you?" she asked. "Please come home and explain this to me. The police just left and I know you're not wanted. Please come back to me. I need to know what's going on! I'm scared." Four more calls went to Rich unanswered.

Hours later, Rich suddenly found himself in Tennessee. He was in a daze, just driving and thinking of Carol. *How would he even remotely explain to her that the people who came in were not his real family?* Tears rolled down his eyes as he thought of his life on this earth without Carol. He was numb. No human had ever gotten to his heart or soul like Carol did. Rich had no clothes or possessions with him, other than a passport and cash, but he didn't care. *How did they find out?* He played in his mind over and over how Carol backed away from him in the kitchen, with fear in her eyes. It crushed him. *Why would her sister say those things about him?* He wondered what Carol was doing, what she was feeling, and even more importantly, what she was thinking of him.

Carol reluctantly welcomed Mary Linda and Bennett's friend, the private investigator. They had some coffee as Carol explained what her sister had told her.

Carol's father had called and was devastated, to say the least. Crying, Dr. Williams told Carol that he was so sorry. He truly liked Rich. As a matter of fact, Dr. Williams was Rich's biggest fan. He was impressed with the way Rich had treated Carol and was actually looking forward to Rich becoming his son-in-law. Talking with Carol, Dr. Williams asked her if there was anything that he could do for his precious daughter.

"I'll be fine, Daddy," Carol said. "I just need some time to find out what's going on here."

"Well, honey, I'll ask Mary Linda to give me a ride to Atlanta in a day or two. Perhaps Bennett and the boys can come, as well," Dr. Williams said.

"Alright, Daddy. I love you. Don't worry. I'll be fine. Let's talk in the morning. I have no idea what to do about Australia. I'm just hurt and confused right now. I love you, Daddy," Carol said.

"I love you too, Carol. Talk to you in the morning," Dr. Williams said.

It was 3:00 am. Her eyes red from crying and her stomach upset, Carol decided to attempt to sleep for a few hours. As her head touched the pillow, it felt like it weighed 50 pounds. Drifting off to sleep, she asked herself, *Where is he? Who is he?*

Driving aimlessly in the night, all Rich could think was, *How is she? I miss her ... I need her ... Carol!!!*

17

Opening her eyes a few hours later, Carol was simply numb. Lying in bed, the thought of getting up was just too much. "God," Carol said, "Why did this happen to me? Why? I don't understand." Mustering up just enough strength to reach for her cell phone, Carol tried to reach Rich again. His phone went directly to voicemail. Hanging up, tears rolled down Carol's cheeks. Looking at her clock, Carol suddenly remembered that in five hours, she was supposed to board a plane bound for Australia.

How can I even think about leaving the country for ten days? she thought. *Poor Caroline … what am I to tell her? This will ruin her birthday. This will crush her …*

Carol finally got out of bed and made some coffee. She felt empty inside. *I thought I had found my soulmate, my destiny.* Suddenly, Carol's home phone rang. *Maybe it's Rich,* she thought as she rushed to answer it. "Hello?" Carol said.

"Hi Honey, it's Daddy. Are you holding up okay?"

As always, Carol was truthful with her father. "No, Daddy, I'm not. I'm so confused. I'm getting ready to call Caroline to tell her that I am not going to Australia. Daddy, she is going to be devastated."

"Have you heard from Rich, honey?" Daddy asked.

"No. I just can't believe this, Daddy. Why me? What have I done to deserve this?" Crying now, Carol wiped her tears as her father tried to console her over the phone. "Well honey, we're all shocked. I found myself crying over this situation last night before I went to bed. I think that he really loved you, but I don't know why he would hurt you so. You know we are here for you. The world is not always what it seems, just like people. The next time you meet someone, take your time and really get to know them first, honey. I love you and this will take some time to heal."

"Since you're not going to Australia, your sister and Bennett and the boys will be coming to Atlanta to see you tomorrow. They're going to pick me up as well. You just hang in there until then."

"Okay, Daddy," Carol said. "I had better call Caroline and explain to her what has happened."

"I am so sorry, Carol. We love you. I love you too, Daddy. I will call you later, especially if I hear from Rich. Bye, bye Daddy."

Getting dressed, Carol decided that she would go for a walk first to clear her head. For the first time in Carol's life her head was truly spinning. Normally, the walks were Carol's private time to thank God for all of her blessings, a time to reflect on her life, her family and of course to sometimes simply just think. This morning's walk was much different. It was the first time that Carol would be questioning her heavenly Father.

"God, I know that you always have a reason for everything that you do. Although this time it is very hard to understand – even remotely understand what the reason would be. The only thing I have prayed for since my divorce, more importantly than anything else, was that whoever would be the next love of my life was an honest man. Someone trustworthy! I thought that I had found that in Rich. I thought that I had found that special bond between two people that comes only once in a lifetime. My daddy thought the world of him, my sister, her family and my friends thought he was great. My life is shattered. I am so hurt, embarrassed and humiliated."

Carol thought about a particular sermon that Andy Stanley had given a few months earlier about how certain people who come into your life are part of God's master plan. Crying now, Carol felt how much she truly loved Rich. "Why didn't I see any of this coming?" She asked out loud. "How could I have been so stupid? I can't believe how much I have been let down again. Did he really love me? Is my engagement ring even real?" Carol couldn't settle this in her heart or mind. *I must find out the truth. Rich treated me like a queen,* she thought. *I know he had feelings for me. I felt it. I saw it in his eyes. He bought me such lavish gifts.*

"God, I need to know who he really is, and who is really part of his family. I cannot stop until I know the truth."

Getting home, Carol sat at the kitchen table and took a deep breath. It was time to call Caroline and give her the disappointing news.

"Mom, please tell me you're kidding!" Caroline yelled. "Mom, you have to be here. All of my friends are coming for dinner! We were going to spend a week together. Please, Mom, don't worry about Rich. Just get on the plane! You'll forget about him eventually!"

Easier said, than done, Carol thought. There was absolutely no way that she could even consider leaving the country. Caroline finally understood the seriousness of her mother's plight. They cried together, and then Carol reassured her daughter that she would make up her birthday to her a thousand-fold. Caroline had not met Rich, so he was just a stranger to her. Hurting her mother was reason enough to disregard Rich.

"Mom, anyone who would bring in a fake family must be some sort of psycho! Call it a blessing in disguise and be glad to have him out of your life."

Caroline could feel her mother's pain through the phone; she also was feeling her own pain. How was she going to explain to all of her friends in Australia who were expecting to see her mother whom she had talked so much about, along with her mother's fiancée. What would she tell them? How could she tell them?

Caroline didn't realize the seriousness for the

depth of her mother and Rich's relationship. She was lashing out, which was understandable. Mom was hurt, so in turn, so was she.

✦✦✦✦✦✦

Rich had been up driving all night. Ending up in northern Tennessee, it was morning and the Porsche was on empty. After filling up the vehicle with fuel, he realized that he hadn't eaten in twelve hours. Grabbing some snacks from the store proved to be wasteful. His stomach was in knots. Rich couldn't eat, or even concentrate. The long drive allowed time for reflection.

The image of Carol in her kitchen with a look of fear in her eyes haunted him. The last four months of his life he had spent every waking hour making the love of his life feel secure and happy and in a matter of moments it was destroyed.

Part of him wanted to head south and drive as fast as he could back to his baby, Carol, to hold her and hug her and make everything okay. Looking at his cell phone, Rich was almost afraid to turn it on; the thought of hearing Carol's voice upset was unbearable.

Realizing that there was nothing for him in northern Tennessee, Rich got back on I-75 south and headed toward Atlanta.

Finally turning on his phone, he could see that there were several calls from Carol. His heart racing a little faster, Rich decided to listen. Tears welled up in his eyes as he listened to Carol's frantic calls asking for an explanation and curious about his whereabouts. The last message on Rich's cell phone from Carol shocked him. Carol commented on how confused she was after talking to Mary Linda about what his real sister had to say. She went on to describe that the things that his real sister said were shocking. Carol also wondered who the girl she met really was; the person she thought was his sister, Lori.

Lori! How in the world did they find out about the psycho – his real sister? Nothing made sense. Rich hadn't talked to his real sister in over three years. The last time he had even seen her was when he had sued her. How could she have known about Carol or any of her family?

One thing that Rich knew: if his real sister was running her mouth to Carol or her family, it would be twisted, terrible made-up lies. Ironically, Rich's sister had absolutely no idea who her brother really was. If she did, the last thing in the world that she would do would say anything derogatory about him, as it could prove to be very dangerous.

Rich in his heart knew that he owed Carol an explanation at the very least. As he continued down the highway, he called her cell phone. Unfortunately, it went to Carol's voice mail. Almost relieved, Rich did not leave a message, but knew that Carol would see that he tried to contact her.

Continuing to Atlanta, Rich reflected on his life. Somehow Carol had managed to do something that no other woman had even come close to doing. She got through ... into his heart.

It was a very guarded heart to say the least. At age twelve, Rich moved with his family from Chicago, Illinois, to his birthplace, Hamilton, Ontario, Canada. His father moved the family back to Hamilton, keeping a promise to Rich's mother. Hamilton was also her birthplace and childhood home. Hamilton was a fresh start, along with a new job opportunity for Mr. Towsley. Mrs. Towsley wanted to go back to

Canada to be near her parents, and with the country's socialized medicine and superior school system, it seemed like a good fit.

However, Hamilton offered something else to an opportunistic and poor young man who found himself on the street at every opportunity…

Rich's home environment was not a loving one. With parents who never told him or any of his other siblings that they were loved or cared for, parents that constantly swore and fought, parents who didn't really pay attention to where a twelve year old boy wandered after school and on late evenings on weekends.

At age 12, Rich was a quick thinker, independent, and hungry. A perfect opportunity to be recruited by the wrong element. Starting with small illegal odd jobs, in time, trust was established and by age 14 Rich found himself working with one of Hamilton's organized crime families.

The praise and compensation overshadowed the fact that what he was doing was wrong. By age 16, Rich was attending high school in the daytime and earning substantial income for a teenager in the evenings and on weekends.

Through fate and a little bit of luck, Rich had an opportunity prior to his 17th birthday to go to Florida. He ran away from home and ended up living with his grandmother in Sarasota, Florida.

Rich did have respect for his grandmother and promised to work hard in school and graduate with a high school diploma. Rich was receiving another kind of education on the weekends, slowly being groomed and learning the ropes from some of the most advanced white collar criminals in the country. Rich kept his promise to his grandmother and graduated from high school. By age 25, Rich had earned the right and respect of his peers in this other world and became a major player; someone who was treated with the utmost respect in this world. Living this double life, in the shadows of society, he was never found out by his grandmother or anyone else outside of this special group of friends.

Arriving back in Atlanta, Rich checked into the Ritz Carlton Hotel. He was exhausted. Still not able to eat, he slowly drank a diet Coke as he undressed. After pulling the curtains to darken the room and putting the radio on low, he fell asleep.

Waking up early that evening, Rich ordered room service and forced himself to eat a few bites of his food. Collecting his thoughts, he decided to call Carol at home.

To his surprise, Bennett, Carol's brother-in-law, had answered the phone. Rich talked to Bennett for a few moments and explained that if given the opportunity, he could explain his reasons for the fake family. Carol's sister got on the phone and told Rich that the whole family, including Daddy and Carol's nephews, had come to Atlanta to be with Carol. She also let him know that they had been talking with Rich's real sister, Lori, and also with Rich's real parents.

Rich could only imagine the nightmare scenario that his sister and parents would cause by talking with Carol and her family. Rich knew what his family was really like. Dishonest, lying, and jealous of Rich's success, they would take this opportunity to try and hurt Rich. Rich had finally had enough of them two and a half years prior, and he had put them in their place.

Before passing the phone to Carol, Mary Linda

told Rich that he had done enough damage and that he should move on. "Rich, you have such a gift of reaching out to people with positive energy. Instead of trying to swindle people in a negative way, why don't you try to turn your direction to Christ and be a witness for Christ?"

Keeping his composure, Rich politely asked to speak with Carol. When Rich heard Carol's voice his heart sank. "Carol, please listen to me. I can imagine how this must look, and if you listen to my family, it will be a big mistake. You don't' know the history of my family. I am finished with them forever. That's why I brought in the close friends to pose as my family. Please let me explain."

"Rich, it doesn't matter," Carol said. Her words seemed to be coached, probably by her family. "I loved you for you and I was honest with you," she said. "That's all I ever wanted from you. You're an amazing person, Rich, but you need to receive God in your life first and foremost if you want to change your life. Please ask God to come into your life. I have to go now. Bye." The clicking of the phone as Carol hung up on him simply crushed Rich.

Keeping all of the lights off in his hotel room, Rich lay on the bed staring at the ceiling. Those words wouldn't stop playing over and over in his mind. "I loved you for you. Please get God in your life."

Meanwhile at Carol's house, the six family members sat in the living room listening to what they thought were true tales about Rich from his sister and father: exaggerated tales of Rich carrying a gun at all times; of Rich scamming numerous women; of Rich impersonating a physician to examine women; of Rich stealing people's identities. Though sensationalized and untrue, Carol's family knew that Rich had brought in a fake mother, Harriet; a fake sister, Kim; and a brother-in-law, Mike, who was not a psychiatrist. They naturally assumed that all of these tales were true, as well.

The next morning, Rich's phone rang. It was Carol. "Hello," Rich said. "Please listen to me. You must know that I love you. You have to know that I love you. You have to know that I couldn't fake that."

"My sister is coming," Carol said. "I have to go now." She hung up on Rich. He knew that making that simple call showed that deep down, Carol loved him still and needed to talk with him.

Carol had texted Rich and asked him to bring back the car that he had bought and put in her name. In turn she would have all of his personal belongings packed and waiting for him. Rich didn't care about the vehicle. He would gladly return it and get his things. But he wanted to look into her eyes and talk to her. He owed her that. After contemplating all day, Rich decided that he would ask a friend to drop off the Porsche to Carol's house and retrieve his things. He didn't want to face Carol's entire family.

That evening while Carol's family listened to more exaggerated tales from Lori, Rich's sister, Rich's friends graciously dropped off the Porsche and picked up Rich's personal effects. Bringing Rich's things to the Ritz Carlton, Rich thanked them and compensated them for their trouble. As Rich looked through his things, many items were still missing: his laptop, his expensive pen, and his Gucci shoes.

Rich texted Carol, telling her of the items that were missing. To Rich's surprise, Carol was apologetic and said that she would set the items out front of her home by the door in the morning and that Rich was welcome to come by and get them then as she was heading out to be with the rest of her family.

The next morning Rich had decided that he would have Carey limousine service drive him to Carol's to retrieve his possessions and then have the limo take him to the airport. He was heading back to Florida. Rich needed to get away and think.

Rich called Carol at 9:00 am and asked if he could come by around 10:00 am to pick up the items. "That would be fine," Carol said.

"Can I please see you for just two minutes?" he begged her. "I guess so," Carol said.

There was no reason to be afraid. After all, Carol's nephews had brought their rifles with them to protect their aunt. They would be watching her like a hawk...

At 10:00 am, a long black limousine pulled up to Carol's house. Out of it emerged an exhausted and distraught Rich. Carol walked out her front door, obviously weathered and also exhausted. She handed Rich his things, which he proceeded to put in the back of the vehicle.

Carol began, "I gave you my heart. I was willing to spend the rest of my life with you. I introduced you to my family and to my friends. You have torn my heart out. Please change your life. Please trust me and get God into your life. Do it for yourself."

Rich hugged Carol tightly as she began to cry asking, "How could you do this to me?"

Rich felt her pain and was equally devastated. "This is not what you think," Rich said. "I love you more than anything on this earth. Never ever forget that. Please don't believe a word my pathetic family says. If you ever really loved me, please believe that," Rich frantically asked. "I will call you in a few days. I will prove to you that you will always be the love of my life. I love you, baby," he said.

"Please get God in your life for me," she pleaded. "Please live your life the right way."

"Okay," Rich said.

Looking in each others' eyes, they parted ways. Both of their hearts were aching.

18

The limousine headed down Carol's driveway taking Rich away from her; it seemed most likely to Rich as the last time that he would ever see his baby again.

Rich reached over to put on the shoes that Carol had handed to him in his baggage when he noticed a yellow piece of paper from a notepad folded in his shoe. Opening the note, Rich recognized the handwriting immediately as Carol's. *Rich*, it said, *Please change your life. Spend the rest of your days on this earth being the special person that I know God wants you to be. Get God in your life, please, for me. I truly loved you ... Carol.*

"Was it Delta, sir?" the limo driver asked for the second time. The 45 minute drive to the Hartsfield-Jackson Airport was over already. Rich was still clinching Carol's final words in his hand. Somehow, while he pondered the thought of losing her, 45 minutes of his life had gone by. Rich knew that the flight to Sarasota, Florida, would also probably pass by as he continued to play over and over in his head what had happened over the last 72 hours.

Rich took his seat in first class. Normally when Rich was flying away from Atlanta, he couldn't wait to rush back to Carol. This time, however, was much different.

✦✦✦✦✦✦

Since the initial shock had worn off and that she had shed more than her share of tears, Carol had decided a change was needed. She needed something to wipe the slate clean and a new vehicle would do just that. Carol's Range Rover was purchased during her previous marriage, and was often a reminder. Now the Porsche would be a daily reminder of Rich, too. Some women when a relationship ends need something anew. A new haircut, new clothes, in this case it was the vehicles in which needed a change; Carol's Daddy and

Bennett would come with her to the dealership to assist her in a new purchase.

Carol's family was still visiting, offering moral support. Carol wanted her daddy and Bennett to come with her to the Mercedes dealership so that she could trade in the two vehicles for a new fresh start automobile. Of course, the two men readily agreed and by the afternoon, Carol was the proud owner of a brand new S550 Mercedes. Carol's family spent the weekend trying to comfort her, explaining to her that this could have happened to anyone, and that over time with the help and power of God that all things heal.

Hugging her daddy, sister, brother-in-law, and nephews tightly, Carol thanked them for their support and assured her family that she was fine. Waving goodbye, Carol walked back into her home, laid on her bed, and cried.

✦✦✦✦✦✦

Rich got out of the cab at his home in Sarasota, Florida. Walking up the driveway, it no longer felt like a home, but like a place he used to call home. In his heart, he knew that his home was with Carol.

Throwing his bags on the bed, Rich changed his clothes and headed to the beach to walk and to watch the sun set. The very thought of his sister sticking her nose where it didn't belong and her lying and hurting Carol enraged him. Perhaps if his sister had even a remote idea of who her brother really was, would have certainly made her think twice about her indiscretion. Rich had the ability to pick up the phone, make one call, and his sister would disappear. Rich knew that at the very least he owed Carol and her family a valid explanation, but what he would reveal would be limited. It had to be.

Rich called Carol from his cell phone as the sun set on Siesta Key Beach in Sarasota. Carol answered reluctantly, thought there were still very strong feelings for Rich. She had no idea how to handle what had transpired. It was too early.

"Hi, baby!" Rich said. "First of all, I need to tell you again that 95% of what you have heard from my lying family is totally false. If it were true, wouldn't I just vanish? That would be the logical thing for me to do, if I were anything like what they had said about me. Are you going to tell me that you don't feel me still? Can you tell me right now that you don't love me? If you can tell me that you don't love me, I promise you will never hear from me again."

"I told you that I will always love you," said Carol. "I just don't know what to think. I thought I knew you, the real you. I thought that I met your real family. I would love some honest answers. The things that your sister said shocked all of us."

"Let me ask you something," Rich said. "How did my sister even get into the mix? If you even remotely understood who my sister is, and my real family, you would understand why I would never expose you to those lowlifes. I promised myself as a kid that I would be the opposite of them and I am, in every way imaginable," Rich said. "For what it's worth, I need you to understand something, Carol. Everything I told you regarding how I felt about you was and is 100% true. I spent every moment cherishing you and treating you like a princess. It's still not too late to spend our lives together. Keep your wedding dress and give me an opportunity to look into your eyes and explain truthfully. Either we will say goodbye or wake up every morning on this earth together."

"Well, Rich, there has been a lot of damage done," Carol said. "I would need you to apologize to my daddy first and foremost, then to Bennett and Mary Linda."

"I understand," Rich said. "But first I need to see you and look in your eyes."

"There is only one way that I will see you," Carol insisted. "I'm not sure if you can do it, but you would need to be 100% honest with me, and I mean about everything!" she demanded. "No exceptions!"

Though Rich agreed to Carol's terms, deep down he knew that he had never been able to be 100% honest with anyone he had met since he was 14 years old.

The two of them agreed to meet in a week. In Rich's eyes just the opportunity to see Carol again would be worth it. A few days later, Carol drove down to her daddy's house to simply talk and see how he was holding up after the ordeal. Dr. Williams was still devastated as to what had transpired.

"Well, Daddy, I am going to meet Rich in a couple of days. He said that other than the fake mother and sister, he can prove that all of the horrific things that his sister said, the carrying of a gun, the scamming women, the stealing people's identities, are all totally untrue and he will prove it to me."

Dr. Williams warned his daughter to be cautious. He knew that she still had feelings for Rich and wanted Carol to think with her head, and not with her heart.

The day prior to Rich meeting Carol, he had thought about his life in great detail. Rich, to most of society, was an educated, clean cut and very intelligent businessman. But to a small group of private, powerful individuals, he was an integral part of a team. He was someone that had been groomed for a specific task, as had others in this private organization. Rich fulfilled his responsibility to this group with perfection. Getting *found out* was not an option ... ever.

Perhaps his actions with Carol being exposed were a blessing in disguise. Living a life of 25 years without anyone knowing the real him had taken its toll. Always covering his tracks, pretending to be someone other than himself most of his life was not easy. Rich knew that he wanted to have a life like that of Dr. Williams, spending the rest of his days on the earth with a family and a spouse like Carol that he could be totally transparent with, being honest with himself. Dr.

Williams also had something else in his life that Rich didn't have ... God.

Perhaps there was something to this so-called Christian lifestyle. The last words that Carol said to him on that note resonated in his soul: *Please change your life and get God in your life.* The only problem with that in Rich's opinion, was that after 25 years of being affiliated with organized crime, his sins were most likely too vast for anyone to wash away.

Carol's neighbors had noticed that her home was not vacant as it was supposed to be since she should have been in Australia. When Carol was in her driveway taking out some trash, they were walking by and exclaimed to her, "We thought you were in Australia!" Hugging her friends who were also members of the exclusive Atlanta Country Club, Carol invited them in and explained what had transpired with Rich. As humiliating as it was, she was still a woman and she needed to vent. *Shocked* was the only word to describe the look on the women's faces.

"Do you believe everything that his sister said?" one of the neighbors asked. The women held Carol's hand and offered to be of assistance. "I'm not sure what to believe right now," she said. "I am actually meeting him tomorrow to talk," Carol said.

"Please let us know what happens," the friends asked. "I will," said Carol. "Wish me luck!"

The next morning Rich and Carol met at the Lenox Mall, upstairs across from the Prime Restaurant were some tables isolated from the busy mall traffic. The two of them embraced, holding each other for a full two minutes. As strong of a man as Rich was emotionally, tears immediately rolled down his cheeks. He explained to Carol that what she was about to hear would most likely shock her. He emphasized that in the event that Carol felt one thing was untrue, she should get up and leave immediately. Rich explained that he had absolutely nothing to lose and everything to gain. Opening the bag that he had brought with him, Rich started with pictures, college transcripts, financial statements, and a series of stories and explanations.

Then came the climax of the events that led to their meeting.

He had been involved for over 25 years as an affiliate of organized crime, but he was willing to give it up – all of it – in order to change his life and be with

Carol.

Yes, he was married, but he had done it strictly for the benefit of his young son, Jack. He had never shared a bed or a full day with his son's mother since their marriage day. And Carol could call her to verify this.

He would prove to Carol beyond a reasonable doubt that his sister was a habitual liar who was not an RN but a high school dropout. She had been married four times. Her son was accused of murder. His brother was not a pharmacist as his sister stated but also a high school dropout who had a menial labor job. His parents were milking the welfare system in Canada and also were liars. His brother also was a convicted bank robber who served prison time.

Rich, now very upset, explained that he worked hard in life and was truly a multimillionaire. He was the only member of his family to graduate high school and go to college. Rich went on to explain his childhood struggle and terrible environment that he was able to overcome. Rich had always been embarrassed and disgusted with his family. He would rather have brought in Harriet as his mother, a woman he had know for over 12 years; and Kim as his sister, a woman he had known for over 9 years, rather than expose her to his real family that he had successfully avoided for years.

Carol explained to Rich that when her father had sent the engagement pictures to the address that Rich had given him for his parents in Canada (which was an old address from seven years earlier) that the current occupants of that residence knew where his parents currently resided and gave his real parents the pictures. They in turn called Rich's sister, Lori, who saw Dr. Williams' return address and phone number on the return label on the envelope. She called Dr. Williams, which started the chain of events that led to that terrible encounter on the evening of June 3.

Initially, Carol took a deep breath and tried to process the very idea that she was going to marry a man who was affiliated with organized crime, someone that was not a Christian as he had led her to believe, and that she only knew partially.

In her heart, Carol knew that she still loved Rich. Not wanting to show that side of her, Carol acted without emotion. "Are you willing to sit down with my daddy and Bennett and show them all of this and explain what you have told me? Also I would like you to apologize to them. You hurt them very much. If things are to ever work out between us that is where you would have to start."

Rich readily agreed. Rich held Carol's hand tightly and thanked her for giving him the chance to come clean. Rich promised Carol that he would contact Bennett and her father when he went back to Florida and just like Rich did for Carol, he would just simply tell the truth. Even if Rich didn't end up with Carol in his life, at least he gave her what he owed her: His true identity and an honest explanation.

Carol showed up the next morning at the Atlanta Country Club for her usual tennis practice. Seeing the group of ladies huddled together as she approached the courts, Carol could see them talking as they looked at her. Suddenly the ladies disbanded, obviously trying to hide the fact that they were talking about her. Embarrassed, Carol smiled and put her head down as she unpacked her tennis equipment. She felt foolish and knew that she would be the target of gossip for the foreseeable future.

While sitting in his Florida home that evening

Rich called Bennett to set up a meeting. The call turned into an hour conversation with Rich explaining everything to him in detail. Bennett said that he understood why Rich did what he did, though he thought Rich should have handled it differently. Bennett appreciated Rich's forthright and honest telling of the truth.

"It may take six months, but I think that in time this could end up being water under the bridge," Bennett said. Pleased, Rich thanked him for taking the time to talk with him, and for Bennett's willingness to explain their detailed discussion with Carol's sister, Mary Linda.

Next for Rich was a much more monumental task. Rich called Carol's father, Dr. Williams, and made arrangements to meet him at his home in two days. Carol's plight had unfortunately become the proverbial "talk of the town" around her neighborhood. Like a wildfire, the news of what had transpired with Rich spread rapidly. Carol felt humiliated as she took her morning walks around her home. Every time someone waved and smiled at her, she couldn't help but wonder what they were really thinking. It was bad enough exposing her issue with her family but to what seemed like the whole world was devastating.

Rich drove from Florida to Macon to see Carol's father. It was very hard to look into Dr. Williams' eyes, as it was evident that the pain and mistrust was present. After a repeat performance of what he shared with Carol, but this time in even more detail, Dr. Williams thanked Rich for his courage to face his demons and also suggested that Rich consider getting God in his life, especially if he wanted a life with Carol.

As Rich discussed the hardships of his childhood and the only life that he had known, the sadness was even more evident on Dr. Williams' face. He had trusted Rich with his daughter's future and was devastated that he had not read Rich better. The very thought of exposing Carol to someone deceitful and giving his blessings for her to marry Rich and welcome him into their family still made him shudder in disbelief. However, Rich's brutal honesty regarding what happened seemed to make it a little more bearable to listen. Dr. Williams thanked Rich for his courage to face his demons.

19

L eaving Dr. Williams' home in Macon, Rich headed for Atlanta to see Carol. Though he kept his word by speaking with Bennett and meeting with Carol's father, Rich wasn't quite sure how much effect it would have on reconciliation with Carol. The drive to Atlanta seemed easier for Rich knowing he was going to see her. Rich couldn't help but wonder how Carol would now view him, knowing of his illicit past. Arriving at Carol's Rich could see the distance in her eyes. Would she ever believe anything he said again? Rich knew that he faced an uphill battle of monumental proportions attempting to win back the love of his life.

After dinner at McKendricks, the two went back to Carol's, Rich pulled up all the information he promised to Carol, proving that his sister was in fact a pathological liar. Rich also pulled newspaper articles from archives showing his brother's arrest for multiple bank robberies. Carol wanted to believe Rich deep down and this certainly was making it easier.

Grabbing Carol's hand, Rich sat with her on the couch and told her that he wanted to give her the opportunity to ask him anything that she wanted. He also assured her that only 100% honesty would depart his lips to her ears.

However, there was something important he needed to tell her. "You need to listen to me fully and understand that what I am telling you is exactly what transpired," he said.

"I told you that I found out about Jack five years ago. His mother was single, and I wanted to be a legal guardian to him. I wanted to put him on my insurance and pay for his college through the 529 college program. In the event that something was to happen to me, I wanted to leave my estate to him as my son. So after talking with his mother and deciding on what would be best for Jack in the long run, his mother and I decided to go to the courthouse and get married.

We didn't even give each other a kiss at the end of the ceremony. We have never shared a night together and knew that we could get divorced after six months or so. We just never got around to it. I can get divorced in as little as three months. So yes, I am married, but I have spent every night with you and four and a half years prior, sleeping alone in my own bed."

Carol bowed her head down and cried. "You're going to tell me that you're a married man?" she asked.

"I am not married like other people who are married. There's no relationship between us, just a piece of paper to benefit a little boy."

"Is there any other shocking news that you want to tell me?" Carol asked.

"As I said, ask me absolutely anything you like. I owe you that."

"Why did you get involved in organized crime?" Carol asked.

"It's a very long story," Rich said. "It all started when I was a young boy, around twelve. The bottom line is that was my life for 25 years. I'm not proud of it, but I didn't grow up in a loving home like you did. I'm not making excuses, but that was my life for a quarter of a century before I ever met you. Now let me ask you a question," Rich said. "Are you even remotely interested in working things out between us?"

"I'm not sure," Carol said. "There have been so many lies. I thought that I knew you!!"

"You do know me. My feelings for you were real, if not, why would I be here? Damn it, I love you. Think about what is important in life. The only thing we have on this earth is time, time to spend with each other until one of us buries the other. Who cares what other people think? They don't pay your bills. They're not going to lie next to you in bed, or take care of you when you're sick." Rich said.

"I'm confused right now. If there is a chance for us, I would need some time." Carol said. "Also, you would have to change your life!!!" Carol emphasized.

"I understand," Rich said softly. "I will give you all the time that you need," he said. "I want to thank you for coming to dinner with me and talking with me tonight. I love you, Carol. And regardless of your decision, I always will." Kissing her gently on the cheek, Rich stood up and let himself out.

Carol had put up a small wall to distance her

feelings in front of Rich, but as soon as the door closed behind him, her heart let out all of the emotions she had held back. Carol sat in her living room and cried. Since it wasn't too late, Carol called her good friend Claire James and told her the details of what was going on with Rich.

"I think I am going to call off the wedding tomorrow and return my dress," Carol said. "I just don't know what to do. My friends are telling me to get rid of him. They say that men never change. What do you think, Claire?" Carol asked.

"Carol, you and I have known each other since you were 17 years old. You have been there for me during the good times and the bad. A friend doesn't tell you what you want to hear, but tells you the truth. The truth is you should follow your heart, do what you feel is right, not what others think. It's your life, not someone else's. No matter what your decision is, I am your friend and will support whatever you decide to do."

"Thank you, Claire. You're a true friend, something I will cherish forever," Carol said.

The last words that Carol said to Rich resonated

in his head. *Change your life and get God in your life.*
For the next two weeks, Rich spent his evenings in
Florida walking on the beach thinking about what
his life would be like without her. Changing his life
was not an easy task. He couldn't simply flip a switch
and become a new person overnight. There was much
more at stake than Carol could ever understand.
Rich had to admit that there were many times laying
next to Carol at night he had fantasized about what
it would be like to live a normal and simple civilian
life with Carol. Walking away from the pressures and
responsibilities of that life was enticing, but that also
meant giving up the benefits that had taken a lifetime
to gain.

As far as getting God in his life was concerned,
Rich wasn't sure what to think. Rich admired Carol's
father, Dr. Williams. He lived an honest life and a
happy life, which he attributed to knowing God.
Dr. Williams seemed to be at peace. His belief in an
eternal life was absolute.

*If there was a God, how would someone like me
ever get to know him?* Rich thought. *With the company
I have kept over the years and the things I have done,*

there's no way that God would even consider forgiving anyone with my past. If in fact He was real! But if there really was a Heavenly Father, as Carol and her family believed... In Rich's mind, he would most likely not be welcome.

Giving up his other life would also mean giving up massive income. When it came to comparing Carol with money, Carol would win that contest hands down.

♦♦♦♦♦♦

Carol was happy that she would be seeing her family today. It was Father's Day. She knew that the day's conversations would be dominated by what had happened with Rich. It was bad enough that the rumors were flying around her neighborhood and the country club regarding what had happened with Rich. The last thing Carol wanted was this to be the main topic of conversation at Daddy's.

Arriving at her father's house, Carol could see that her family had already arrived. After hugging everyone and saying hello, the first question posed to her was, "Have you talked to Rich?" Carol politely asked her family to forget about Rich today and celebrate Father's Day. The last thing Carol wanted to do was to inform her family that she had gone out to dinner with Rich and sat and talked with him afterwards.

Leaving Daddy's house late in the day, Carol's sister, Mary Linda, made a comment that Carol brushed off as silly, but it bothered her the whole way home. "Well, I know his family was fake, except for Mike. I hope the engagement ring he gave you wasn't fake as well," she had said.

The next morning after her walk, Carol went to the jewelry store that she had patronized for many years, the Jewelry Artisan, and asked to speak to the owner. Carol discretely asked the owner, Jamie, to look at her ring and tell her if it was real or not. The owner came back within five minutes, telling her not only was her ring real, but it was of superior quality. Carol's ring had never meant more to her than at that very moment. It solidified to Carol that Rich must have loved her. But she had to be sure, just saying goodbye to Rich would be so much easier, but could she go on the rest of her days without him?

There was only one way to find out. Carol had joined a dating service in Atlanta about a year prior to meeting Rich. Through the service, Carol had met a few men and gone on some dates, but the result was nothing more than some company during dinner. *Perhaps I should call the service and see what happens,* she thought.

Carol set up an appointment at the dating service. She updated her picture and profile and filled out the appropriate paperwork to seek a match of her interests.

✦✦✦✦✦✦

Rich flew back to Atlanta, because he needed to be near Carol. Rich called Carol and asked her if he could attend Buckhead Church with her on Sunday. Surprised, Carol said yes and welcomed the thought. That Sunday Rich sat in the Buckhead Church with Carol and listened to the sermon. Ironically, Andy Stanley's sermon was about being the real you and that God knows who you really are and what you're really thinking. Going to lunch after the service, Rich told Carol that he still wanted to spend the rest of his life with her and that changing his life was something that he was interested in doing. If she decided not to be with him any longer, he still wanted to become a better person.

Rich called Dr. Williams and had a heart-to-heart talk with him and explained that he wanted to take Carol to dinner once a week. Rich didn't want word getting back to Dr. Williams that he was back in the picture without Dr. Williams' approval.

Dr. Williams told Rich that he could see his daughter and Rich together in the future, but it was going to take time. In his opinion a very slow approach was needed.

Rich told Carol the following day that he wanted to talk to someone, perhaps a pastor, about a few questions that he had regarding religion and God. "That's great, Rich. I am proud of you for taking the first step," Carol said. That night the two of them went to dinner, and then back to Carol's house to talk. The evening turned into a confessional for Rich. Not holding back, Rich told Carol intimate details of his past. Finally Carol could rationalize somewhat as to why Rich ended up going in the direction he did. Carol also told Rich details of how God had helped her throughout her life and the comfort she felt knowing that He was in her corner.

After their intimate and lengthy talk, Carol went to get some more coffee. As Rich walked back into Carol's room to look at their picture, which she had on her dresser, he realized that what she was saying made sense.

Rich went to glance out of Carol's bedroom window to look up at the moonlight and chills shot down his spine. On the window staring back at him with the moon as a backdrop was a cross — a perfectly shaped cross had somehow formed on the window made from natural elements. Call it a miracle or one of life's coincidences, either way, it was a sign to Rich … perhaps a sign that he was doing the right thing.

Rich yelled for Carol to come into the room. Taking her by the hand, he showed her what he had found. Carol put her head down and prayed. She also knew that this was a sign. Her powerful God had once again spoken to her. On his way driving back to the Ritz Carlton, Rich, for the first time, thought that maybe there really was something to this God and his son Jesus. That night in the dark privacy of his hotel room, lying in bed alone, Rich closed his eyes and talked to God for the first time.

The next day Rich went over to Carol's house to pick up his wallet that he had taken out of his pocket while sitting on the couch the night before. Carol was not yet home, but knowing where she hid her extra house key, he helped himself in. Walking out the door, Rich noticed a piece of paper next to Carol's home phone. It was from a place called The Right One Dating Service.

As Rich read the paper, his heart broke. Carol was going on a date with a man the next day at 12:00. They were meeting at Goldfish Restaurant at Perimeter Mall.

There is no way that she will go through with the date, Rich thought, *not after last night.* Putting the paper back exactly where he had found it, Rich left. *How could she have wanted to see other people so fast? He thought. Did I mean that little to her?* Rich was more hurt than mad, but he reminded himself about the deceit, the pain, and the hurt that he had caused Carol. Rich had no room to complain.

The next day Rich took Carol to breakfast. He said that he needed to jump on a plane and head down to Florida for business when they were done. During breakfast Rich asked Carol what she would be doing afterwards. "I just need to run a few errands," Carol said. Rich hoped that this would really be the case.

Walking Carol to her car after eating, Rich hugged her tightly. Looking in Carol's eyes, Rich told her that he would miss her. "When will you be back in Atlanta?" Carol asked. "I could return as soon as tomorrow night," Rich said. "Okay then, have a safe flight," Carol said.

"I love you," Rich said. "I love you, too," Carol said. Although she was not sure if she felt that way again, it seemed like the right thing to say. Instead of catching his flight, Rich knew he had to see for himself if in fact Carol was actually going to meet someone.

Carol got home and looked inside her closet. She was very nervous at the idea of going on a date. Rich had consumed her life up to this point.

Rich arrived at the Goldfish Restaurant about twenty minutes before twelve. He asked the hostess if he could sit upstairs where it was quiet as he had several business calls to make. The hostess obliged. Rich's heart was racing and his palms began to sweat. Rich had much more dangerous assignments in his other life, and he never seemed to get nervous. In this case, he was emotionally attached. At five minutes until twelve, Rich's fear was realized. Carol walked in the restaurant without wearing her ring that he had given her. She was directed to a table where a man in his late fifties sat waiting. Rich was numb. He now truly understood what it was like getting his heart broken. After watching the two have lunch and conversation, Rich called Carol on her cell phone to see if she would answer. Her phone was off in her purse, and she was unaware that the man she was supposed to marry was watching her intently from above.

When the lunch date was over, Carol walked back to her car and tried to call Rich right away. Rich had been on her mind the entire lunch date. The date served its purpose – it proved to Carol that her feelings for Rich still lingered inside her heart.

"Hello," Rich said. "Where are you?" Carol asked. "I'm on my way to the airport," Rich replied.

"When will you be back?" Carol asked again. "I will be back on July 3rd," Rich answered.

"Can we go to dinner when you get in on the third?" Carol asked.

Though Rich didn't understand Carol's sudden willingness to meet, he told her of course. Returning on the third, Rich picked Carol up for dinner. Carol could tell that Rich's eyes were not as inviting as normal.

Rich seemed distant. After dinner, the two of them went back to Carol's for coffee. Rich sat close to Carol holding both of her hands. "Is everything okay?" Carol asked. "You seem different, like something is on your mind."

"You know, Carol, I know that you said I love you to me when we said goodbye the other day. But I was wondering why you would say that to me and turn around four hours later and go on a lunch date with a man through a dating service?"

Carol froze. The only thing she could think to say

was, "How could you know that?"

Though Carol had every right to go on that date, guilt came over her. "Were you spying on me?" she asked. "No, not spying but I did sit and watch you hoping that you wouldn't go through with it."

"I want to know: how did you find out? Did you have one of your organized crime friends bug my phone, or follow me?"

"No, I didn't," Rich said. "Regardless, why did you go on a date so soon?"

"I hope you believe me when I tell you this," Carol said. "I loved you as much as a woman can love a man, and you hurt me more than you will ever know. Even with that said, I wanted to see if I could forget about you, if I had to."

"Well, are you going to forget about me? Is that what your intentions are?" Rich said.

"No, I realized that I want you in my life forever. ONLY, and I mean ONLY if you are honest. And I mean honest with me every day of your life."

"Carol, I told you that this was going to be an uphill battle for me. However, I am willing to stay and fight and work hard for your love as long as that is what you truly want. I know it is going to be hard for you regarding your family and all the neighbors, especially the Atlanta Country Club crowd, but who cares what they think," Rich said.

"The only thing that matters is that we want to spend our lives together. I will never tell you a lie again, and if you truly want to spend your life with me and commit to making us work, I will 100% walk away from all of organized crime," Rich firmly stated.

"Are you sure you want to do that and that you can do that?" Carol asked.

"You would be surprised what I can accomplish when I put my mind to it," Rich said.

"Please don't hurt me again, Rich. I want to trust you for ever." Grabbing Carol, Rich pulled her into his chest. Holding her he whispered in her ear, something in Italian. "What does that mean?" Carol asked.

"It means you and me against the world, forever!"

After a long, deep and very passionate kiss, Rich dropped Carol off at her home. She had made arrangement three days prior to meet her friends to return her wedding gown and their bridesmaids dresses, but she didn't want to hurt Rich's feelings, so she kept quiet about it.

The next evening was the fourth of July. A movie and dinner was the plan for the two of them. Driving to dinner, Carol asked Rich a question, "Why did you put your profile that you had $44 million, lived on Longboat Key, and had eleven cars?"

"Carol, when I made up that profile, with my friend standing behind me, I thought that the people on the site most likely were a bunch of gold diggers. I had bought a home in Atlanta, and I truly thought that whoever I met I certainly would not end up with them. Perhaps I would meet someone through them or through you. I had no idea that I was going to meet someone that I would fall in love with. In my world you didn't even exist. It backfired on me."

"Okay," Carol said. "I just had to ask."

Dinner at the Cheesecake Factory was nice. Each of them had the spark back in their eyes.

Carol asked Rich another question. "Are you really going to give up all of your organized crime business? I mean, all of it?"

"Yes," Rich said, "For you, I am finished."

"Will they let you leave?" she said, obviously

concerned.

"You let me worry about that. I'm not Italian born. I am what they refer to as an honoré, someone who does business day to day with them. Leaving is something that I will take care of," Rich said.

"I want to understand more about God," Rich said. "I have a hundred questions in my mind."

"I'm not sure that I can answer them all correctly," said Carol. She was obviously thrilled that Rich was taking a genuine interest in God. "Perhaps we can make an appointment at Buckhead Church and talk to someone, someone that can guide you properly," said Carol.

"Okay, let's call tomorrow," Rich said.

That night, Carol thanked God for the first steps that Rich was taking to change his life. She prayed that he was strong enough to carry through with it.

Rich ended up getting an appointment with a pastor at Buckhead Church. He asked Carol if she would accompany him, and gladly she did so.

Telling Carol the truth was hard enough, but opening up to a stranger, even one who was a representative of the church, was very difficult for Rich.

The two of them met Suzanne, a long time pastor. Rich felt that Suzanne was respectful, knowledgeable, and didn't push the religious issue to hard. After a two hour meeting, Suzanne knew that Rich's circumstance was unique. She recommended a Christian counselor in Marietta, Georgia, who as a licensed professional would have to remain discrete regarding Rich's situation. Prior to Rich and Carol's departure, Suzanne gave Rich a New Life Application Bible. Although Rich offered to pay for it, Suzanne insisted it was a gift.

Carol couldn't believe that Rich willingly went to speak to the pastor and went back home to immediately book an appointment with the Christian counselor. Next came the real monumental task that had to be done by Rich alone. Leaving a lifetime in organized crime was something that would have to be orchestrated very carefully. In his other life, Rich understood the rules in which to live by; he knew how to act, what to say and what to not say. Religion was as foreign to Rich as anything he had ever experienced in his life. But he was eager to learn.

Rich would have to go straight to the top of the

ladder to do this task properly. Rich opened his Bible and read different passages. This was an entirely different world for Rich.

Dr. Williams started calling Rich twice each week to check on him. Rich looked to Dr. Williams as a father figure. Rich had always admired what *Doc* had to say, and the phone calls were appreciated immensely by Rich.

John Dotson, a Christian counselor, was not what Rich had expected by any means. He was laid back; he had longer hair; he was soft spoken and caring. The only word Rich could think of to describe him was "cool."

John had been in a rock band in Los Angeles as a drummer. One night he overdosed, ending up in an emergency room. The ER physician asked him if he believed in God or not. When John asked why he wanted to know, the physician explained that John should have been amongst the dearly departed. Through the years, John subsequently became an ordained minister, and then a licensed therapist and psychologist. Through a series of weekly meetings, John explained to Rich God's infinite grace. John also explained to Rich that though it was hard for Rich to believe that if he truly asked God to come into his heart and mind, that even the monumental indiscretions that Rich had done for a quarter of a century would and could be forgiven. To ask forgiveness and be cleansed if he truly repented seemed almost too easy for Rich. With Carol by his side, session after session, Rich Towsley's heart and mind slowly were convinced that an eternal life was his for the taking. Carol reminded Rich that he should share his knowledge of the Lord with some of those constituents with whom he had previously shared a lifestyle, and to never be afraid to share the word of God.

20

It was a beautiful, crisp autumn Sunday morning. Carol sat out by the pool area of her home. Rich would be coming over to watch Joel Osteen, then the two of them would be going to church. For the last six months, this had become their Sunday morning routine. This particular Sunday had a slightly different twist to it.

Daddy and Carol's sister, Mary Linda, were up getting ready. They had slept over at Carol's for this special occasion. Today, former organized crime member Rich Towsley was attesting to the cleansing of his soul at Buckhead Church.

Rich was going to be baptized this morning in front of three thousand parishioners. Rich's video would be shown prior to the baptism, a testimony of the triumph of grace. Carol was thankful to her mighty God. The man she called her fiancé had all of the criteria that Carol had prayed for all of her life. They say that people don't change, but Rich did a complete, 180° turn. He had not only walked away from his illicit past, but every day he was walking with his partner: the One who lives inside each of God's children.

Many months prior, Dr. Williams had a long talk with Rich. He explained to Rich that the devil would always put temptations in front of him. After all, Rich had been plucked from the devil's team and traded to the other side.

Dr. Williams emphasized that Rich would have to jump in with both feet, to burn the ships, if you will, and commit fully to Christ. "You can't get a little bit pregnant," Dr. Williams said. "It's all, or nothing." This statement stuck in Rich's mind. To say that Dr. Williams was proud of Rich was an understatement. Not only had God welcomed one of his children to walk with Him for eternity, Dr. Williams felt as if he also had welcomed a son into his family forever. Rich had not only changed his life, but he had also changed the life of Carol, one of Dr. Williams' most prized treasures. When Dr. Williams looked at Rich, a heartfelt smile followed because he now knew that destiny had been fulfilled.

Rich had met with the head of the crime family where he had been affiliated to make arrangements for his departure. He did something unprecedented: he gave back more than a million dollars he knew were ill-gotten gains. He said goodbye to a family that groomed him and to friends who were most loyal, more than most would comprehend.

Rich changed his address and phone number and burned his Rolodex. Next came returning a brand new SL500 Mercedes that he had purchased for Carol as a wedding gift: it had been purchased with tainted money. Rich had truly severed the cord of organized crime.

Rich had also taken what Carol had asked of him to heart. Though he walked away from the only world he had known, he told his story of change to many of his friends from his past. He explained the massive weight that had been removed from his chest. The peace that he felt knowing that an eternal life was awaiting was a treasure he shared with anyone who would listen. He explained that he would proudly spend the rest of his days on the earth as a different kind of warrior, a warrior for Christ.

Some of his past associates took what Rich said to heart. Slowly, they started changing their lives, as well. What Rich had was contagious and some of them wanted more of it.

The domino effect all started with a five foot four, one hundred and five pound Atlanta socialite and mother of two. She was slowly and inadvertently changing the face of organized crime, one soul at a time. Carol was leaving a legacy.

Daddy, Mary Linda, and Carol took a seat in the large Buckhead Church audience. Little did the three thousand attendees realize that they were about to witness the true power and capabilities of their Savior. Rich's video testimony received a very loud applause.

When the actual baptism took place, Rich felt as he was rising from the water that the hand of God Himself was pulling him out of the water, washing away all of his past transgressions. Those in attendance cheered, whistled, clapped, and yelled.

Good had prevailed. One of Carol's good friends, Kathy Wagner, who was a witness to this triumphant moment, hugged Carol and exclaimed, "Praise God!"

Dr. Williams somehow knew that Rich would now be okay. Walking with the Lord was the surest bet out there.

Carol Greenbaum had done her part to help make the world a better place. Rich knew that this pivotal moment in his life was owed to Carol. By demonstrating kindness and forgiveness; by not giving up; and by believing in the Word of God, Carol had contributed to helping save a soul for eternity.

Carol's life was also forever changed. Rich had taught her over the last year and a half together about how the world really worked. The two of them knew that together no obstacle could stop them. By putting God first and letting Him lead the way, they would be together for eternity.